The Girls of Nevada

The Girls of Nevada

by GABRIEL R. VOGLIOTTI

The Citadel Press   •   Secaucus, N.J.

Second printing, January, 1975
Copyright © 1975 by Gabriel R. Vogliotti
All rights reserved
Published by Citadel Press
A division of Lyle Stuart, Inc.
120 Enterprise Ave., Secaucus, N.J. 07094
In Canada: George J. McLeod Limited
73 Bathurst St., Toronto, Ont.
Manufactured in the United States of America
Library of Congress catalog card number: 73-90953
ISBN 0-8065-0378-5

Contents

Introduction

THIS IS THE story of a state's idea—the stubborn idea that if a man wants a girl he should be able to go out and hire one, an enduring idea that probably began with the beginning of time and certainly runs throughout all Nevada history.

It was first reported by Mark Twain when he was a lusty newspaper editor in Nevada's first real town, Virginia City. Twain thought it delightful that Virginia City should have a girl market. Girl markets appeared in the squalid camps where wagon trains stopped, and there would be a girl market in every mining camp within three weeks of the discovery of ore.

Today, a hundred years after the Virginia City strike, the vast, barren state has become one of the nation's great Air Force bases, its skies criss-crossed by every plane in the nation's arsenal. It has also become the world's major gambling mecca. Nevada still has only a sparse population, but it has such a disproportionate number of brothels that the pilots of the supersonic F-111s have their navigational jokes. Since the red lights of the Nevada houses stand out in the clear night air, a pilot will advise another: "You can forget the beacons. Bear north at Cindy's and pick up the red lights at Dora's, Jackie's, and Billie-May's. If you miss Dixie's, you're in Utah."

When Benjamin Siegel became the first Eastern underworld

man to open a Las Vegas casino, he started the industry which has always considered prostitution a part of the business. In the years since Siegel's demise, Las Vegas has built more hotel rooms than there are in New York. In February 1973, Las Vegas Sheriff Ralph Lamb announced that he had arrested a hundred and fifty prostitutes that month (a number which is estimated to be about five percent of the total working any routine evening) and Lamb added angrily that the Hughes management was getting brazen because exactly half of the arrested girls were caught in one Hughes hotel—the Frontier.

Girls swarm in Nevada in time and space. In the north, outside of Reno, a man is now rounding out his second decade in the first American county to legalize prostitution. He is the ubiquitous Joe Conforte, who, with thirty-five girls in his Mustang Ranch, is impatient to conquer new worlds. His firm aim is to secure legislation making the "profession" legal in Las Vegas and then work on California and the nation. He maintains that government is rarely abreast of the needs of men and that in fifteen years prostitution will be a legally accepted institution.

In the remote past of 1971, Joe's forecasts were considered insane. People are now less certain of the future. This past spring bootleg film prints of *Deep Throat* were selling in Las Vegas and Los Angeles high schools, and sheriffs' deputies now know that Las Vegas is beginning to market Lolitas. Joe's forecasts no longer bring ready laughter because, in the momentum of the sex revolution, it could be like betting that the airplane would never be invented.

G.R.V.

The Girls of Nevada

1

The Deal: Billions If We
Can Look Legitimate

WITH ALL THE policing of Nevada—by federal task forces, by resident FBIs, by Nevada's own gambling police, and by the seven hundred deputies of Sheriff Ralph Lamb—no one ever thought to make an elevator count to find out just how many whores go upstairs in any one hotel in any one night. Not, that is, until the idea hit Jack Golden, a security man in Howard Hughes' Sands Hotel. The count came after Hughes had fired the little army with which he had entered Nevada, the army of his top man, Robert Maheu, and replaced it with another. In the turn-over, Hughes also fired security boss, Jack Hooper, and hired James Golden in his place. Golden, a former Marine, was tall, brawny, handsome, and silent, every inch the super-cop. James had a younger brother, Jack, a free soul, taller, wider, handsomer than his brother, and a man with an unexpected turn of mind. James made Jack his assistant in charge of ultra-secret chores; within weeks Jack was scaring the whole Hughes establishment. One Saturday night, when the Sands was a-throb with people, Jack was struck by the number of mini-skirted cuties who, looking neither left nor right, were entering the elevators. He bought a copy of *Time*, found a couch and tried to make himself small. He

13

slouched there, pencil in hand, from ten to a little past midnight, during which time anxious Hughes men watched him, wondering what he was up to now. For they remembered him as the boy who had set up the unsuccessful garbage operation.

The new Hughes team wanted to get something on the deposed chief, Maheu, and Jack had come up with the idea that Maheu's garbage might produce something incriminating. Jack took charge: he bribed the proper truck drivers and arranged to meet them in the predawn to sift through the cans. An alert newspaper boy stopped peddling his bike one morning to stare at what was obviously a garbage-sorting going on in the middle of the street. He saw that it was Mr. Maheu's cans that were being dumped. The boy told his dad and his dad told Maheu. Maheu called photographers and Jack's future with Hughes went dark.

Now Jack was making a count on the cover of *Time,* and after two hours he had numbered eighteen. His estimate for the Sands' upstairs traffic was fifty per night, which is higher than that of the Vice Squad, and lower than that of Joe Conforte, operator of the world's most celebrated brothel. Jack explained, "You see, the elevators serve only the Sands tower, but the hotel has eleven other buildings spread out over the lawns, and the cuties who serve them never go near a lobby. Also," he said, "a lot of broads don't like to go up the elevators alone, and they have their guys go up with them. I must have skipped fifty couples where the gal is just too gorgeous to be any wife." His estimate for Las Vegas as a whole sounds a little like that of Joe Conforte, who, speaking of Las Vegas prostitution, says, "You don't compare it to big cities like New York or Los Angeles, where it's spread out. For concentration you got to compare it to Antwerp and Hamburg, the places where they *really* got whores."

The Golden brothers are gone now, moved by whatever forces keep the Hughes empire in turmoil, its bosses in musical chairs, men who are powerful in January and ex-kings in June. New Hughes managers struggle to learn the gambling business, to penetrate its secrets, and are in perpetual reorganization. William Gay, the new Hughes supremo, could be a football coach who keeps shifting players to get a working combination. This floundering would be irrelevant except that, in their confusion, the Hughes managers also floundered on whores.

For, after Maheu, the new Hughes bosses came on brash and strong. While they were new to the business, they were quick to learn that pretty whores do pull in the men, and that a lot of pretty girls are as good a way of attracting males as paying Frank Sinatra $1000 a minute. The Hughes bosses were making confetti of an old, unwritten law, that Las Vegas must not be too offensive and prostitution never too obvious. The Hughes managers, with appalling ignorance, did not know that Las Vegas' twenty-five-year growth had been one long siege of fear.

Las Vegas, to which nothing can be really new, now saw something different. In the Frontier, which had long been the Hughes headquarters hotel, the prostitutes working the lounges, the bars, and the lobbies were as obvious as those of Times Square.

Sheriff Ralph Lamb, a man who has suffered under twenty years of attacks on Las Vegas, who grew up in dread of the FBI and of J. Edgar Hoover, who spent years in fear of a Washington crackdown, tried to warn Hughes' men that such big, crass, whore stupidity was not the Las Vegas way. He tried to explain that, the sexual revolution notwithstanding, Las Vegas still controls whores. But to Hughes' men, he must have sounded like an old scold. So many girls continued to roam the Frontier that people thought they were a convention of visiting Thetas. At this point, Lamb, prodded by the other hotels, started the raids, hitting all of the Strip, and making sure of the Frontier. Through the night for some weeks, police vans would unload dozens of cuties at the station, girls who jammed the corridors as they shouted for lawyers and bondsmen. Even these roundups had no effect on the Hughes managers. On top of which, there was the Frontier orgy. It was not that orgies were new to hotels, or that they weren't almost pathologically wild, but what Lamb found irritating was that everyone in town seemed to have heard about the one put on in a Frontier suite—by six girls and a German Shepherd dog. Lamb did something unprecedented; he called a news conference to announce that of one hundred fourteen whores arrested that month, fifty-two were nabbed on the carpets of the Frontier.

Nevada's older bosses marvel at changing times, for just a few years before, such raw, open, don't-give-a-damn prostitution would have brought in the United States Marines. Things have changed in Las Vegas and there is now a whore inundation that raises new problems, but the sheriff and the hotel owners still retain their old fears. To understand their edginess, one must go back to the Carson of 1962.

In tiny, lovely Carson City, Nevada's capital, a car backfiring at noon can be heard at the city limits, and in 1962, when the town was even smaller, the sound would echo over empty sagebrush. In the offices of the Attorney General, Roger Foley, a call came in one morning, announced by his secretary with some worry as "The Attorney General of the United States." From Washington, the high-pitched voice of Robert Kennedy carried bad news. Kennedy told Foley that he was coming to Nevada with a force of seventy federal agents. He was going to clean out what he called the "bank of America's organized crime" and, failing that, he would press Congress to close down gambling. Kennedy explained that the men could hit harder if, in addition to being federal police, they were also Nevada police. Would Foley please deputize them, make the seventy men Deputy Attorneys General of Nevada?

Foley is a native Nevadan. He knew that in Nevada most gambling owners loathed Robert Kennedy, that they considered him both anti-Nevada, and even a little unbalanced.[1]

Foley, today a federal judge, would no more cross Bobby than he would call J. Edgar Hoover a homo. "I went quiet as a mouse pissing on cotton," he says, "and I said, 'Sir, could I please check with the governor?'" The office of Governor Grant Sawyer was across the street, so close that at times Foley could see Sawyer's outline through a window. He tried not to run as he made tracks there.

---

[1] The differences between Kennedy and the Nevadans were basic; Kennedy was sure the eastern underworld had taken over Las Vegas gambling, while Nevada insisted that only a few bad types had come in, and that most of these had been forced to sell out. Kennedy believed that Nevada exported hundreds of millions in "skim" (money not declared as income and piped to the underworld). Nevada's governors argued, instead, that skim was light and that what there was was small, garden-variety tax evasion. Kennedy said gambling was dirty and rotten, and Nevada's answer was, "It's a living." Nevada owners thought him naive, a dilettante on crime matters, and a bit paranoid. As put by Eddie Levinson, celebrated boss of the Fremont, "The guy's views would not have mattered except suddenly, the son-of-a-bitch is Attorney General and his brother is President."

Four days later, an east-bound plane carried the men who hoped to appease Washington. Sawyer and Foley would meet with Bobby Kennedy himself. Nevada's two senators had been told of the threatened occupation and were working on President John Kennedy, whom the Nevadans considered saner than the fire-eating Bobby. On the plane were members of Nevada's Gaming Commission who were to meet with Bobby's assistants. In Washington, in a huge room of the Department of Justice, the Nevadans argued for three days. One memory of their little Versailles was that Bobby attended the first meeting in his shirt-sleeves and barefooted. The Nevadans, addressing a roomful of federal attorneys, insisted that they were as fiercely determind to ban hoodlums as Washington was, that they had a bigger police force than the FBI, that Nevada was in control, that gangs were not running the state, and were not even a strong force. They kept cool when Bobby or his assistants asked about Anastasia, Dutch Schultz, Luciano and Genovese—hoods whom the Nevada men had only read about—in tones that showed loathing for the dirty state. Still, by the third day, the Sawyer team had managed a reprieve: Bobby would call off the big invasion. Instead, he would send a small group to Nevada, men who would come in secretly and study Nevada for gang content. If they found that Nevada could handle things, the invasion was off; if Nevada had lost control, the seventy men would only be a start. Bobby did not get into prostitution, but his assistants did. One of them recalled that in a supposed division of territories by the mobs of the 40s, there had been a settlement, as between Sicilians and Jews, the Jews to take the nation's gambling and shystering, and the Sicilians its narcotics and prostitution.

"That man," said Sawyer, "showed an understanding of ethnic crime like that of Gracie Allen. He said nastily that Las Vegas was not sticking to its own dirt and was preempting whores, too. "It was," said Sawyer, "unbelievable crap, incredible innocence, the stuff that Nevada's own FBI men would laugh at. But those bright young fellows in the Department, a year or two out of law school, all in their Brooks Brothers grey flannel, and hell-bent on careers, had read it somewhere and believed it."

One assistant made a parting shot. "You'd better shape up," he said. "In the next showdown, the boys on the Hill will have the votes to shut you down."[2]

Back in Nevada, Sawyer confided in only a few people; the state had just escaped disgrace and the less the newspapers wrote about it, the better. But he did talk to the gambling owners.

No man can become governor of Nevada unless he is installed by, or endorsed by, the owners, and in his first term Sawyer was as close to them as cousins. He spoke to Moe Dalitz, leader of the Desert Inn group, and long the most influential man in Nevada gambling, to Eddie Levinson, boss of the Fremont, to Major Riddle of the Dunes, to Kell Houssels of the Tropicana—the big ones. He told them that Nevada now stood pretty well alone, and that it was always possible that Congress could end its gambling. The owners knew all about the Nevada hatred in Congress. They knew that at the beginning of every session, new senate groups automatically introduced new anti-gambling bills, and they knew that a well-managed bill can be run through in a week. The owners, however competitive, had long understood that they must act as one. They might compete for Dean Martin, Barbra Streisand, or Sinatra, but they knew they must now be as close as oil companies, as well-knit as the farm lobby.

Bobby's threat, which was only one of many paralyzing scares, put a final seal on policy, on the grand design for the owners of Las Vegas. They would have to become discreet, subtle, self-disciplining businessmen. They must perfect ways to run the hated gambling business. Las Vegas must be a town without gambling-connected murders; there must be no scandals, grand jury indictments, arrests, discoveries; no trials that might support any accusation. If even one Lansky were found to be a hidden owner, it could renew the boil in Congress. If Las Vegas should become a narcotics center, if even one hotel provided one trial that proved "skim," all the accusations would seem confirmed. If they were smooth, they would survive and preserve a business that was already pulling in a gross of a half-billion a year. As this discretion extended to whores, the Las Vegas hotels should show no more girls than those who stroll through Los Angeles' Beverly-Wilshire,

[2] He was referring to the House attempt to close Nevada gambling in 1951.

not because of any nonsense about morality, but because big prostitution would bring the charge that Las Vegas had let a Luciano move in.

But making prostitution inconspicuous was a little like trying to de-roar Niagara, like trying to slip freights through town without rumble. Even in the 60s, several thousand men were arriving daily, and hundreds wanted a girl that same day. Still, until quite recently, the handling of girls was fairly clandestine and not too visible. It was a considerable performance by the earlier managements, and prostitution got out of hand and became open only recently.

Fourteen years after the clash with Bobby, in the summer of 1974, the owners of Las Vegas gambling were troubled by changing times. They were getting a fantastic closeup of the sexual revolution, and wondering how to adjust to some of its more cruddy throw-off. For Las Vegas had tripled in population, and so had its prostitution. But where gambling was under control, the prostitutes and pimps were not. It had streetwalkers, which were new. In Bobby Kennedy's time, the shortest distance between hotels was the two long blocks between the Desert Inn and Stardust. But the boom had filled gaps and created hotel clusters. The intersection, first selected by Siegel for the Flamingo, was chosen three more times, by the Dunes, by Caesars Palace, and finally, by MGM, and the four-hotel crossing became a pedestrian mall. Whores discovered that thousands of men crisscrossed between the hotels and the teeming sidewalks brought a new type, the streetwalker, who can charge as little as $10.

Change, indeed. Formerly, few men would ask for a "Lolita"; buying a fifteen-year-old was not done. Now Lolitas come in two colors. The men who want a child whore need only be a little more careful. The girls come, two or three to a car, from the neighboring small towns of Utah; they come for weekends, and are back in Mormon junior highs on Monday. Their counterparts from California, cute, leggy kids, have, at fifteen or sixteen, more sophistication. They know that hotel guards dread the teenage whore, so they avoid the bars and work the swimming pools, trying to look like guests. They manage to find motels whose clerks will take a chance, even with children.

Sheriff Lamb was discussing the problems with some deputies one day—the new inventiveness of pimps, the new age groups that were getting into the business—when one of his deputies said, "Ralph, there hasn't been time to tell you, but there's this new twist you haven't heard about." Lamb looked doubtful. After a lifetime in Las Vegas, he thought there was little between Sodom and Portnoy he had not handled. "Well," said the detective, "you know the parking lot back of the Dunes and, for that matter, it's going on back of Circus Circus . . ."

"What's going on?"

"Well, we got five-six complaints in two days, a new way of rolling. There's these girls—they can't be more than thirteen-fourteen years old—this bunch happens to be all Negro. Well, they proposition the guy soon as he parks, or else when he gets into his car to leave. The price for then and there is five bucks flat." Lamb blinked: it sounded like the prices of Reno's Alamo in the time of Harding. "They only offer the quickie," the detective went on. "The guy stays right in his seat, or maybe he gets away from the steering wheel, maybe in back, and the gal goes down. Then, while the guy is worked up and feeling his pleasure, she starts reaching up; them arms go up, right during the act, she takes the leather out of his coat or his pants, and the snatch comes at the peak, when the guy wouldn't know if the car turned over. Made me think of a new name," the deputy added.

"What's that?"

"Parking lot fellatio."

In the new inundation there was also the problem of the pimp, and how to circumvent him. For new parasites had come in to work the fringes of the industry and the old restraints were hard to enforce. Pimps had burgeoned. They were sharp young men who sat at the bars, among the throngs of the newly-opened MGM, and in bars the full length of the Strip. They drank and tipped well, and their heads swiveled to spot the man whose vibrations show he wants a girl. They were at the tables, betting modestly, they were on foot, working the sidewalks, and they were cruising in Volkswagens and Cadillacs, cheerfully putting the offer to men, even at intersections. Las Vegas does not like the pimp, not because of any objection to his product, but because he does not confine himself to it: most of them go for the sudden chance. Since they are outside the law they diversify, and are heavily involved in narcotics. Few have any sense of outrage about crime; they cultivate criminals and pick up sidelines, robbery, burglary, fencing stolen goods. They see girl-hungry men who can be easily robbed, in bedroom or parking lot.

The pimp is a nuisance but, as Las Vegas knows, only a symptom of today's strange anomaly; in sex-obsessed America, sex is still hard to get.

It is hard to get despite so much evidence that man is jaded, living in a coital surfeit. The sexologists say that most young men now get two to ten times the sex their fathers did. Single men go to singles bars and leave with a girl in casual pairing for the night. It is a time when college men seem to have no problem getting partners for a weekend, a term or the four-year run. A time when high school sex is measured by the figure that ten percent of any class will get VD each year, a time when married men have easy office affairs, where some indulge in wife-swapping, and where many are casual about their mate's extracurricular affairs. High school boys have steadies, or one-night stands, and presumably masturbate less than the one-per-day estimate of Masters and Johnson.

In the spring of 1973, the principal of a Las Vegas junior high school called police and asked that they send someone over to try to catch whoever was selling shoulder patches. The teachers could see them on the girls' blouses through the windows, and also the convulsed laughter of the kids, but they could not get close. Police collected a few. They were made of felt, 4 x 4 inches, with an adhesive backing, so they could be pressed on and pulled off quickly. Police don't know whether they got all the patterns or not. One patch, taken from a teenager's blouse, showed a penis in erection with the caption, "The best pacifier." One showed a vagina with the caption, "Taste me." One said simply, "Let's fuck."

Still, for the majority of men, sex was still hard to get. The evidence was everywhere. Why were call girls all over the nation getting $50 to $150 for one visit? If men had enough, why the hunger for pornography? If sated, why the boom in X-rated movies? If wives and girl friends gave fellatio readily, why the excitement over *Deep Throat*. "If it's easy," says Joe Conforte, "how come one hundred to four hundred men come to my place each day, some driving five hundred miles, and pay up to $500?" If sex were adequate, why is there such a demand for the infected prostitutes of the Times Squares of most cities? If men were still not hungering, why do the millions of married men, who have it available any night, go to Las Vegas and pay $50 to $100 for one episode? Why do some pay $1000 for a showgirl? Why, at another level, is there so much rape?

But the marketplace—in America and in Las Vegas—has become a mess. Procurement was not only against the law, but was considered degrading. As a result, the business was taken over by those middlemen who were willing to deal with the illegal, willing to take the arrests, the chances, the trouble, the furtiveness. And they were charging for their brokerage. A man willing to pay $25 or $50 or $100 for a girl had to add something for the pimp. Which was right, in a way, because pimps and whores have high costs. Customers made a human stream at McCarran airport, and jammed the freeways with their cars. Entering Las Vegas they spread out. And while they found industries that were geared to give them rooms, to give them food, gambling, and shows, there was only chaos for procurement. It was a great, complicated black market, much of it as rule-less as buying narcotics. It was a vast exercise in illegality, ranging from the smooth procurement by which a big player gets a $500 showgirl free, all the way to the parking lot scene, where a pathetic little tramp invites a man into a car (not her car, but one she finds unlocked) for a five-minute, five-dollar episode with hands or mouth.

The great whore boom in Las Vegas—it really became obvious at the start of Nixon's second term—was quite a contrast to the more orderly ways of Nevada tradition, its old system of houses on the highways. They are such different whore worlds that we might hold the Las Vegas story to look in on the road houses first.

2

Forget the beacons. Bear north at Cindy's and pick up the red lights at Dora's, Jackie's, and Billie-May's. If you miss Dixie's, you're in Utah.

Airline Pilot's Joke

Carol and Margaret
and Some Brothels

MOST PEOPLE have felt the tug, the touch of sadness when, leaving a city with its totals of the wonderful and unexplainable, they see how fast a plane can carry them into other worlds. Those who leave Rome are startled that the lands beyond the magic city should be the barren, brown Umbrian Hills. Minutes out of London, one looks down on villages that have horse-drawn wagons, and minutes out of Paris, is the set of a thousand movies —the farmyards, the tranquil geese. The planes that lift out of Las Vegas enter another world fast; it could be the Gobi or the Negev. Five minutes out, one sees unending sage, infinite sand, serried mountain ranges, an infinite nothing. Now the groins, the breasts, the naked girls of the Lido must seem like hallucinations. Here are alkali, cobalt and slag, a world where the sun hitting the creosote brush gets so hot that the leaves give off a faint crackle, where heat makes a shimmer that creates a false infinity. The Dunes nudes, indeed! Below, the roads are ribbons in a gray universe. Still, they are a little different from other roads because, down there, a man in a car can find a whorehouse every twenty-five to fifty miles if he is on the road to Reno. If he is driving 93 to Ely and Salt Lake, the intervals are longer.

25

The houses of the highways are inconspicuous and shabby, sometimes derelict, as befits the grubby poverty of the villages. Some are plank-walled, others are sided with shingles, and all are nondescript. To enter one is to be hit by the immediacy of sex. Most of them have a little bar, and the girls on stools turn to smile when the door opens. As bars go, they are ordinary, with illuminated beer signs, glass-lined packages of pine nuts and sometimes a mounted rabbit head with miniature deer horns. The calendars have nudes that are never pornographic. Inside—places that may show cracked linoleum and dead beetles in corners—they still manage to catch some suggestion of the boudoir, some magic of love, because, though the girls may never be as much as $500 ahead of life, they do buy the exotic aids. They use Joy, Shalimar, Arpege, Chanel, no cheap, acid imitations, and they sit with a man, soft-voiced and agreeable in their Patou and Lanvin imitations.

Two highways head north out of Las Vegas, a great "V" joining Nevada's famous highway 80 further north, and forming the triangle that takes up most of the state. It is the highway triangle that carries most of Nevada's towns and has (excluding Las Vegas) 99 percent of its whores. One highway, 95, goes northwest out of Las Vegas, clings to Nevada's western border, and joins Highway 80 at Reno. The other, 93, heads north, but hugs Nevada's eastern border to join 80 at the tiny town of Wells. The great east-west 80 carries what is certainly the densest per-mile count of whores on earth.

Heading north on 95, the first house is Ash Meadow, which is so far off the road, so lost in its own Death Valley desolation, so hard to reach over miserable roads, that one wonders how men ever find it. But its owners say that they draw from a five hundred mile circle. Its landing strip is used by well-heeled Californians in private planes, who can come and go while their wives think they are on a training flight. A little beyond the Ash Meadows intersection, 95 produces a cluster of tiny houses. Lathrop Wells has nine dwellings, one of which, the Shamrock, offers three girls. Driving on, one crosses the Amargosa desert and, after a time, gets to Beatty, a town no more than three streets wide, whose house on the outskirts is called Fran's Star Ranch. Some sixty miles beyond is another crossroads, the tiny trucker's station called Lida, and not far from it, skulking in tall brush, is the Cotton Tail Ranch. Continuing north, drivers come to the shrunken remembrance of the once booming Tonopah and, perched on a pile of ore tailings, the pleasant bar house called Bobby's.

After Tonopah, few places could match the all-is-lost, windblown sadness of the shacks of Mina, a run of weathered houses spread out along the highway for some three blocks, one of which is the Lucky Strike; depending on season, it may have three girls. Another forty miles raises the sizeable town of Hawthorne which has one house, the Green Front. Then, some twenty-five miles north, is the valley of Nevada's capital, Carson, in whose brushy outskirts there is a considerable change of management, so that its houses may vary between two and four; the more permanent are the Starlight and Moonlight. Beyond Carson comes Reno—death on fixed houses but well served by Joe Conforte, whose Mustang is the first house on east-west 80.

The other highway out of Las Vegas, 93, heads north, and intersects 80, some three hundred forty-five miles east of Reno. It is all desolation, and its houses are few because people are few. Some twenty miles out of Las Vegas, in a desert named after the obscure Pahranagat Indians, are two houses which, despite the distance, get their men from Las Vegas. One is Sheri's, a place of some pretention, and the other, a few miles away, is Betty's Coyote Springs Ranch. Continuing north there are no towns until you reach Ely, sizeable for Nevada, with four thousand people. Its side streets have three houses, the Stardust, the Big Four, and the Green Lantern. Beyond Ely, it is a long one hundred twenty-five miles to Wells, a tiny, windblown town dwarfed by surrounding mountains. But it is quite a crossroads because it also sits astride 80, and its two houses, the Hacienda and Dona's, can be arrived at by either highway. From the California border to Utah, 80 has sixteen towns and some twenty-five houses that have operated through war, peace, pestilence, and plenty.

Joe Conforte, easily the greatest girl-broker in American annals, has hired about twenty-six hundred women since he started. If, to this army, one adds the girls of some twenty-five houses along Highway 80, and if one goes back to the many years of operation by his predecessors, 80 produces a ghostly parade of something like fifteen thousand of what were once called "soiled sisters." On any given weekend, there are about fifteen hundred girls in Las Vegas, most of them birds of passage who may not stay three months. The police estimate implies an annual turnover of something like ten thousand. The figures were lower in the earlier years, of course, but since the start of houses, in the days of President Lincoln, the cumulative total might add up to the population of today's Idaho. To ask a girl, in the year 1860, why she did it, and to ask one today, is to be met by the same thing—a shrug. They don't know. In his more Huxleyish moments, Joe says that in every era there are girls who are more perceptive, more honest, more aware of the hypocrisies, and that these are the clear-minded ones who turn whore. But then he wrecks his syllogism by adding, "Of course, lots of them just like to screw."

Carol Smith is an assumed name. She took it as her whore-house name when she started in Elko, and then changed it again when she married. Carol left a beautiful home in Burlingame, California, to become one of the girls of 80. This makes her somewhat unusual, because few girls come from homes of wealth. Her story is told, not because she is typical—there is no typical whore—but because she remembers the days and the hours as though they were on film. She took her drive along 80 in 1965, in the first faint dawn of the sexual revolution, and her approach to Nevada started with a near arrest.

She was wheeling down the beautiful canyon that opens out of the Sierras into Reno when she was spotted by police. Two patrolmen had been parked back in the pines when they saw her go by in a car fitting a description from the California police, a red Jaguar convertible with big tires. They touched the siren off and reached her just as she was slowing down for the city limits.

But Carol had cards to prove she owned the Jaguar. She was seventeen years old and of legal driving age. "She was gorgeous," Officer Jennings remembers, "like a damned shampoo ad." He stared at her youth. "Your tires are pretty smooth, Miss, and you were going too fast for those curves. I should give you a ticket."

He saw the worry in the blue eyes. "But your dad will maybe raise hell? You take it easy if I let you go?"

Demurely, Carol said, "Cross my heart."

He was about to wave her on when he had a thought. "You all right? Going far?" "I don't know," she said brightly. "My first stop is Joe's." It didn't tell Jennings anything. He knew of no taco bar, no pizza hut named Joe's. "Joe Conforte," she explained.

Jennings was no innocent: years on the force had given him some new facet of the sex thing almost every week. There were the complaints on incest, the calls on rape—which some assistant D.A. would not take seriously unless the gal was so beat up that there could be no question of teasing or consent—and there was the sadism which got you into the damndest man-wife refereeing. Cops saw a lot of sexual invention, but Jennings still could not believe that seventeen-year-olds were ringing the bell at Joe's. He was still figuring it out when the red car was lost down the road.

Carol drove some three hundred miles beyond the point where she was stopped, barely pausing in Reno. She had a sandwich at Dennys, avoiding the hotels because she had been told that Reno is tough, and hell on prostitutes. On the freeway she held to the right to catch the turnoff for Joe's, the place which Joe Conforte has made the most publicized house of modern times. Joe was nowhere around when she arrived. She passed through the parlor where girls do the lineup, and into the kitchen. Five girls in bikinis sat at the long table eating, intent on their plates, without laughter or talk. She saw the other table where, day and night, the girls make their written entries on the chart, a time-and-money code for the services they are about to perform. In this all-purpose room a kindly Negro cook told Carol they weren't hiring that week. As Carol left, she glanced back at the girls. She had a sudden feeling that a lot of what she'd heard about Nevada was wrong.

A half-hour beyond Joe's, Nevada goes unbelievably desolate: 80 runs through a sage greyness where even the occasional ranch can look abandoned. Carol stopped for gas in tiny Lovelock. She looked around, struck by the silence. A dog slept on a sidewalk.

Where a store broke the line of one-story buildings, it became two stories. Yet tiny Lovelock, she had been told, had two houses, and destiny might just see her wind up here. She was headed for Elko and hadn't thought of any other town, but she stopped now, curious to see whether anything could be as stark as Joe's.

She knows now that few girls arriving in these towns ask directions. Most of them know where they are going, and have been given explicit directions by someone. But Carol had had no coaching, so she asked a taxi driver, one of three in the little town. He stared at her, at her car, then back to her, and shook his head. He told her how to find the street, and drove off.

This place was entered through a bar and was as plain as Joe's had been. It was when she asked for the gentleman who ran the place that the lady bartender smiled. "Honey, these places is all run by dames, exceptin', of course, for Joe, down the road." Carol learned it was true; some twenty-five houses on 80, and all except two in Nevada, were the worlds of women. Back home, hearing about Las Vegas, about girls who marry casino giants, of Conforte girls who wind up owning apartments, she had assumed the owners were men. She had no idea that Joe was unique, almost alone on his own pinnacle, and that there is something about a houseful of girls, in twelve-hour shifts of cunnilingus, fellatio, coitus, with every possible variation, that demands the compassion, the how-to-deal-with-everything ability of a woman.

The Lovelock cottage was owned by a lady we'll call "Ruby," who had no interest in hiring Carol, whom she spotted right away as a beautiful, problem-causing amateur. "Hell, these kids rassle a few guys and figure they can take the beating of this business." But the kids kept coming, and Ruby tried to let them down easy. "You know, sweetie," she told Carol, "there's no way you can get in if you're a minor. And them damn phony driver's licenses you kids buy! Not worth a damn here. Tell me, you done it? You sure this is what you want to do?" Carol said yes, which settled it for Ruby. So many of them lied. Of course, you would have a magnet hiring a gorgeous young thing that looked untouched, something right out of a movie lot, but men could lose enchantment fast in the back rooms, when the little beauties went scared or drew some line. "Honey, these places don't fool around. You do everything? You French?" Carol had begun to realize that the California she had just left, though pretty gooey with sex, was still far from this. She had puzzled Ruby because, when asked why she wanted to go into the business, Carol had not offered any of the usual explanations. She said she didn't know. Which leads us to the discoveries of Julien Vestergaard, a veteran editor on Highway 80, that the girls themselves don't know.

Of all the towns that are strung along Nevada's Highway 80, those that have more than fifteen hundred souls have at least one whorehouse, and two towns, Elko and Winnemucca, have as many as seven each. Elko sits alone on its own summit, with seven houses and two newspapers. Of some forty houses in Nevada, about twenty-two fall into what Vestergaard calls the "category of higher amiability," that is, "bar joints." They are houses whose business, while not entirely flesh, in terms of income are about seventy percent flesh. In these, a man can walk in, buy a drink, brood over it alone, or he can be joined by a girl or two, where they discuss things as uncarnal as Congress. They can talk through one glass or ten. These stand apart from "parlor houses," and the difference is vast.

The biggest house in Nevada, Joe Conforte's Mustang, on Highway 80, is a parlor house. A man entering it, or any parlor house, slams into the crisis of immediate decision, the realization that he is supposed to have his clothes off and be palpating any two of four to sixty breasts facing him, and this within minutes. For in a parlor house every available girl lines up on the signal that the door is opening. The man who enters, who may stand frozen and undecided on the threshold, will stare at the line of girls in bikinis, who stare back at him, each wondering if he will choose her. But a man who enters a bar house need not reach the rear at all. On entering, he may cover his shyness, or his newness to whorehouses, or any of a dozen sexual blocks by first going to the bar.

It gives him time. The girls sitting around will smile and, if he is in the great pattern, he will ask one or several if he may buy them a drink. The bar houses are more civilized. They allow a man and a girl to start by talking. And because the house is making money, sometimes more than if the man reached the rear, there is no pressure to get him there, no push to get him onto the chenille bedspreads.

Over the years, the editors along 80 have learned that there can be few secrets in small towns. No prominent local dares take a girl in back unless he is willing to have his moment become known to everyone. But it is safe for local men to visit the places, if they stay in front and buy a few rounds to show good will. Most editors have been in them countless times, sometimes reluctantly, when they must play guide for visitors. To Vestergaard, who has been interviewed by men from the *London Times, New York Times,* and the *Frankfurter Zeitung,* by writers from *Figaro, Time,* and *Life,* the remarkable fact is that so many writers have the same curiosity as other men. They seen eternally fascinated with the question, *why does a girl do it?*

"Somewhere, sometime," says the editor, "maybe in the Carthage of Hannibal, maybe in the Mycenae of Homer, a man first asked it. 'What's a nice girl like you doing in a place like this?' showing surprise that a girl can be both lovely and a whore. In a hundred versions it is still asked. It is a compulsive opener, when buying a girl a drink, an ice-breaker that shows shock and a desire to be nice. It is the innocent gaucherie, a poorly concealed regret that the girl should be a whore and yet so like the girl she ought to be. The girls don't get mad because the insult is kindly meant, something like the man who says, 'Gee, you don't look like a Jew or an Italian.' Most girls will look beyond the language to the clumsy kindness and let it go."

But asking a girl what she's doing in a whorehouse can be irritating, as it was to one girl who is still remembered in Ellie's, in Elko. Figuring the man who questioned her for only beer, she answered, "Well, we fuck mostly, but there's days when it's Frenching from morning 'til night." After four thousand years of hearing about prostitution, and with the whores of Times Square outnumbering cab drivers, men can't hide their shock. They still want to know why girls get into it.

Carol walked into Ellie's around five in the afternoon. Like most of the houses in Nevada, it was not designed for its present

business. Someone had put up the three-bedroom stucco bunga-
low in the era of Taft and it was showing age when the first of
several madams took over. Now, under Ellie, it could handle
twenty men at a time, in the rooms and at the bar, but poorly,
because it was tight. A girl wanting to get into one of the two
bathrooms with the pan and soap needed after the "check" might
find she was second or third in line. The houses need private
entrances and they have them. In Ellie's, it was the back door off
the kitchen. It served for deliveries and, as Ellie told the police,
was something of a problem to burglars because they'd have to
fight their way past a defense of garbage cans.

Several men looked up as Carol came in the front door. Ellie,
recognizing a job-seeker, motioned Carol toward a closed door. It
served as her bedroom and office. She was not encouraging. "You
looking for a job, kid?"

"Yes, I was hoping . . ."

Ellie didn't let her finish, "Jesus another Ann-Margret." Carol
winced. She had been told often enough that she was a double for
the actress. To Ellie, these doubles were rather pathetic. "Christ,
this must make the fourth or fifth Ann-Margret this year. All over
the country is these girls who get a hometown rep for looking like
somebody, Elizabeth Taylor, Audrey Hepburn, Raquel Welch.
Some of them go to Hollywood and find out it's no dice: the
resemblance kills any chance of acting. There's these others who
get the idea they'd be a sensation in a house. They come in, complete with three wigs." Along 80, reaction to doubles is mixed.
Some madams turn them down, possibly because they want no
more laughs than their houses are already getting. Some will hire
a double, reasoning that the world has so many ordinary guys who
can never hope to get near Hollywood's or TV's famous ladies,
that it's smart to give them the chance to ravish a celebrity for
twenty dollars. Ellie had hired Grace Kellys, Jackie Kennedys,
and one Tricia Nixon. She patted Carol, "Well, honey, I wouldn't
let that matter, the real problem is you're too young."

"Ellie" is a pseudonym. She came from a town north of Stock-
holm, which she remembers as silent and depressing, a place of
long winters, her home a place where the gramophone always
seemed to play the somber stuff of Grieg and Beethoven. Her par-

ents, middle-class and comfortable, had a disenchantment with life that pervaded the household. Ellie, with little schooling, was pretty sure that life was meaningless, without logic or pattern, certainly without justice, and she had come to believe this without knowing about the scores of writers who try to convey the same idea in books. She didn't read. Landing in Hoboken, amid the squalor of the New Jersey waterfront, she became a hooker within a year. As with many such girls, there had come the day when, "Out of maybe two thousand guys you've fucked or sucked, you do it with one guy who seems special. You know, friendship. So there's a lot of talk and, Christ, you even talk of love. He goes on about forgiveness and understanding and you get married. Then, bam! First time he's drunk comes the crap; he can't forget." In the dreary room, in the New Jersey tenement, this meant drunken nights when, dependably, her man would go into his "once-a-whore-always-a-whore." She left him and fell into what is called the "hooker's cycle." This is a succession of moods in which, one day, the profession seems as good as any other, and on another, unbearably degrading. The girl leaves it to try something else; like serving table or driving a school bus, but finds that integrity at $65 or $80 a week is grim too. So she returns to the business.

By the time she was thirty, Ellie was firmly convinced that life was futile, that it was impossibly hard to make a living, and insane to think in terms of luxury. She remembers alcoholic talks with friends when it seemed Socialism might be the answer. The system was cruddy because it applauded the bastards. Few people were kind. In her case the system seemed to have a ceiling; never a job that paid more than $3 an hour. By the time she had drifted west to Denver, to different bars now, servicing men whose leather jackets smelled of sheep rather than coal smoke, she knew one thing. She would stay in the business, but not use her own body. She would get girls. To sell the body was the final low, like those bums in Hoboken, those derelicts who would travel all the way to Saint Elizabeth's Hospital in Manhattan to stick out an arm and sell their blood.

The autumn when she met Carol, Ellie was pushing forty, and

was known to thousands of men in Nevada. She was "Ellie" to
both of Nevada's United States senators, to many state senators, to
its governor, to county commissioners, judges and police. She
knew them as occasional visitors, men who would come in to buy
a drink, and some, with elaborate secrecy, to have a girl. Virtually
every politician would look in before election time to show that he
was urbane and tolerant and to accept any help Ellie might give
them. To Elko's banks and merchants she was top credit. She was
known to most of the men of the town, and particularly to some
fathers to whom she had spoken about their sons. The town's
women were harder to know. There were two wives who had
approached her, both a little drunk. They had asked, with some
indirection, whether they might sneak into her place for one
night. One had developed hate for a husband who was playing
around, and the other had thought she might indulge an old
secret yen; have four or five men in a marathon without going all
the way to those distant Sodoms of hearsay, San Francisco or Los
Angeles.

Ellie was only one of several madams in Elko; though she knew
the others, she did not trade many secrets with them. Like all
madams, Ellie was in good ecological adjustment with her town.
She knew what was expected by Nevada tradition, by customs as
clear and settled as if they were law; what was expected by the
city police, the highway patrol, and what was understood by the
county commissioners. She knew how to seem humble, particularly
to the church people. She could handle the unexpected; the local
man who might get carried away at the bar—she would get him
home: she had a way with the high school boy who was too
young to be served but who would come anyway, usually when
some cutie-pie had been with him in the back seat of a car, leaving him with an aching groin and nothing to show except a girl
scent on his hand. Most boys she turned away with a friendly pat.
A few she sent to the cottage of a waitress who would allow herself to be seduced, a woman who was careful not to discuss money
and who would look to Ellie for payment later.

Carol had bothered Ellie. The lovely girl had come in, polite,
mannerly, unsure; one of those who come along now and then to
make you wonder whether you have really seen everything in the

business. As a general thing, Ellie didn't think much of her girls. She had dealt with several hundred, God knows, and her fifteen-year memory was of creatures who weren't too bright. They tended to be dull. And some you had to turn down, because they were so ignorant that the legal possibilities scared you. What attorney could help you if some sadist bit the nipple off of a girl who was a minor? Ellie knew, of course, that for many girls whoring was an easy settlement of problems, girls selling, literally, the only thing they had. She would sometimes stare at them as they sat at the bar, feeling both sympathy and contempt. That the girls would take so much customer abuse, accept the claustrophobia, live in the little pens, docile as rabbits, as isolated as nuns, she could not understand. Some were easy to hate. "Take a girl who's dumb, real stupid, but who's gentle and kind and, well, its' just sad, but take one who's dumb and mean, you get rid of her fast. You see, to fight the boredom they keep busy, get as many customers as possible; fuck to fight boredom, really, and they get into these weird situations which nobody on the outside would believe. Like this little Darlene. She was here maybe six months. Darlene was only medium-pretty, but she was peaches and cream, and she had this fantastic mouth—men called it voluptuous. In back, Darlene's work was almost all the one thing. But then afterwards, instead of Lavoris or Listerine, she found that what she wanted was a Hershey bar. Christ!" Ellie could not get over it. Darlene had put on thirty pounds in ten months, had become a mass of swollen curves like a Kewpie doll.

Ellie had an old, recurring reverie that she turned off because it was so absurd. But it kept coming back. It was such a lovely way of becoming really rich. There was this insurance man, the one who had the business in Sacramento, and who would make the long drives to Elko every few months. He liked to sit with Ellie and talk, happy to buy drinks for anyone around. Sometimes he would not reach the back at all, and he would leave after giving every girl a ten or twenty. They became friends. Ellie knew that he was building up to something, and waited. One day he asked her to take a drive and told her about his dream. He wanted girls, but a special kind. He had a hidden yearning for young things, beautiful and innocent. "Quite honestly," he said, "these little dolls you see coming out of junior high. Ellie, they are the girls who, for a man my age, are out of reach, even to talk to." Ellie only half-listened. The man had described what was one of the best hidden yens of millions of men, the hunger for a "Lolita." If she could only manage it, if she could get around the toughest of laws, get lovely, teenage kids—twelve to sixteen years—God! It would be like selling Cadillacs for a hundred bucks. She could set the price at $100 minimum, and there would even be buyers at $500. For every kid she could recruit there would be a hundred buyers. The demand would give you a business as big as you cared to handle. If ever the time came when the country relaxed on this, when the laws weren't so violent, she would say goodbye to the $10 and $20 business of the highway and set up in a city. She would deal with men to whom money didn't matter, or for that matter, even the poor ones, who would still hock their furniture to have a Lolita. Maybe it would come some day, such an open market, but not in her time. The country still considered corruption of a minor in the same category as murder. The little fifteen-year-old angels might be in their second go with gonorrhea, but the law said *no*. Handling junior high cuties was a fast way to make the women's ward. "Well," said the Sacramento man, "if you ever have one come in for a job, you might give me a call." Carol was pushing eighteen and was too old to be a Lolita, but she had the look. The Sacramento man would probably have paid $1,000 to have her for a week. But that would be inter-state business, and to hell with that. "Hell," says Ellie, "there's such a thing as being ahead of your time."

Outside it was getting dark. Elko is like most desert towns. Night brings almost total silence, and virtually every house fights it with radio or TV. Ellie didn't want Carol going to a hotel because a girl that green could find trouble fast. "Come on," she said, and led the way to the kitchen. Ellie could turn off reality by cooking a stew the way some people might open a bottle. As she breaded pork chops, she put Carol to work peeling potatoes. Around seven, when the girls had been called to supper, Ellie robbed her bar of a bottle of sherry and took Carol to her own quarters. When the bottle was empty, she knew a lot about the beautiful applicant. She told Carol to think things over for a few days. Then, if she were really determined, "Well, you put that damn fire engine in storage—don't sell it yet—get yourself a driver's license, and you come back."

Carol explained that she had a driver's license.

"Not one I seen," Ellie said. "The one I see has to show you're eighteen. There's a bartender over in Reno, here's his name. You go talk to him and you'll have a driver's license. Then, if you still want to do it, we'll see. Tonight, I'm sending you to a rooming house I know."

Carol was back in Elko in a few days, coming this time by bus, and she had gotten the driver's license. Ellie led Carol to the rear. "With the pros you get to the point on everything, but with the beginners you don't try to crowd a lifetime into one night." She explained that, for a few nights, Carol would not have to take on every man who wanted her. She showed Carol how to stall. When she had a man who was beginning to press, and whom she didn't want, she should ask whoever was tending bar for an aspirin. "You get a headache fast," said Ellie, "and go to your room." If you had a man you wanted, you made sure he understood about price. Ellie did not have the complicated scale invented by Conforte. In her place it was ten dollars straight and fifteen for half-and-half; she offered only a few variations. The girls collected the money just before, and took it to Ellie or Minerva, the maid, in breaks between customers. "If a guy hands you a twenty and has change coming, give it to him right away." There was no holdback against possible extra services. If, afterwards, he showed signs of wanting to sleep awhile, and go again, he should understand it could be expensive. "Now then, Joe, over in Mustang, he goes in for the way-out stuff: movies, two girls, putting on a show with the customer watching. We don't go for that here, so you don't have to worry. We do go for doubles, but no sweat about what girls you like or can't stand, I mean to go down on, or have them go down on you. You do only what you want. Now about the check, I'm sure you don't know a damn thing about that either?"

"No."

"Well, it's squeezing mostly." Ellie explained it, and Carol had a fleeting wish that she could get into the Jaguar and drive away. She asked, "But doesn't this check embarrass them?"

Ellie considered. "Yes, to some of them it's embarrassing, especially if he don't check out. But there's those who've had it done so many times they actually get worked up by it, get hard as a rock."

On her first night, Carol took advantage of her leeway and managed to remain aloof. She saw what seemed to be a lot of unwashed men at the bar, and she went to her room. The other girls smiled as they remembered how beginners can be. Around midnight, however, Carol asked for a glass of straight vodka and had her first man. She remembers her first, as do many pros. He was better dressed than the usual run, a passing easterner. He kept her at the bar an hour, studied her, and after a while, said, "I'd rather you didn't lie, there's no point, really, but aren't you new to this?"

"You're my very first." He was stunned. "Ask Ellie, ask anyone." Three hours later, he told her he wanted to marry her. The night cost him something like $100.

Carol's seventeen years were spent in the California house where she was born. It was a house with status, even in the rich Palo Alto area, and real estate men coded it as "$200,000 upwards." Her father died when Carol was only two. His widow, Laura, was left with a small child and a considerable estate. Laura was young, beautiful, and giddy, insistently aware of sex. Her circle of friends ran to the same pattern; money, parties, drinking, sexing. It was not long before she remarried. Her new husband was the colorful David Bruce, a handsome, woman-chasing man who ran an insurance business, but his real interest lay in the after-hours life of the peninsula. David went into a pattern of sexual assault on his beautiful wife, livened by partying and a run of girls on the side. He seemed to find his wife attractive only when he was drunk.

By the time girls reach the age of twelve, they have a pretty good sense of the sexual practices of their parents. Carol knew that her stepfather could be counted on, after imbibing heavily, to drag her laughing mother upstairs where they indulged in sexual excesses they barely tried to disguise from the child. Afterwards, Dave would sit through his wife's chatter as if she were not there. During this period, Carol was left alone a good deal. When her parents went to Paris, one year, they made the happy discovery of French creativity in sex. That was when Laura and David coined the word, "Rodin." For years, art students had been intrigued by Rodin's statue of the two nudes in their chaste kiss. Apparently, Rodin was easy to imitate because the Paris shops featured fine "Rodins," right from the student garrets, all displaying various twists on love; they had miniatures of a stallion mounting a mare, and one, so common it must have been the graduating test, of a moronic stallion belaboring a cow. Laura brought home a statuette and kept it hidden. One night, Carol, hearing the screams of laughter at a dinner party, came down to see what it was all about. She carefully kept out of sight, and while she could not make out what the adults were passing around, she did see where her mother hid what seemed to be a small object. Later, she tiptoed down the stairs and went to the linen closet. She stared down at two bronze bodies; a woman lying on a chaise longue, and a man whose head was lost between her thighs. Sometimes, when they were all sunning themselves at the pool, David would ogle his bikinied Laura, smile fatuously, and say, "Honey, I'm Rodin-y as hell."

As far back as she could remember, life had picked up and brightened with the arrival of her Uncle Bart. Every few months, when the mud-spattered, white Cadillac pulled up, there would be laughter and stories, and the exciting pictures her uncle painted of his ranch country. Bart owned some shares in one of the few big ranches of Nevada, dividing his time between the ranch and some vague mining deals, which must have done well, because her parents said he was rich. After months at the ranch, he would suddenly get an impulse and take off for New York, Paris, or the Mediterranean. Carol loved to hear his stories of famous people, his drives in France, where he declared the French make better pasta than the Italians. Almost anything he did or saw became exciting to Carol.

The Bruces teased him a lot because he was a bachelor. They would observe that his Cadillac passed the towns of possibly two hundred girls every time he drove to Reno. Carol knew about the houses when she was ten, and when she was fifteen, her uncle grudgingly agreed to talk about them in front of her. He insisted he frequented only the bars, where men could drink without sin. Carol thought of Nevada as a romantic state, with its deserts, its lost mines—all of it dotted, apparently, with these little houses.

With Bart gone, Carol's loneliness grew worse. There were times, of course, when her family seemed normal, with dinner on the table, and all three present. David would talk about his business, the money they were making, and even make plans for the future. But it was as though neither of them could stand normalcy for long. By evening, the house would sound like a tavern. People would arrive in droves, and there would be a sudden rush to someone's party, the club, a dance.

There were some good times in high school: it seemed as though every kid had a car, and there was much rushing around to beach parties or, maybe, to supper in the hills. She knew girls who were as alone as she was, and she had the bad luck to run into an unusual number of bright, bitter, young analysts in high school, boys who were cynical, and in constant challenge; they were forever trying to show that life was grotesque, ridiculous. The pretty world of Burlingame was going through something of a Camus cult, students who thought the pessimistic Frenchman was right, that life was not worth the long try. When she was fourteen, she got it from the brother of a girl she knew. He had taken her for a drive to Pebble Beach, talking most of the way. "It's all so crappy," he said bluntly, "the same things that create life make piss."

In 1964, when she was a senior in high school, the percentage of girls who slept with boys was said to be 50 percent. Most such girls paid for it with a special status. Some might have known ten or twenty boys intimately; a few already had the sex routine of the married. Carol felt the usual pressure; the need to have dates, the imperatives of making so-and so's party, the games, the dances, the beach affairs, finding a boy who did not hassle you, or going with one who automatically assumed you gave. She could not lean on the argument that girls don't do it. You woke up mornings thinking of the game in Berkeley, the trip to the beach, who'd be going with whom, which often meant who would sleep with whom, what country house or motel, what back seat, what station wagon or sleeping bag. The few times she had tried to discuss these things with her mother were a disaster. Laura's put-offs were puerile homilies, "Don't bother your pretty head, dear, you'll find a nice boy and marry." "Fine," thought Carol. "After my second pregnancy or my fifth?"

The last week had been the buildup to graduating; everything exciting, with hope lying in every ring of the phone. Everyone had plans: some girls were going to Switzerland, some backpacking to Yosemite. There was the comparing of colleges and, what are you wearing for graduation? The Bruces, for once, had shown some understanding. "Darling," said Laura, "It's so important. Now you just sit down with those catalogues and decide what college you want to go to." That evening, going upstairs, she passed her parents' bedroom. The door was wide open, and the five-second exposure imprinted itself on her mind; David, sprawled in an armchair, and her mother's blond head lost between his knees. Carol packed in a few minutes and was on the freeway within a half-hour. She didn't stop until she was high in the Sierras. Why she headed her car into Nevada, she could not explain. In the stretches between the Nevada towns, she wondered why she had not thought of confiding in someone; there were several boys who had given signs that they would like to marry her. In speaking about it later, she admits she cannot explain her motives and that she has conflicting feelings about why she left. Part of it was the undeniable impulse to push Laura's blond head out of the way....

That night, lying on the bed, feeling the ridges of the chenille on her back, she thought of her first hour with its fear, nervousness and the hidden pleasure she got from the man's lavish tongue; his ecstasy, which he seemed to confuse with love, when he told her how wonderful she was. Once, he proposed that they dress and leave, forget this, and get married. "My God!" she smiled ironically. "My first man, a talkative cunnilinguist." She saw what had not hit her before—that sex was funny. It was what she had felt talking to the first two girls she had met, Annie and Fay, girls who were not too bright, but who laughed a lot and saw all the groaning, the agony, the ecstasy, as funny. Men were slaves to (what in the world was the plural of penis, penii?); anyway, they were slaves. They would do things they knew were ridiculous, but do them because it was beyond their power to stop.

Carol had read enough to recognize her neurosis. Her mind was dominated by a single theme—she saw every man as he would look in a hunched position, the coital crouch. She would leaf through a movie magazine or *Newsweek*, and see every pictured man on his elbows and knees. She had not got into it willfully. Her fixation had moved in when she had experienced her first trauma in the back bedrooms.

Most girls remember some first shock. It varies enormously from girl to girl. Whatever their earlier experiences, whatever their callousness, the first day could cause some to vomit and some to quit. For some, it was the need to wash a man. For some, it was the order to go down in her first hour for any male who entered, and the sudden realization that she had lost all choice. In Ellie's, accident made Carol a spectator, spending a rather passive half-hour in a room with a man and another girl. And while the houses would live in her mind for the fantastic inventiveness of people on a bed, the variety of things that thrill different men, the biggest surprise was not the occasional violence, not the occasional orgiastic wildness, but the ugliness.

The girls, she learned, fall into patterns of what they prefer, and when the man himself is undecided, the girls end up with their own preferences. A favorite, if the man agreed to the cost, was the double, an affair with two girls. Girls liked it because it meant more money for each one and, generally, less work. But the unexpected result for Carol was the many times she saw men from a position that was above and behind.

Talking to Ellie one day, she observed that lovemaking did not show man at his best. Ellie laughed, "Honey, you know, when they do portraits of presidents, they show them at a desk, or if it's athletes, maybe holding a football. But no artist ever done a man humping. You know, actually, it's ridiculous for animals, too. Take chickens. Christ, the rooster gets completely on top, not part off and part on, but on top, and he keeps falling off. To hold the hen still, he bites her on the comb; son-of-a-bitch is cruel as hell. I never see a rooster screwing that I don't want to grab a stick and take his head off. Sadistic, bites her comb so hard it can bleed. And bulls? They heave and wobble up on their hind legs, they stagger and lose balance, trying to keep up with a cow; she's got good traction because she's on four legs, but the bull, he's got to keep up on two." But even that, Ellie concluded, was not quite so silly as men. "They don't look bad on a horse, and they can be OK on a diving board, but when they have to make a bridge, up on their elbows and knees, well, you walk in on him, and see him from above and behind, Christ!" Carol knew.

On her second day, she was at the bar with a man, a local, who apparently did not want to go in back, who wanted to drink with someone who would listen to him talk. It was while she was with him that the other man came in. He looked around, looked at Carol, assumed she was taken, and nodded to another girl, Millie. But he kept glancing at Carol, and it was clear that he would have preferred her. Carol describes him as young, tall, nice looking, but not athletic; with his clothes off, he had a fat, roly-poly, non-muscular build. She would get to know him as a repeat customer, a man who came every few weeks all the way from Provo, Utah. That day he had gone in back, and was making love to Millie in an unhurried way, when Millie had a thought. "Sweetie, I seen you looking at Carol. Now maybe you'd like to have a party with her too. She's a gorgeous dish, and me, I'm not jealous." The Provo boy had never had two girls before. "Let's go," he said, without asking about price. The money was Millie's purpose, since the price for each girl was $25 minimum as against $10 for a single. Millie had gone to the door, opened it a crack, and told a maid to tell Ellie the guy was going for two, and that they wanted Carol. For Ellie, who was tending bar, this was no problem. She poured a drink for Carol's man. She was sure he wouldn't mind if Carol left him for a while. The man was propelled into instant politeness, "Oh sure, I got to be going anyway." He left, and Carol went to room C.

They were waiting, side by side, the experienced Millie keeping up his fever with a slow manipulation of her hand, the man clearly in the controlled wildness which, while it lasted, would have him in that transport where the wildest act carries no shame. The man's first knowledge of two girls pushed him into a frenzy that ended everything in minutes, a short delirium that left him gasping like a man recovering from sickness. He got up, with no interest in the short convalescence that some men want. What he did want, like thousands of others, was nowhere available on

Highway 80—a shower. The veteran Millie supplied the last service, an affectionate once-over-lightly with washcloth, before the man, wrung out and anxious to leave, brushed her away, and buttoned his pants.

It led to the girls saying that Carol was great for doubles, not for what she had done, which was little enough, but because of her indifference to money. In Ellie's, the double was theoretically an equal affair, with the $50 fee split evenly, but it could lead to problems. Often, though two girls were chosen at the same time, one might become something of a stage manager, thinking up the best ideas, and even being the main performer. The girl could argue that it was she who had done the most. Ellie tried to cut such arguments short with no-nonsense rules as to who got what. But while she might silence bickering, she could not stop the pouting. Doubling could lead to accusations that so-and-so was a chiseling bitch. It was Millie's idea that, as salesman and main performer, $35 of the $50 should be hers, and to her delight, she found that Carol could not care less. With money, Carol had the indifference of habit; a knowledge she had had since she was ten, that on reaching twenty-one, she would come into the estate left by her father. She knew that a phone call could get her anything she needed. So the story went through Ellie's that the new kid was not only nice, but loaded, and while the shy little beauty pulled her share of tricks, she wouldn't compete. Carol became the girl to be called when a man was talked into a double.

The girls of 80 don't think much of writers, and neither do those of 95, or 93, or those in Las Vegas. They see the typewriter guys as men who find $100 mind-boggling, and no girl remembers a reporter doing what a trucker will do, hand a girl a twenty at the bar and tell her to go buy something. "Matter of fact," says Ellie, "the writing creeps are inclined the other way. They feel that since they are writing about your place, making it immortal or something, the booze should be on the house." She remembers writers who weren't writers, pushy lads who got hold of a card from the *New York Times* or *Reader's Digest*, and persuaded madams to let them interview the girls. "They ask a million questions and then they leave, and that's the end of that. Even when the writers are genuine, they hold that mike up to you for days, thank you and leave, and then, whatever the reason, no article. Besides, after a girl has talked to hundreds of customers, she can tell when a man is talking sex for kicks. There's giveaways that show when he talks about erections and orgasms just to get a bang from the words. The girls lose all respect when they realize they're with some writer who's putting on the intellectual front, talking all the sociological crap, just as an excuse to corner a girl. 'Now then, Miss Lola, you say the last time you had an orgasm was when you were thinking about your father? Now, can you explain . . .?' " Ellie concludes, "You know, writers can be sort of oh, shit." Still, now and then, she had to endure them. She would get a call from a sheriff or a county commissioner: some reporter was dying to do a story and would like to have the freedom of the house: he promised to disguise all names. Ellie had let them talk her into it a few times, something that was unpleasant for herself and the girls. But she refused to give them the freedom of the house and managed to see that reporters talked only to girls she selected. She warned the girls to steer away from talk of money, because you could never tell who was a plant of the IRS. Ellie hated the days when a reporter was sitting around, but it could be funny, too, like the time she turned the reporter over to Betty Jo.

Betty was a veteran of twenty-eight who looked twenty, and was pretty even in her bad moments. When dressed and ready to leave for her time off, she could be the girl in the soap commercial waiting for her beau. The girls knew that Betty had spent a couple of years in some university and that she read a lot. Also, they had discovered that she was an inventive bitch. When Betty was in the mood, elbow to elbow with a customer at the bar, prompting him into another round every few minutes, other girls liked to listen in because Betty, talking about her past, was straight *Tobacco Road*.

"How did I get into it?" she would say in a soft voice. "Well, I had no choice really."

"How's that?"

"My step-daddy. I guess I wasn't no more than fifteen: you see, we lived in this little farm, way off from everything. My uncle was out working on the highway all day, and no one was home, exceptin' for dad and me, of course. My mother, well, after she washed things and made the beds, she was off, drivin' the pickup to town. She worked in the textile mill, rayon, and like that. So that left me alone with my dad, my step-dad, really. He worked the farm but he was in the house a lot, and well. . . ." Betty Jo almost believed her own stories. With a customer listening, she would recreate the hot, steamy afternoons of the magnolia country outside Mobile. Her stepfather bought her secret gifts; he would take her for drives: they would sneak off to movies; he kissed her a lot. Then one day, a hot afternoon, naturally, her father had come into her room and found her sleeping wearing only a pajama top. He had sat on the edge of the bed, and Betty said she was actually sorry for him. The summer was a long one; things got bad when she began to swell. They finally placed Betty in a home for unwed mothers that was recommended by the Salvation Army man. Sometimes, the man at the bar would ask, "What happened to the baby?" Here, Ellie and the girls would have to bite down hard, because depending on her mood, Betty's baby had been given to well-meaning folks from Mobile all the way to New Orleans. "Anyway," Betty would say, "I never went back. I got jobs, and every new job, some boss wants to make babies. I'm nice to a few of them, and then I say to hell with that, and I start making them pay. I still write to my mom, but my dad, well, he took off after a while. Maybe my mom finally took the shotgun down off the wall. I think he was beginning to fool with my sister. She was coming on to twelve herself, and the kid had boobs like this," and Betty would pull back her bikini bra.

Carol, thinking about Betty, was sure that many girls experienced incest at home. Even though Betty had found that her story was fun, a school burlesque of *The Long Hot Summer*, the fact remained that many girls did come from houses where incest was the family secret. Why doubt it in girls, so many of whom had been lesbians before drifting into the business? Why doubt anybody's story when she had stepped so casually into her own kind of incest?

Carol stayed five months in Elko, and from that convulsive time, days that never ended—the middle-aged man who fainted while being frenched, a man who kept calling his wife's name as the frenzy increased—days that produced every sexual style— her central memory was of the girls: so casual about sex that they didn't see anything as abnormal. They accepted things; they did not recognize the word "abnormal." They were almost totally tolerant.

In Ellie's, for example, you were on the chenille beds on-and-off for ten hours before, finally, your day was over. At two or three in the morning, when the men had stopped coming, you went to the kitchen, had something to eat, then went to bed. But to a bed that you had used ten or fifteen times since noon, a bed that never saw the hand of a maid, a bed which you made different by pulling off the spread, a bed you made a little your own by getting into sheets that had not been used and were free of sperm. In Ellie's the spreads were kept on during working hours. This little touch of fastidiousness was the point which, when Carol made it to a psychiatrist years later, had the man muttering. "Imagine," he said, "that this should be the thing that became important when you went to bed." She had gone to the psychiatrist, at the urging of her Uncle Bart, after Bart himself had spent weeks in his unhappy attempt to find out why Carol went whore, why any girl does. For Bart had come to Ellie's and taken her away.

On the morning after her flight from Burlingame, Carol felt that Laura would certainly call the police. She had not left a note, and any of the police cruisers on the road could wave her down. In the Sierra town of Colfax she decided to call her mother. Laura was in a state, already into her sherry flips at nine in the morning, confused and petulant. But she had not been too hard to handle. Carol told her that she wanted to get away, that she was nervous, and that she needed to think things out. She said she might look for a job. She threw her mother off by saying that she was driving to Oregon. She would phone again and write.

Her story had worked with Laura and had barely interested Dave. The only person who was really concerned was her Uncle Bart. The disappearance of the girl from the house had him baffled. He kept calling from his ranch to ask if there had been any letters. After five months, he called in detectives. Blond girls in Jaguars leave a trail. The detective traced her to Reno in two days and then, working the gas stations, traced the car to Elko, where he lost it. By the fourth day, he found the car in a Reno garage. He found his hunch hard to accept. This girl type should be off with some boy, in some resort town, maybe the French Riviera, maybe beach-bumming in Hawaii. But the leads said "80." The detective, who had memorized Carol's face from photographs, thought it might take a bit of drinking to do all the stops on 80. He asked for another man. They worked the highway, and one of them went to Ellie's. He had been at the bar a half-hour when Carol came on shift. One look was enough. The men reported to Bart, whose first reaction was to go on a long drunk. He considered going to Ellie's, but decided against it. Finally, he decided on a letter. In it, Bart begged his niece to meet him at the Stockmen's, Elko's main hotel.

To Carol, Bart was a surprise. The man crossing the lobby was now a well-dressed easterner. She felt a sudden warmth that this distinguished man, the closest thing she had to a father, was, apparently, the only person on earth who gave a damn about her. "But the poor man hesitated," she said. "There he was, dressed like a banker, and so worried. Didn't know whether to kiss me or not."

On his part, Bart had no idea how to handle a niece-prostitute. His idea of a whore was a girl who came from a vaguely horrible background—slum families, or Okie families—girls who went whore for money. He thought Carol might have become a mental case, that puberty had turned her into a psycho something-or-other. Bart thought to feel her out slowly. He suggested that they take a drive, and was relieved when she agreed. Driving, he was elaborately off-hand, afraid that a wrong word might prompt a child-schizo to jump out of the car.

Carol thinks of that drive as the first run, a preview of an argument that would come often—unending arguments as pointless as those on divorce or religion or abortion. She had heard them all —that a whorehouse is the ultimate depravity, the total of everything anti-nature, the final low in commercial debauchery. She had also heard those who argued instead that the little houses point the way, that they accept now what will eventually become common; that they serve a great, primal need.

Once, after some general questions like . . . did she know this country . . . did the girls take drives . . . and, finally, "Do you know why you did it?"

And Carol's answer, "If that's the big question, it's going to be hard. Most girls don't really know. They get asked all the time. But they have so many answers, they really don't know."

After a time, he said, "Was there anything in Burlingame—did anything happen there that set you off?"

"I told him it was hard to explain. How explain that suddenly, somehow, I thought the world had gone insane?" She wound up telling him about Laura and Dave.

Still, Bart could not see that the incident could justify her going to Elko. He began to fear that the girl was some new kind of monster, a sane, beautiful, cool, teenage, revolutionary monster. Impulsively, he pulled off the road and sat there, looking ahead, his hands on the wheel. "Look, I won't scold, or moralize, or anything, but can we talk about it? Without tempers, or hurt feelings? I would like to get some things answered. After that, well, we can put a cut-off date on it, no more questions, we can stop it at sunset tomorrow."

"Tomorrow?"

"Yes, I hope you will leave Ellie's. I'd like to take you to Europe, change everything. Maybe you can go to some school. You could go to Switzerland, England—hell, anywhere."

She liked the idea. Why not? She had come to Elko on a senseless whim, why not move on the same way? He went on, "Don't even go back for your things, call Ellie and tell her to burn them. We can be in Salt Lake tonight, and buy everything you need. We could catch a plane and be in New York next day." He was pushing. "Throw away the Salt Lake stuff and buy in New York, my God, the shops . . . ."

"Fine," she said.

After a while, "Look, I take it you've not even tried to talk to your mother?"

"No."

"Why?"

"Bart, you know she's an idiot. Mother doesn't care about anything outside of her own little body. It's like talking to a cat."

Then, the next question. "Could it be that maybe you ran into more than your share, more sex than other girls?"

"I doubt it. Half the girls at school were trading pills before noon. Most boys wanted a shack-up. Every movie was pure sex. Look, your world may have been different, but mine, it's a sex binge."

"So you decided that, as things stood, a whorehouse just might be the ultimate university?"

"Something like that."

Carol remembers her anger then. Bart was trying to be clever rather than understanding. "I didn't know it then," she relates, "but Bart changed when he drank. When he couldn't solve something, when logic didn't work, he'd go for the bottle. We were getting near Wendover, that's a little nothing of a place right over the line in Utah where the ground begins to show that salt crust, and he said, 'My God. Utah's dry.' We came to a bar and he ducked in and came out with his old friend, a bottle of Old Taylor. And soda, warm soda. He made drinks in paper cups. I don't drink, but I took it. He must have had six in the next fifty miles."

"As I understand it," he said, "you did it, really, as a kind of defiance. You think the world is crummy, nothing makes sense, so you go for the Camus thing."

"Camus may have had something!"

"But you," he yelled, "you go prostitute as a way of sticking your tongue out at the world. To get even, you go to Ellie's, and you hold still for every stupid, drunken bum who comes in!" He tossed down another drink. "How long were you at it?"

"Five months, with a week off every month."

"That's how many men? Five thousand?"

"It was that type of sadism that made me angry. I told him, 'Not five thousand, but one thousand, for sure.' He was boiling. He kept filling his paper cup. It was around nine when we got to Salt Lake. He said there was a good hotel there, and then had a sudden thought. 'By the way, how in hell do we register? I'd like a suite with two bedrooms.'

"It gave us the first laugh that day. He said that if he signed me in as his daughter, the clerks would laugh, and if he made me his wife, it would be as funny. Then I made a mistake. I said that if any of the bellboys had been at Ellie's, they would laugh, too. It made him furious. 'Nothing like riding up an elevator with a bell-boy who's fucked your wife,' he said. After that, he hardly talked. Anyway, we registered as man and wife. It was wonderful to be in a hotel. He fell asleep dressed, and I took the other room.

"Next morning he was another man. He looked like a British duke, dressed in tweeds and ascot. I bought some clothes and made him promise not to hit the Old Taylor until evening. We started driving around noon, and like the day before, we talked about everything else before he started, 'I take it the cut-off is sunset, so I'd better start.' I told him it was nonsense about a cut-off, and that I'd tell him anything he wanted to know. But it was hard to talk. We were far apart. He was forty-three, had traveled a lot, but there was so much he had never thought about. He had had girls, but he hated talking sex, so he never had."

Bart was thinking that if he could take Carol to New York, he could persuade her that it had all been a crazy aberration. Maybe travel, the smells of Scotland or France, would do it. He sensed that Carol's mind was more analytical than his, more aware of the sex comedy, of its ironies. He did not know if this was common with young people or not, but he realized that bromides sounded stupid. It was hard to talk to a girl who had just lived a hundred years.

At Ellie's, Carol had put in more time at the bar than in back. Soon she began to see that all but the simplest men were troubled. So many had the familiar syndrome; to be one way before the half-hour of sex, and different afterwards. They would come in, educated or not, articulate or not, aching for a girl. But then came the reaction. And for so many, the new need. So many showed a comic loneliness, a reluctance to say goodbye. Some would pull you right back to the bar and hold your hand. They would ask questions, almost helplessly, thinking for some reason that a girl who deals with penises all day must be an authority on human sex history and all its complications. She had seen them stare into a glass, trying, in confused, drunken ways, to find out about themselves. They would talk about their fears of little homosexual twinges; they were bothered by yens for their daughters; bothered that they should want to betray their wives, not occasionally, but all the time. Some were bothered that they should be unheroic little nothings who masturbated while looking at girlie magazines. Some were so bad at describing their feelings that Carol could only nod and smile, making occasional sounds, and only half-listening. On the other hand, she had also met delightful men, wise and whimsical, who were vastly amused with the whole sex thing.

How could she tell this to Bart? Once, she caused him to swerve the car when she said that whoring was not so different from the acts of mothers. "Look, to be mauled by a man who has paid may be bad, but what's so noble about a wife, a mother, who has had five, or ten, or twenty men before she married, and every possible kind of sex, and being mauled by a husband, who himself has indulged in maybe three, four thousand—what shall we call them—sex acts; where he has played with fifty or a hundred vaginas before he married, and who probably doesn't consider his wife his last woman, by a long shot?"

Bart drove on grimly. He asked, "Is that how the girls talk?" Heading for Denver on roads he knew well, Bart hardly noticed the country. He was unhappy that a girl of eighteen should make him feel so stupid, that she should have been thinking of the slaggy realities, where he had not. He began to speak to Carol in a different tone, not quite so patronizing. Her ironies were hardly new to him by this time, but she had a way of making them sound like revealed truth. By evening of the second day, he began to wish they could get to New York faster. Two days, closed in by the upholstery of the car, had been too much. He wanted a new setting. This whore to his right, who looked like a vestal virgin, who never used an obscenity, was a voice from another planet. In Denver, he moved fast. He was up early next day, and by noon had sold the car and bought tickets to New York.

Her uncle, it developed, favored the Hotel Pierre, and for Carol it was a shock to discover how nice things could be. After Ellie's kitchen, where each girl ladled her own stew, she had almost forgotten that food can be served with such perfection. Bart was two men, she learned. When he was at the ranch, he would be seized by a fit of restlessness and leave for New York. For a few weeks,

his life was almost an orgy—not of girls or drinking—but of theatre. He would sometimes see two shows a day. He liked the
whole ritual, the dragged-out feel at the last curtain, the restaurants frequented by stage people, some of whom he knew, and the
nightclubs afterward.

Carol remembers the time in New York as carrying them to a
new stage. Bart was often lost in thought, staring out of the
window for long periods of time. Then he would turn to the dis-
tractions of the city, almost desperately. "Let's catch a play" or
"You'll like the Persian Room." He tried not to mention Elko. He
seemed to assume that the decision was made, and that Carol
would go to school. Carol, adrift in a pleasant limbo, without
much will of her own, was quite ready to follow any idea he
might have.

"We were there ten days," she recounts. "He was sick over what
I had done, and I felt sorry for him. He was miserable, it was like
losing a relative, like being told he had a child in prison. We
would be in a nightclub, laughing, drinking champagne, and we'd
see a girl sitting alone, obviously on the make, and suddenly he
would act as if he wanted to vomit. Once he was standing at a
window and he whirled around, 'Carol, you could have no way of
knowing about Elko, except when you heard it from me. My God,
am I the one who got you thinking about Elko? Did I put it into
your head?'

"He kept asking what my state of mind was, could I adjust, get
interested in something, did I lean to anything—art, nursing, or
what? And then he could be mean. He asked if I could ever get so
normal that I would want to marry. 'A lot of men don't seem to
mind,' he said sarcastically, 'I hear there's quite a turnover in
Elko, so many girls getting married. Some men would blow their
brains out if they discovered their wife had been a whore. Others
don't seem to mind, in fact, they propose right on the whorehouse
bed.'

"Once I asked him, 'Bart, you'll never get over it, will you?
Nothing can black it out?'

"He said, 'No, and let's not have any Goddamn regurgitation
about how right you are, and how the world stinks. I'm shocked
as hell and, no, it won't go down. You want a drink?' It put him in

a mood to go out. He called the desk and we went to a play, then a restaurant. That was beautiful too, and then, back in the hotel, he said, 'Goddammit, don't you see how it could have been? You could have married and kept discovering wonderful things every day of your life.' He was again at the window looking out. I went over and put my arm around him. He put his arms around me, led me to his room, and that was it. It was as if he hadn't had a girl in a year. Well, with a man like that, it was really the start of something bad. Next morning he was gone early, as usual, and when I saw him it was around four o'clock. He had had quite a few. He kissed me.

" 'Darling, do you know the lowest name, the word that packs the worst insult, the word used by Chinese and Eskimos, for the absolutely lowest?' I waited. 'It's motherfucker. Well, as part of my mission of rescue, it seems I have become a daughter-fucker.'

"I told him it was not that bad. 'After all,' I said, 'you hadn't seen me for a year, and when you did, well, I was grown up. It's not as if you crawled into the bed of a daughter you saw every day.'

"He was stubborn. 'It's not that simple. Suppose I married, had a daughter, and suppose, when she's fourteen, I walk in on her and . . .' He laughed. 'You see? I've lost everything.'

" 'You just be normal,' I told him. 'When its all told some day, it will come out that every father who has a goodlooking daughter has wanted to . . .' " It turned into a long day. There were Martinis before lunch and a lot of wine. He was getting red-faced and mean again. Bart, she saw, was another of those men who had so huge a conflict that it amounted to a split personality. There were men who had a violent urge to do things, but who developed a kind of self-hatred for wanting to do those very things. "Up to now," she said, "I had been willing to answer his questions, but I was developing an ear for his turning point, the point which was always heightened by the amount of whiskey he drank."

Carol thought she might tell him something that would infuriate him even more—that he was not so much an individual as a category. She had learned, at Ellie's, to spot the men of that special category, the men who were not so much jealous of wives as they were jealous of certain acts—a kind of memory jealousy.

They could accept the fact that a wife had been married before, that she had had men, and possibly two thousand bouts in bed. But they wanted to think that their wives' sexual history had been conventional.

"Bart took me by the chin and ran a finger over my lips. 'That gorgeous mouth,' he said, 'who the hell would ever dream that it had serviced so many?'

"That's when I decided. I caught him the next morning when he was completely sober, and he agreed that it was all ridiculous, and that we should end it. We were having coffee. He laughed, 'Actually, we are really all through arguing anyway. You've won, you know, every point, every damned one. I mean, about how people are. I'm forty-three, and I've just fucked my sister's baby, and I've wanted to ever since we left Elko. I'm in love with you, and I would marry you over any woman on earth. But I'd want to blow my brains out every time I looked at that mouth.' It wasn't even ten o'clock, but he went to the table and poured himself a whiskey. He downed it and it seemed to make him feel better. He said, almost cheerfully, 'How about making it Columbia University, right here in New York?'

"I said, 'Fine, but why Columbia?' "

" 'Well, Christ, you couldn't go the archery route at Vassar!' "

Margaret Grey explains, "Mister, there ain't anywhere a young, beautiful, well-hung guy counts for less than in a whorehouse." The girls call him bad news, physically, sexually, financially. They call him a beautiful stud, and that's all. He just can't accept that he is simply one of maybe fifteen you've had that day, one of two-three hundred that month. He's got to be the one you remember. He loves that body. He comes on like a wrestler and, what's funny, seems to want the admiration of a whore. We girls don't care for the guy because he's in you too much, not like the ordinary guys you play with, excite, and get rid of fast. These guys are a marathon, in you like a machine, and for so long they leave you sore. They're the ones that really force you into defensive fucking."

Margaret, now twenty-four, still beautiful, with only a trace of the grimness of the veteran, lucky to have escaped all but small infections, says, "You know, sex doesn't show. Or rather, it needn't. If a girl is lucky, if she doesn't get sick, doesn't drink, well, it won't show."

Margaret can't forget the book by James Jones, *From Here to Eternity*, which gave a picture of the Honolulu of another era, before Pearl Harbor. It was a picture of the life of men in service, the boring, frustrating days in a peacetime army, and the emptiness for men whose homes were their barracks. Jones wrote of the rush to get to town, to the bars and cafes, the rush by men who were sick of the dormitories, and who made a mass charge on Honolulu's houses. One character in his book, the lovely Loreen, worked for two years in the New Congress Hotel, which was a production line for soldiers. Loreen might have totaled ten thousand men. With Pearl Harbor, the houses closed, and Loreen was on a ship headed for the United States. A woman passenger stared at her, child-like, lovely, clear-skinned, and accepted her as a *nice* girl.

"Ever watch a military parade?" Margaret asks. "Do you know how long it takes for ten thousand men to march by? It's true, sex doesn't show. Or it doesn't have to. You know, Joe has a girl, maybe she's still there, she looks healthy, clear-eyed, actually, rather lovely. She doesn't show she's forty. She started when she was seventeen. What's crazy is that she's a girl who never got away from it for more than two, three months. Try multiplying twenty-three years by three hundred sixty-five days, or make it 300 days—because nobody can stand it every day—and give her eight tricks a day, average. Remember, for every ten-minute guy, there's three or four who bang you a half-hour. What do you get? Over fifty thousand." Margaret's admiration for Loreen and for Joe Conforte's veteran, is the professional awe of women who can have fifty thousand invasions and not show it.

Margaret had survived some years in the business by then. She had come through her first year of prostitution in Gilroy, California, without running into any real sadism. There were men, of course, who were rough. How to handle the power boys, those with endless endurance, who got lost in the rhythm of powerful thrusts, guys determined to prolong their ecstasy? She had gone to doctors. One said defensive sex wasn't covered in medical school.

It was years later, after she had been in Ely some months, working in Mabel's Alamo, that another doctor coached her, after the
rape experience.

Some of it was right out of a southern script. The Negro was
big and a little drunk, and took her violently. Afterwards, knowing that he could be arrested, if not lynched, he had shown fear.
He was handsome and educated. Margaret had the feeling that he
might be a professional football player, until he told her it was
baseball. Why he should be driven to rape when black athletes
had their pick of girls, black or white, she did not understand. He
had come into the little bar and silenced it. At 8 o'clock, Ely's
little Alamo[1] could be crowded. There were some fifteen men in
the place, some drinking with other men, some with girls. Margaret was at the bar with several girls, free for pickup. This was
1966, when the Negro's admission into the white world was in
what the Ely editor, Jay Steed, calls the "middle Johnson period."
That is, if you listened to Governor Wallace, Negroes should be
happy for having achieved complete integration; if you listened to
Malcom X, it would be twenty years before Negroes would know
50 percent integration. The Negro entered the Alamo at a moment
when Ely's own rules were wobbling but still in force; a black
could drink at the bar, if he could ignore the room's hostility, but
he could not go in back with a girl, white or black. The rule
endured, not so much from Mabel, as from the customers. There
were whites who did not mind the lubrication of an untidy girl,
who had not washed from her previous man, but who were
repelled by the thought of any lingering sperm from a "nigger."
To blacks, who didn't understand such distinctions, blacks already
explosively angry, the idea that white revulsion should extend to
sharing a vagina was, for the more violent, another reason to think
of machine guns.

This one took a stool at the bar, and his eye caught the sign,
"We reserve the right . . ." Mabel, behind the bar, didn't try to
hide her fear—that frame, those arms. She wondered if this was
the time to signal Smitty to phone for the cops. Instead, she tried
what had worked before, the pitch of friendliness. "Look, friend,

---

[1] After Reno was closed down, a number of towns named their places after
the defunct Alamo, Mohawk, and Green Lantern. Ely's "Alamo" is fictitious.

it's nothing I invented, it's nothing to do with me. Hell, you know the situation. Will you let the house buy you a drink, or ten of 'em, and get me off the hook?" The man thought a moment, and his smile was mean. He took the whiskey standing, sipping slowly, aching for someone to make trouble. Mabel filled his glass twice more before he refused a fourth. He looked at the roomful of men and said softly, "What a bunch of shits." Seeing that no one took offense, he left.

Margaret borrowed Mabel's station wagon that night and went into town to the drug store. She was getting out of the car, ten feet from an arc light, when she felt the grip on her arm. "Get in and don't make a sound." Margaret says that while you don't reason with panic, it still doesn't stop thought. My God, a whore being raped, how awful! From the first she was sure he didn't have a gun or knife, that if he killed he would do it with his hands. If she could have controlled the panic she would have tried to make him laugh, to tell him it didn't have to be rape. But the nearness of death was paralyzing. She cowered in the seat until he stopped the car.

Margaret did some reading on rape after that, and once talked with the District Attorney of White Pine County. He looked in on the Alamo now and then, bought drinks, but never visited the back. On rape, he had a tired knowledge.

"Honey," he explained, "there's the rape where the girl enters into it, willing as hell, and then changes her mind. If they fool around, say, for fifty minutes and she only consents for forty, it can be rape. Then, there is the kind where it begins in fun, and the guy goes rough and he won't stop. It's the roughness of the last five minutes that makes it rape. Then there's between an adult and a sure-as-hell consenting minor. Hell, all kinds. I knew a case where the guy couldn't get an erection and still made the pen. Why, you ever been raped?"

Consistently, Margaret said no. It had begun violently. The black had spread his corduroy jacket on the ground, pulled her down and made a ritual of taking her clothes off, piece by piece. The doctor told her she was hurt mostly because there was no give in the sand. Several times she was near fainting, less from the pain than from the weight. He was on his back finally, and she sensed that he was no longer angry. On an impulse, she kissed him. The result was unexpected; he almost cried.

"Why did you do that?"

"I just wanted to tell you I understand. And I'm not mad."

"Oh Christ!"

Back in the car he drove for several hours. As the mountains began to show a rim of light, he spoke of Negroes and his time. He drove with one hand and held hers in the other. When it was fully light he said, "I'll drop you at the edge of town. If you call the police, they'll have me fast. Up to you."

"I told you ten times," she said, "I'm not calling anybody. Actually, I'd like to see you again." She kept her word, and it had meant trouble. Mabel got worried when Margaret failed to come back: the girl might be hurt, or she could have picked up a trick in a bar or hotel, which was trouble too. Her understanding with the town fathers was that she keep her girls in the house and not let them tarry in town. By two in the morning, Mabel asked friends to make a search, bars, motels, the hospital. By dawn, she called the police. It was one of the town's three patrolmen who spotted Margaret as she was backing away from the curb, only minutes after the Negro had walked away.

Her story was that she had been going crazy with the confinement and had taken a drive. The story went over with the police but not with Mabel. It was after Margaret had gone to sleep, waking up with pains, that Mabel guessed. "Honey," she said, "you been raped." Angrily, Margaret said no, but Mabel's intuition went further. "Was it that black?"

"I'm all right," Margaret insisted. "And I haven't been raped." Mabel thought about it and decided that this might be the best answer after all. A manhunt, an arrest, maybe lynch talk, all centered around her Alamo, was no good. But she called in the doctor, a man who had been attending girls for years, and it was he who added to Margaret's education in what is known as defensive fucking.

Margaret's own look backward—why she got into it, why any girl does—she finds no crazier than why they stay after they know what it's like. She does believe that since pros face the damned question every day, having to explain themselves to every eighth or tenth customer, the girls are forced to invent something, to rationalize, to work up a logical reason. Actually, they can no more explain themselves than they can explain the electoral college, or how a carburetor works.

From reading, Margaret knows that most psychiatrists have taken a stab at motives. "Like the ones who say that whores have this self-hate, and are deliberately trying to get their bodies beat up and their egos trampled. They ought to get together with the ones who say that it stems from a basic hatred of men, that girls get into it to get even with men, to make the bastards pay."

Back in Gilroy, Margaret remembers that she would lie awake, hearing the bedsprings in the next room, finding that her real disgust was with her mother and father. Margaret has a theory which she wishes someone would check out; that few kids pick up first knowledge about sex on the street or in school. She gives the credit to the home experiences. "Were the walls always that thin? How about the log cabins, or those stone houses, in the days of Franklin and Washington? Most houses," she says, "show thought about a lot of things—dishwashers, hot water throughout the house—but not much concern about the sounds of love."

Margaret has had no occasion to meet Tom Pursel, the Las Vegas attorney who decided to represent prostitutes, and who, like Margaret, is struck by the gap between the prohibitions put on kids and the fantastic, often orgiastic, sex of their parents. Margaret's point is that of Attorney Pursel.

"In the millions of matrimonial nests that line every street, there is a father-mother team that tries to hide its coitus, people who profess sexual continence and even indifference in front of the kids. Yet, nights, they retire to beds that squeak, metal springs that sing, wood frames that creak, headboards that touch a wall and thud, bedrooms so close to the kids' rooms that, in the silence of the night, even with doors closed, the little gasps of mama, the groans of dad, wouldn't fool a moron. In the bright light of breakfast next morning, ten zillion parents try to deadpan some bright fourteen-year-old, not realizing that the kid was listening and saw the thing almost as if he were standing by the bed."

On the day that Margaret's parents gave her a bike for her eighth birthday, she knew that her folks were in such copulation that, coupled with the graphic fill-in of kids at school, she believed they should be walking bent over. Their stricture, that sex was not nice, was something they said, for some reason, while doing it all the time.

Gilroy's streets have cottages that are almost covered with vines, backyards that are choked with peach trees, porches with grapes over the door. Her father and mother were off at jobs all day; he worked a fork-lift in the freight yards, and she worked in a store. Margaret remembers their marriage as an argument as to who got which car when one broke down. She calls her father "Dumb, hell, stupid," and speaks of her mother as a woman with little conversation beyond comments on TV. They tried to be good parents and scolded and moralized about drink and sex. As with Carol, her best times were in grammar school and one short year in high school. Gilroy, with its vineyards and orchards, was strangely free of the young toughs that infested Sacramento.

At ten, she was putting a pillow over her head to close off the sounds of bedsprings, the gasps and groans of adults in their own transport some fifteen feet away. At thirteen, it was a short progression from the day when a boy took her out, and in a parked car acquainted her with what he said was "French kissing," to the night when he taught her everything. Her life could have followed a stencil, the boy becoming her steady, and then her husband, but he left town. It left a void which she filled with other boys.

In her last school year she was talked into copulation by six boys, always so consistently in a back seat that she wondered whether there would ever be a change to beds. In later years, when she was asked what influence in the slow-moving town led her into prostitution, she could not explain. Her parents were nearly always broke, but not destitute, so it was no desperate need of money. She was a year in junior high when someone told her she could get a job as a car hop, an idea that her people thought fine. She doesn't know whether it was because she had no talent or because small towns have so few openings, but she had several part-time jobs in two years, all depressing, with low pay; a sequence as waitress, salesgirl, carhop, babysitter. Like so many girls, she saw rescue only in meeting a boy and marrying, which didn't happen. She remembers amiably that her own road to hell was casual, even pleasant. She was now a waitress in a restaurant roadhouse, and so obviously a minor that they would not let her near the bar. But Louie, the bartender, was the one who made the proposition.

It was after a couple of months of running—"Hash slingin' is almost constant running," she says—and earning $60 a week, that Louie drove her home. She could beat that 60 bucks in one night, and no tax withholding crap. He told her his customers were "All right Joes, no different, really, from the guys you're screwing now for free." Her parents never thought to question her about her new hours. By Christmas of 1965, Margaret had bought a used car and was already being stared at by police who knew that the kid was home-based, that she got her bookings through the bartender, and that it was a toss-up whether they would pick her up first for narcotics or prostitution. She was safe on the narcotics count because she had a horror of dope.

She was a clever and stealthy visitor to hotels the night they picked her up and took her to the home of the juvenile officer. In the little parlor, the overworked man told her that if she were caught again it would be reform school. He seemed to know that her parents would be no help. He offered to help her find a job, an idea that opened up a vista she hated, living in a town where, sooner or later, everybody would know. She ran away. She worked as a prostitute for almost a year in California towns before she decided on Nevada. Once, impulsively, she telephoned her people. They were pleased that she should be alive and well.

Her closest brush with friendship, the man she still remembers as the only man she would have married, was a detective. She met him in the lounge of the St. Francis in San Francisco. Margaret had come in and ordered a drink, hoping no waiter would order her out. She told an indifferent waitress she was waiting for a friend. Then came the glimpse into the other world, the moment when she was mistaken for a college girl.

A "Smith girl," from neighboring Smith College, was getting married that day and the lobbies were noisy with collegians, all in cutaways and white carnations, and all a little drunk. One boy, who was meeting a blind date, grabbed her arm, and headed for the elevators. "Pam, darling! So sorry I'm late, let's get to the brawl and be properly introduced." He was let down when she said she was not Pam. The brush with the quality left her saddened. In the lounge that same day, she met the man who would get her out of California. He was about forty, beginning to gray, and quite ordinary. He sat down at the next table. She was a moment realizing that he was talking to her because he was looking over her head. He didn't want any waiter to see the pickup. "Miss," he said, "I'm a police officer. Do you want to see my badge, or can we go outside?" She felt the deep fear. She had never been arrested.

"I'd like to talk to you," he said. "Come on, let's take a walk." She followed him to his car. He didn't take her to the station but took the freeway to Palo Alto. He was bothered and wanted to talk. He hated his job. He thought that a grown man who winds up as a detective hasn't done very much, and the vice detail, that was the lowest rung. He was unhappy for himself and for her. The world was lousy if it offered so little to a girl that she had to sell her body. He had arrested hookers, he told her, many of them not worth much, stupid, man-hating babes who were best locked up, but he felt bad when he saw a young one just starting. Margaret felt that he should have been a social worker.

It was the first of many drives. Margaret liked him so much that she tried to get him to her motel. He laughed, "Some answer, the station house joke, the cop who uses sympathy to get the girl." She stopped working and saw him practically every day. But after some weeks they saw that it would lead nowhere. It was on a drive on the coastal highway that he gave up. "Look, I can see that I'm not going to change anything. You're going to do this, and that's that. I think, though, that you should go to Nevada. It's legal there and you can get into a house. Nobody will roust you. You won't get a record there and there's no pay-off. Maybe, after you've got a stake, you'll work it out." She would have married him, but he wasn't marrying, so she left. Her detective had said that the only town he really knew was Ely. "Little place, so far from anything you wouldn't believe it. It's maybe three hundred miles from Reno. But it's a rich little place, with the Kennecott mines keeping it going. Who knows, you might even marry a miner."

3

The Hustler State

IT WOULD BE nice to know how many members of Congress have looked in on the little whorehouses, hoping no reporter sees them, perched on a stool, talking with girls who, clad in two strips of cloth, might as well be naked. The editors on 80 know that hundreds of FBI agents have looked in on them, reasoning soundly that everything American should be known to the Bureau. The editors have spotted cabinet members, congressmen, governors, police chiefs, ambassadors. Most American columnists have had a drink with the girls, and reporters come by the thousands. The houses are something to see, like Williamsburg or Yosemite. Nevada reporters know that John Kennedy used to drop in on Reno when he was a less conspicuous senator. There is the story that J. Edgar Hoover was so revolted by Nevada that he would not set foot in it, which is not quite true, because, while disapproving, he stayed in the Sahara Hotel as a guest of owner, Milton Prell, in Prell's own suite. Many of the nation's eminent have parked their cars in downtown Lovelock, Winnemucca, and Elko, thinking it smarter to walk than have their license plates seen in front of a whorehouse. They ask about the places, and bartenders smile, "Sure, as you step out of the door you . . ."

For a quarter of a century, the question asked by Americans has been, *why*? Why, out of forty-eight states, later, fifty states, why here in Nevada? How did it start? There are men who know whore history. They agree that, oddly enough, today's traffic is not the highest, that the peak hit just before World War II, a time when Reno and Las Vegas had huge, open girl markets, and almost every village a market of its own.

After Pearl Harbor, military camps grew up everywhere. The War Department, noting the vastness of Nevada, its clear weather, chose it for two of its biggest air-training bases. One, called Stead, was on a flat ten miles north of Reno, and another —today, the biggest air base in the world—Nellis, was nine miles north of Las Vegas.

Nevadans were delighted. Outside of the honor, people saw that the bases would mean thousands of airmen and an enormous payroll; much of it impoundable by merchants. With dependents, plus maintenance forces, the soldier population near Reno would be a third that of the town itself.

The war boom was on, but there was a problem. Reno had the biggest concentration of officially tolerated whores in America, girls in three compounds, strung out along the Truckee River and known all over the west as the Green Lantern, the Mohawk, and the Alamo. In Las Vegas, the whore district, while not so awesome, was big, a string of houses that occupied an entire block, and was called Block 16.[1]

For the Commander of Stead, it was one headache too many: the road to Reno could become a coital express and, if Reno responded to demand, the town could wind up even with the whore district of Hong Kong. With men coming up for off-duty passes in rotations of five hundred per night, that riverbank could become the pubic center of the West; this at a time when syphilis took weeks to check, and when gonorrhea could cripple a company. Moreover, the War Department had already heard from wives; no whores near their men. The ladies had many arguments: venereal disease, men who were called to arms should not receive federal help in sex betrayal, the War Department should

---

[1] Whatever the significance, the houses of Las Vegas were as obvious as City Hall; the celebrated Block 16, while off-limits to nice people, was there for all to see. In Reno, the houses were hidden, nestled in a tangle of cottonwood trees that made a forest of the riverbottom.

not debauch men and cheapen womanhood. The Department ordered a crackdown and in Reno, the commander summoned the mayor and told him every bedroom was to be closed within thirty days. If Reno wanted to be stubborn, the War Department would simply declare the whole city off-limits. Reno's mayor lost all will to fight. He met with the owner groups and, well before deadline, the girls were gone.

The same blow struck Las Vegas. There the base commander delivered his ultimatum, and the famous block of houses went dark. For the duration, thousands of airmen would drift into the bars of Las Vegas for near-beer and cokes, to listen to the radio voices of H. V. Kaltenborn, Gabriel Heatter, and Edward R. Murrow. Las Vegas and Reno were no longer fun cities.

But the state is vast, so vast that people have always had to reach for comparisons. "It's ten times the size of New York . . . just a little smaller than Alaska . . . big as the Sahara . . ." Within months, little houses were sneakily reopening. The first, to the east of Reno, was in the farm town of Fallon which, for a time, was run by the lady who is today Mrs. Joe Conforte. In Lovelock and Winnemucca, they served locals and tourists and those GIs from Stead who could sneak off and race the distance from Reno. There was the same "business as usual" in the tiny houses of Battle Mountain and Wells.

This stubborn determination of a state to have prostitution, to have it openly, to have houses in the villages, and whole blocks of them in cities—fascinated America. Of course, most American cities of any size had their districts, their houses, streetwalkers, and bar girls, but they operated with some stealth; none could match Reno with its uniformed police standing at doorways. Nowhere did mayors explain their value to visiting reporters.

Nevada's way has caused American editors to write scathingly about the state for fifty years. The anger peaked in the years 1960-70, when Nevada's gambling reached a point that nauseated the FBI—and many in Congress. Nevada first created a scandal with its bid for the divorce trade; it added new shock with its open prostitution; it affronted again when it built its life around gambling, the business which, so many believed, was run by crime syndicates. This combination produced a torrent of books and magazine articles. It created a literature—the most vitriolic diatribe ever directed at a state since the founding of the union. (See Chapter 8.)

There was a moment in Nevada history when J. Edgar Hoover was so personally fed up with Nevada that he determined to force the state to remove a number of owners, despite the fact that Nevada's governor, its Gaming Control Board, and its legislature could find no legal formula by which to comply. It was a dilemma with no solution. The problem prompted the head of the Hotel Association to fly to Washington to see whether any act, within Nevada's legal powers, might bring a moratorium. There was a meeting in the Department of Justice. The specific question was, "What can Nevada do to appease J. Edgar Hoover?"

The official leaned back in his chair. "That would be a little tough," he mused, "because you'd have to erase so much of your history. You'd have to make Congress forget how consistently, how totally rotten your state has always been. You'd have to explain why you were the first state to create a divorce industry, to milk, exploit the miserable. You'd have to explain why you are the only state with a hundred-year history of whorehouses. You'd have to explain why you are the only state to legalize gambling when every other state makes it a crime. And why you let millions go outside to finance narcotics, prostitution, murder. You'd have to explain why, right now, in the biggest hotel in Nevada, call girls know which phones the management wants them to use. You'd have to explain why, today, there are men in your little legislature who want to make Nevada first in still one more cesspool, the first state to legalize prostitution. What do you Nevadans want, a national franchise to put trailers outside of every high school?" After this, he relaxed a little. "Frankly," he asked, "can you yourselves explain it? How come your fucking little state has gone in for what is outlawed elsewhere, dirty elsewhere, illegal elsewhere?"

The Hotel Association man had a theory, in answer to the many who loathe Nevada, a theory inspired by cartoonist Al Capp. As Sunday readers know, Capp once invented a country called Lower Slobbovia, a place that is unbelievably poor. Capp never shows an interior. The people always stand waist-deep in snow. Wolves, starved and gaunt, lurk behind trees, eyeing babies clutched to their mothers. Drooling bears hungrily eye the wolves. Capp's country catches the situation of Nevada, a land that was always a problem to its legislature, always so far behind in the human parade. It was poor even as a territory—but then it didn't matter.

In the division between California and Nevada as to what beauties, what marvels, what lushness, what moutain ranges and rivers and canyons and valleys should go to whom, it was all California. It was never a division in the sense that two groups meet at a table. Actually, the westward wave that produced California came some years before Nevadans would get their own idea to form a state. But when they did, their western border was frozen, a line that marked what California did not want. California was already the four-hundred-mile strip, paralleling the Pacific, that contained so many riches, such a vastness of growing things, whether redwoods or asparagus. Being first at table, California took everything up to and including the lovely Sierras. Where the mountains end, where they flow into desert, Nevada begins. A Nevada editor, Bob Richards, of the *Territorial Enterprise*, once pointed out that, "Since Californians liked to say they had some of everything, they took some awful bad Badlands when they took Death Valley and the Mojave Desert, but even here California outsmarted Nevada—even its deserts are more picturesque."

This desert stretches east a thousand miles, and its first four hundred miles are Nevada. The state, twice as big as England, has a bleak beauty of its own, but it is a land that would never attract many people. Crossing it, are four seemingly endless highways. To drive on any one is to see rabbits, lizards, the occasional coyote, and the eternally circling hawk. It was the Spaniards who, crossing the Sierras saw the mountains as two lovely images, the "Mother Chain," or Sierra Madre, and the "Snowy Mountains," or Sierra Nevada.

The state, which can be buried by snows that reach from Montana to New Mexico, was destined to be different. It was a land whose ways were as tortured as the quartz formation of its rocks. Whatever cosmic mixer put coal in Pennsylvania, oil in Texas, timber in Oregon, put little in Nevada. Geology, climate, and men seemed to agree that Nevada was a joke; at least three of its historians have held their noses. Nevada has never produced many writers so it became inordinately proud of two who tarried for a while, the writing partners, Dan DeQuille and Mark Twain, who came with the Virginia Strike to become editors of the *Territorial Enterprise*. But the writers did not return Nevada's love. DeQuille said, "After statehood the borders were vague, but considering what they enclosed, who cared?"

Travelers crossing the sagebrush have always looked for that western silhouette, the steer, and been disappointed because it is not cattle country; the stories of Abilene and Dodge City, of cattle drives and cattle barons, were about other states. As to other industries, there have never been any. The ebullient Governor, Grant Sawyer, was stung once by a writer who said that no self-respecting industry would set foot in Nevada. Sawyer told an aide to make up a list of the companies that had moved in during his term. The aide produced a list, but the fifth largest was Rocketdyne, a company with twelve employees. It has no forestry or farming to speak of, and its little legislature has been known to debate five hours over a $7,000 budget item. But for a time there was some money in mining, a run of bawdy years that left no money behind but gave Nevada its heritage of whores.

In the spring of 1859, two friends, Peter O'Riley and Patrick McLaughlin, set up rockers in a gulch, the pine and sagebrush trough called Six Mile Canyon. They had been crushing rock, holding it to the light, testing it, even tasting it, and were digging a reservoir when they uncovered the vein that would become the famous Ophir Bonanza. Within days, they were sacking ore and finding, at sunset, their rock was worth another $1,000. Virtually every western strike is a story of a badly kept secret. Pete and Pat were spotted by other prospectors, and the stampede to their canyon emptied several California towns. Mark Twain thought the surrounding wilderness should be called a federal foetus, a part of America which was no longer Mexico, and was just orphaned space. In giving the figure for the population of what would become Nevada, writers have been known to repeat the number so that typesetters would not think it was a mistake: it was ten. The stampede to Six Mile Canyon assembled the people who later would make it a state. In their first enthusiasm they gave the region three successive names before settling on Virginia City. Within ten years they had built eighty ore mills.

The men who rushed to the strikes whipped their horses and mules into hauling the rails and ties for a railroad. The train, in turn, brought the bigger stuff for a city that would have fifteen thousand homes, an opera house, one hundred saloons and, depending on the historian, thirty to one hundred and fifty whorehouses. It was all there was to Nevada. Its mobs included murderers and gentlemen, a vigilante police, and fourteen fraternal orders.

Virginia City lived at a high whine for twenty years, and then wound down. But it had put out satellites. Whenever the west had a strike, men would rush in to find every hill and valley crawling with prospectors. So they fanned out and produced Nevada's next seven cities. Ten years after the world first heard of Virginia City, prospectors had ranged over a hundred ridges, creating the boom towns of Austin, Unionville, Aurora, Belmont, Pioche, Hamilton, and Eureka.

Then it was over. It was all accident. Virginia City became a wasteland of empty houses with some three hundred stragglers; Abandoned totally were Unionville, Aurora and Hamilton, while Austin, Pioche and Eureka survived as ghosts, whose reason for lingering became lost in their own mystique.

Tonopah came into being in more recent times. It has fairly modern hotels and rail lines to Las Vegas and Reno. Again Nevada's population soared. Tonopah, too, begat satellites, one of them Goldfield, which had a ten-year boom that produced $125 million, making it one of the great gold finds of history. Goldfield attracted men who spread out, their explorations producing the "one-year" towns, Bullfrog, Rhyolite, Rawhide. The towns were noisy and bawdy, and their stories were like those of atolls in the South Pacific, lands that rise from the sea and sink without trace. A number of writers saw these deaths and their stories became requiems for towns. Men would leave. One in a hundred might own a horse and buckboard, but others would load their things on the wagon freights, which were already cutting down their services as the towns shrank. Some would lash together a version of the Indian "travois"; load everything onto an axle between two wheels and start pulling, possibly to abandon it in a day or two. Towns would show a few empty cabins, and many acquired the "smell of emptiness," the musky odor of packrat droppings. Ranchers and miners came from great distances to pick over what had been abandoned—furniture, dishes, doors. Prospectors would drift in to live in what had been the boarding house or the jail. When a gale moves through a ghost town, banging doors and bending surviving trees, it is the ultimate sound of hopelessness.

We have it on the word of James Scrugham, an early Nevada governor, that the girls of the camps were as basic as food. "In towns without wives, they substituted. The camps were not for wives. They just couldn't put up with the roughness. Hell, many camps didn't have water. I don't know when it was that Virginia City, for example, first got flush toilets. The few wives in the camps had to break up branches to get the stove going, and buy water to make coffee. But on those slopes, where many tents and shacks had no heat, the cribs had stoves. The miners, some coming in from a day in the drifts, some coming in from months of prospecting, hands callused, boots worn, having smelled only sagebrush and sweat, living like Indians, why, the poor bastards knew the one place they could get a welcome, a smile, a bed with springs, clean sheets, the smell of perfume, was the crib. So the cribs were the place. There were men in the camps who did no work beyond salting a mine, and there were high talent guys who sold phony stock. But in the camps they all had it the same. Come evening, the card-sharp and the blacksmith took the same walk down the street of whores. The girls understood; they played the phonograph, and they had pictures on the walls, and maybe a bottle of sherry, because whiskey was not as refined."

Then new towns came that had no connection with mining. They appeared along the highways, and their general store had shelves that were set up for ranchers; for men had managed to get ranches going, even in Nevada. As soon as a valley numbered a thousand people, a madam would get clearance to bring in some girls. Take a typical town on 80. The year is 1880, and the Presi-

dent is Rutherford B. Hayes. It is twenty-five years before the
Fords will replace horses, but the highway is already the reason
for being. It has about five hundred people, including the farrier
who shoes horses and will soak a wagon wheel in water to tighten
the rim. Its cultural mold is set. It has a hotel, whose counter is
also the post office, and two small assertive buildings, the Protestant and Catholic churches. It is three or four streets wide, three
or four long, and among the bungalows are stores, a school, a volunteer fire department, a doctor, a weekly paper, and saloons. On
the edge of town is the house with the girls, with a name like
"Dolly's" or "Dora's." An elder will decide to run for office; he will
hitch his team, cross unbelievable distances (Humboldt County is
almost exactly the size of Sicily) to find, on election day, that he
is a county commissioner. Now the worries—money for the dirt
roads, for a hospital, money for a bigger jail. And some time
during his term he will get into the argument between the minis-
ter and townsmen as to whether "Dolly's" should be closed, or
moved farther out, or even be allowed to expand.

Actually, the "Dollies" were a small problem. The commissioners knew, of course, that most of the town women hated Dolly, and
that the churchmen did too, although the pastors and priests
should have blessed her for providing the sermons for their Sunday
anger. Sermons of soiled sisters and cheapened love. But they
knew, too, that it was the majority will that there be a house.
There were many single men out in the back country—cow-
hands, miners, sheepherders—who would come in after payday
with one driving need. The town realized they should have a
Dolly, if only to avoid the men's hanging around the schools. So
the thinking of the mining camps carried over. Today, there are
houses strung out in most towns between California and the Utah
border. Lovelock has two, Winnemucca seven, and Elko seven.
Such crossroads as Battle Mountain and Basalt have one each,
houses so small, tawdry, and shack-like that, in them, assignation
hits the levels of *Tobacco Road.*

From the beginning every madam was given the order—which
exists even today—she must not advertise, not in newspapers, not
on signs. Her only leeway was the symbol, the red light somewhere near the door, technically illegal, because it was advertis-

ing, but permissible. Some madams wanting to make sure the light was seen, and finding no rule on wattage, used big bulbs. The result was that the red glow could be seen from the air, and this produced the navigational jokes, "Forget the radar and the beacons and just fly low. You pick up your first light at Cathleen's, near Wendover, bear south ten degrees at Lola's in Battle Mountain, then pick up Deedee and Klondike Belle's. When everything's black, you're in California."

The lights, seen by the pilots of Ford trimotors and today's F-111's, do not signal rich interiors; no movie sets where waiters pour champagne and Marlene Dietrich bats her lashes on a satin couch. Most had the unfailing feel of furniture that came from the Salvation Army. In the face of the town's contempt, the Mabels and Ellies would not spend money to make things swank.

One editor, who has watched the girl business for years, writes:

> The town's ministers, the mothers, hell, everybody, would have raised hell if, in towns so modest, where the fanciest room is the hotel dining room, the bordello should be the one place with walnut paneling. Remember, it is a part of the country where, as Lucius Beebe put it, "You may drive from San Francisco to Denver, crossing thirty towns, and never find a waitress who has ever heard of Bordelaise Sauce. If, in these towns a madam had the brashness to put in carpeting and paintings, she would have the only place with style. She knows better, she knows her place. The madam is nicely adjusted. She smiles as she chooses secondhand chairs; she smiles when a friendly customer tells her that nothing goes on in her place that isn't going on in every cottage around. The madam knows that the wives, the Mayor's lady, the saloon keeper's wife, spread their legs and have their own way of washing off sperm. From drunken customers they know such sexual detail as would be familiar to Professor Krafft-Ebing. So the madams accept the double standard. When, on Sunday, a minister thunders about harlotry, it is to the upturned faces of a congregation in which some of the ladies are

only hours removed from whatever acts so offend the pulpit. But they leave church in swathings of corsets and camisoles, safe in the knowledge that a respectable married woman can know every writhing sensuality and still carry that air of virtue. Her personal intercourse is rare and done in prayer. The madams know this and want to laugh, but they have to be discreet, so they go along with the charade. In this dark age of sex, they take what comfort they can from knowing which husbands sneaked in to give endorsements of their own.

In every year of the last fifty, there have been writers who saw red at the mention of Nevada. They are angered by Nevada's insolence, its refusal to conform, its tin-faced amorality. Such a one was Clyde Billings, reporter for the *Denver Post*, who passed through Nevada in 1929, the first year of the Depression, and who gave a picture of Highway 80 as it was about twenty years before Carol and Margaret were born:

> As for those places along the road, you would have to have the eros of a demented bull, a lust that would hold up while standing in a freezing lake, a hunger that would hold through carnal knowledge of a cadaver. Entering one of those damned places, a man might have in mind the delicate maid of a Shelley sonnet, or he might want a repeat with the bawd with loose bridgework. But he must have a libido that will hold up under terrible assaults. He must not retch at the smell of the bathrooms, not be bothered by soiled carpets or cabbage smells, and he must stay doggedly romantic while sitting on a cast-off couch with the springs coming through.

So much for admirers. It was in 1931 that Nevada gave up any thought of holding to the respectable poverty of such neighbors as Idaho or Montana. Nevada now faced the facts of its poverty and it passed the laws that would make it permanently notorious, the laws that put Nevada on the road that paid off so well that, by the time Howard Hughes arrived forty years later, it would be so brazenly rich that many states debated whether to copy its practices.

In 1931, when the Depression reached Nevada, the gold and silver glories of Virginia City and Tonopah had become boring stories about the "old days." Nevada had hit bottom: the sorriest state in the Union. Its pathetic assets were ghost towns. The cattle business was elsewhere. Farming was in states which somebody called the farm block. When the Depression hit, the joke was that there was so little to recede from, no factories to close, no skyscrapers to go vacant. The Depression hurt in the sense that it cut down even the trickle of California and Utah lads who used to drive in for the illegal gambling and the girls.

Nevada's little legislature met in Carson every two years to take another look at its poverty. Carson is at the western edge of the state, in the shadows of the Sierras, and for the men of such northern towns as Battle Mountain, Ely, or Wells it meant a drive of two hundred to three hundred miles. The roads were two-lane macadam or gravel, and to follow one was to discover the rhythm of its troughs. For the entire state is a washboard of mountain ranges, all parallel, generally running north and south. In between are swales, some a mile or two across and some fifty miles from rim to rim. The traveler, whether on a horse or in a car, has always tried to kill the tedium by guessing the distance from one summit to the next, and to top any summit is to see a panorama that is faintly lunar. Blurry specks may become ranches or towns. Even today, in much of Nevada, one can drive an hour without meeting another car. What strange blight covered this vastness that it should be bypassed by everyone? After eighty years, Nevada had the industry of Albania. The Nevada of 1931 was a still-life, an endless expanse, seen by the writer, Paul Gallico, as "Like parachuting into Iran." As they got within sight of Carson, the men could understand the worry of the movie cowboy who, approaching a waterhole, is afraid it will be dry. In the hotels the men carried their own bags to their rooms. As they shook hands in the speakeasies that night, they needed no committee to tell them that things were bad. They had read about the Depression, but only in four dailies, for of Nevada's twenty-eight papers, twenty-four were weeklies, one with a press run of two hundred.

It had been Nevada's way, every time the legislators needed

money, to come up with something unavailable elsewhere, something considered dirty or illegal elsewhere. Nevada had first jolted America, in the time of Theodore Roosevelt, with its divorce law. Nevada had had girl houses so long that it was generally assumed that the state had legalized them. Nevada had long permitted gambling rooms which, though illegal, were condoned. But none of the attempts to bring in money had worked for long, and now its solons were meeting in desperation.

After months of hand-wringing, they decided to legalize gambling. They wrote the "Wide Open Gambling Act," hoping to persuade a few investors to open more gambling places, and bring in a few more tourists. This done, they got to worrying: would gambling do it? They added another law: they opened the divorce gates wider with the amendment that cut the residency requirement from three months to six weeks. When the *San Francisco Chronicle* asked angrily why Nevada's legislature didn't go all the way and legalize opium, the story made the wire services, but the sarcasm was lost in Nevada. No Nevada paper carried it.

This done, the men drove home, and nothing happened. Nevada slept through the four-year depression and through the years before World War II with the metabolism of a sleeping bear. When the gambling law was passed, the men who would make Nevada notorious were still kids in the alleys of Cleveland, Chicago, and Detroit. Except for a few small, carnival-type operators in Reno—Harrah, and the Smiths of Harold's—no one seemed to have heard about the law.

Gambling was off to a puny start. It would not be until the fall of Japan that the eastern boys would discover Nevada's "come-and-get-it" gambling law. It was in 1946 that Nevadans themselves heard about the opening, in the hot, improbable desert, of a place called the Flamingo. People wondered if its builder, Benjamin Siegel, were sane, picking a flat that was torrid, treeless, and without people. But Siegel's guess changed Nevada history. The Flamingo was followed soon by the Thunderbird and the Desert Inn and, within ten years, American columnists were writing about the Sands, Riviera, Dunes, and Stardust, often without bothering to identify the town or state. Later still, they wrote with the same easy familiarity about the Sahara, Caesars Palace, and the International. In a run of twenty years, America found itself possessed of something new, a gambling city. The nation read that not only was Nevada the center of gambling, but that gambling had a parasite, the derivative industry of prostitution. In newspapers of two generations, people who read the *Saturday Evening Post, Collier's,* the *Reader's Digest, Cosmopolitan,* and *Life* were told and retold that the strange state was a Mecca for prostitutes. They already knew something of the Ellies and Mabels, but now they read that Las Vegas, too, had become a whore city. Nevada's open tolerance reached a man who, in his way, has become a Nevada force, a man who is now advocating that Nevada become the first to legalize prostitution, a man who now joins Nevada's Who's Who, together with MacKay, Siegel, Hughes, Del Webb: This is Joe Conforte.

4

Joe, His Start

ON A MARCH morning in 1954 Reno people opened their papers to read about the death of a local woman who worked the grave-yard shift at Western Union. A young man, described as a hand-some, darkhaired Irish type, had gone there to ask about a money order. He was a visitor from Chicago, a compulsive gambler, and had lost all his money at Harrah's. Something snapped in his mind and he plunged a screwdriver into the woman seventeen times. An hour later, police arrested James Cleary and brought him before the only eyewitness, a fellow worker at Western Union. The case had Reno divided because so many people said that Cleary was a soft, gentle, normal guy, an argument that brought the reply that the dead lady had been nice, too. Years later, Jim Cleary admitted to friends that he had killed the woman, and that he had pleaded innocent simply to save his life. He described his act as a "crime of passion." In his long prison years he made a study of such killings—acts committed by men who are sane, but in a kind of frenzy—which Cleary believed had its own psychiatric connotations.

Cleary hit into one of the tough prosecutors of the west, William Raggio, then an assistant D.A., young, capable, and so ambitious that people meeting him for the first time wondered at his calm assurance that he would wind up as a U.S. senator. Raggio admired Tom Dewey, the New York D.A. who had almost made it into the White House through his fame as a prosecutor. Young Raggio saw his own Nevada as confining, but still a state in which he could build a name. In his summation, he went after Cleary with a cool ferocity that was described by one reporter as "overkill." Cleary was given life in Nevada's penitentiary.

Until quite recently, it was said of Nevada that a man could stand in the center of any of its towns, shoot a rifle into the air in any direction, and hit into sagebrush waste. This is no longer true of Reno and Las Vegas, but Carson is still small. The state prison, three miles out of town, stands, half hidden, in the eternal brush. The grey fortress is in the architectural style of so many prisons built a hundred years ago, a square, granite mass. The prison hit its capacity of two hundred in the time of Cleveland, but was never enlarged, and it has been overcrowded ever since. Its cells have seen little change, though the ironwork has the usual electronic additions. Cells used for solitary were as barbaric as in the days of Victor Hugo—holes dug into the rock of a hillside.

Wardens have had to deal with the stranglings, the stabbings, the unending homosexual assaults, and the plottings to escape. Every warden has known that the stone horror should have been torn down, but no legislature would vote millions to ease the lot of felons. So the wardens make do. By 1962, the year when Joe arrived, many wardens had tried to ease the anger of the inmates and, within tight budgets, provide them with some diversion. This being Nevada, one warden thought to set aside a room where prisoners could do what other Nevadans do, gamble. He scrounged for layouts for dice, 21, poker, and Panguingue. It became the world's only prison casino and an instant success. It got wide publicity. Writers came from Europe and Asia to see it. Some wrote about it with wonder, but others, those who thought Nevada unchangeably dissolute, wrote with their usual contempt. But for the warden, the idea was inspired because it relieved pressures to a large extent.

Into the greyness of the century-old fortress there arrived a man who would dispel a lot of the misery of prison life; Joe Conforte, dynamic, volatile, imaginative, generous, and pathologically egotistic. That first day the grapevine buzzed: this was the guy with the world's biggest collection of beautiful broads, the guy who beat the system, the guy who made Nevada lump it, who had made the state accept his whorehouse. His money was anything that imagination might invent, $500 an hour, $2,000 per shift, day and night, rain or shine. He was not in for long—three to five years—so anybody who got next to him could figure on help when he got out.

The man they shook hands with in the yard was short, compact, swarthy, with the slightly bulging eyes and challenging stare that movie casting directors give to Sicilians. He was friendly and his movements were quick and nervous. Warden Fogliani, retired now, says, "He talked like an intelligent man with little education, but he had the fluency of the self-taught." Conforte made so many small loans in his first month that his image was set. Those in need managed to corner him, and for quite some time every pitch got something.

It was instant affinity between Cleary and Conforte. Joe had become interested in Cleary even before meeting him in prison, when Erle Stanley Gardner, the mystery writer and attorney, considered intervening in the Cleary affair and came to Nevada to study the case. To Joe, Cleary was a nice guy who had lucked out, a man who had lived a good life but who had hit into one bad hour. They liked each other. Cleary, who would be paroled and become a prison consultant in penal rehabilitation, was an amateur psychologist. In Joe he saw an interesting case of the superego, a basically generous guy full of complications, an intent man fiercely set on his own climb toward his own summits. They became friends, and within weeks were a team. After four months they were in charge of whatever self-government was allowed by Warden Fogliani.

At first Joe reacted badly to the walls, the claustrophobia that could reach the edge of terror. He had always found it hard to sit still, even to eat. He was used to money, to alligator shoes, the suits of good tailors, to long escapes in Europe, to weekends at San Francisco's Fairmont Hotel. Prison was tortured pileup, disinfectant, cells, bleached denim; the smells and sounds made him miserable. He brooded for some weeks and then, with the sudden release that is possible to some men, he licked claustrophobia by taking on a new ego-target. He would take charge of the prison, or that part of command which the warden was willing to delegate. Joe conscripted Cleary as his No. 2 man and, with the eagerness of a quarterback who has had a good rest on the bench, he started the moves that would put him in charge of the casino. Joe already had some money, if not the money of his reputation. Gambling tables must be bankrolled—it is a known fact that players don't like a game where the bank is weak. Joe was able to guarantee the payoff of every game in the casino by putting up less than $2,000. Since the banker always becomes something of an owner, Joe became a prison version of a Nevada licensee. Soon the grapevine said that the guy was a wizard at gambling and absolutely straight. Joe laughs and admits both rumors. "I've took rubes in my time, but Jesus, who'd trick a con?" Under Jim and Joe the casino became as popular as the mess hall. Joe would have gone farther, would have pushed for what in Mexico is called the "connubial room," where prisoners got a bed and an hour with their wives, but Joe had to stay with the possible. What really gave him status was something he invented in self defense, "the fund."

The prison had a lot of hardship cases and while Joe passed out considerable money, the touches became something of a strain. Joe thought the handouts should be spread through the general membership. "In any gambling game worth a damn," he explains, "the house has got to win." This was as true, of course, of the prison casino as for the Las Vegas Dunes. Joe's idea was to share the win with selected inmates, to make all senior prisoners stockholders. Cleary remembers, "You know, so much of this penology stuff is nonsense. It's not all tough derelicts in there at all, but a cross-section, same as outside. You jail a doctor, and over the years we had several, and you've got a cultured guy with money. You jail a man who's been making $50,000 a year, and he still has plenty. A lot of inmates had money and there was no problem getting it in, right into the cell. Some of these guys could have walked into Harrah's and been good for $5,000 credit. Of course, we kept the play low. We had dollar chips and then, so as to cut in the guys who were broke, nickel chips."

With so many good players feeding the casino, Joe set up the cooperative. Its capital was whatever the casino counted as win. The stockholders were those prisoners who had already earned some seniority, those who had what are called "compensation" jobs. A prisoner working in the laundry and making five dollars a month rated five points in the pool. A man driving a commissary truck and making ten dollars got ten points. Every two weeks came the dividend. Joe and Jim would retire to the captain's office, count the money on hand, deduct enough for the bank and for reserves, and then go through the alphabet of eligible prisoners to make up the packets. "Damndest morale builder you ever saw," says Cleary, "so many of the guys knowing that every second Friday there's that little bit extra." That was only the start. There were little emergencies for which prisoners needed money, so Joe created the "special account," which was separate from the dividends from the casino win. For this fund, money was held back from dividends and kept for the committee on emergencies, its chairman, Joe. "For example," says Cleary, "suppose that convict, John McGee, is due for release and he needs bus money to get to Seattle. Well, he gets word that on his last round of handshakes there will be an envelope with fifty bucks."

It was live and let live and help the next guy. In addition to running the games, Joe and Jim ran a betting pool which caught most of the big sports events, horse races, fights, baseball. Cleary explained, "A guard would come in and ask, what's the price on Notre Dame, or maybe some horse in the Preakness. We had to be up on the Las Vegas odds because some of these smart cons knew like they had shortwave radios. Well, comes the Fulmer-Robinson fight and there's a lot of betting. Now it happens the captain of the prison is a Mormon, and so is Fulmer. I forget this and we're chewing the fat, and I say, 'You know, Robinson is going to castrate that carrot-snapper.' The captain goes up the wall. He's so mad he asks for a chit and he bets $400 on Fulmer. Naturally, we got to cover. So Robinson wins and now it's funny, the captain can't pay. Which is bad, because an official who welshes can be unpopular. But Joe covers for him; he puts the dough in the fund and tells the captain, "Don't sweat it, sir, pay when you can."

Joe, generous, restless, obsessed with the need for applause, was Lord Bountiful. One time he raked Cleary. "Christ, there ain't no fruit around. Here it is, the peach and cantaloupe season and no fruit. Why don't you order some?"

Cleary was helpless. "There's no budget for it. Prison is supposed to be austerity. You go buying fancy stuff and pretty soon there's committees raising hell." But the following week the gates opened for a truck that was loaded with fruit, enough for all four hundred men for several days. Joe told the warden it was a donation from the Wadsworth Fire Department, which is a story that made the cons want to run Joe for governor. What happened was that Sally had been arranging for this truckful of fruit when her girls heard about it. Right away they insisted on passing the hat. But they figured it was too much to say the stuff came from a cathouse so they invented a fire department. Actually, Wadsworth didn't have one. For the rest of Joe's stay, that truck came every few weeks.

The prisoners thought Joe a hell of a guy. In the way of prisoners, there was not too much concern with what got him there, where he had slammed into society. His fellow cons knew, generally, that Joe had tangled with the D.A., that SOB, Bill Raggio, and that the state had charged extortion. But what the hell, all D.A.s are bastards.

Joe had slammed into society early. Whatever the astral influences, the pull of destiny that got him into what he calls "my lifetime fuckup," they began early.

The story starts with Agostino Conforte who, in 1920, was another of those Sicilians who had found the island to be "the mother of poverty." Agostino was several years putting together the steerage money to escape, but, eventually, he left for America. His destination was Dorchester, a suburb of Boston, where other townspeople had preceded him, and where they found a job for him working a fruit stand. But, from the first, Agostino worried about the wife and two daughters he had left behind. He found no peace and saved up for a trip back to Sicily. But the money and jobs were in America, so after some weeks, he was back in Dorchester. They were bad years for Agostino. When would he be able to bring his family to the "promised land"? He made a second trip to Sicily, and this time he stayed for two months. After he was back in Dorchester, his Francesca wrote him that he had a son now whom she would name Giuseppe.

Seen from a distance, Sicilian towns can be breathtakingly

beautiful, with the soft grays of stone, the red of the roofs, half-hidden in groves of olive trees. Rocky cliffs rise jaggedly against the landscape. Flowers grow in abundance. But up close, there is wretchedness. The slate roofs cover houses without running water; some homes have an electric cord hanging from a beam; some get light from kerosene lamps. Joe's house had an outside privy and a stove that was two depressions, where his mother fanned coals with a turkey wing. Joe does not remember her too well because she died when he was four. The local doctor, called in after her pains had lasted for weeks, diagnosed cancer, and could do little more than call the priest for the last rites. Relatives took Joe in. At six he had his first job delivering bread, and such was the poverty of the time that he decided that all theft must be judged by circumstance. "It was a big day when I managed to steal or beg some olives, so we could eat bread and olives. I stole the bread, too, but it was sort of understood, if it was only what you could eat, it was not a sin."

Joe's father was living in the Massachusetts of the Cabots, the Lodges, and the Kennedys, but Agostino knew little about them. He would learn little English during his lifetime, and never own a thousand dollars. He did make a living and he remarried, a Sicilian widow with two daughters of her own. In the household it was understood that he should go to Sicily once more to gather up his own family. Agostino made the last trip to pick up his children, and the son who was eleven years old when he first saw his dad. In Boston, Joe did not find much of a home. He and his stepmother developed an instant dislike for one another. Joe thought she favored her own girls, while his stepmother found him overbearing and obnoxious. "My family environment was shit from the start, and the situation outside wasn't so good either."

Dorchester had sections almost solidly Jewish, with islands of Sicilians. But the Irish, whether shanty or Kennedy, surrounded the suburb. Joe was the same age as his fellow townsman, Robert Kennedy—who became aware of Joe, years later, when a U.S. Attorney in Nevada would ask Washington for help in going after Joe. Bobby was attending military academy when Joe entered school to start his own twenty-month school career. He showed two facilities, a rather fast pickup of English and a talent for mathematics. Joe ran away from home twice, before he made it the third time. You find home hell, so you leave.

Joe's wanderings, the thousand-mile jerks of impulse, the years with the compulsive consistency of movement, in buses and at steering wheels, are a willed chaos. Joe remembers the smell of the ship that carried him to New York, the urinals of Grand Central Station, the color of the sky in Fallon, Nevada. His trail, land on which he cast a shadow, is important to him. Each zig and zag is fraught with meaning—the times he bought gas, or eluded a cop. He was reluctant to tell this much of his story because he believes that whenever he chooses to disclose the full richness of his wanderings, the hourly diary of his hungers, his ideas, his whore management, he will be launching one of the great motion pictures of our time. He is as enthralled by his own experiences as by those of Churchill or Kissinger.

"We was living with my stepmother and her daughters, which is silly because, naturally, she favored her own children. My sisters could take it, they have a different character, religious, took after our mother. But I took after my father, a flamboyant-type guy, going forward all the time, not caring for anybody. I was in one fight after another. I learned English fast. This neighborhood is so Jewish I had to learn English, because these Jewish kids sure wouldn't try Italian.

"First time I run away I go to Boston Common, sleep there for two nights, and the second night I'm lonesome, so I write my sisters. If they want me back, put an American flag on the porch. If I see it I come in, if not, to hell with it. Two days later I sneak by, and there's the flag. I snuck in by the fire escape that night. I put in another year, but it's bad. I run away again with another kid. We hitch a freight for New York, reach New London, and the train stops. It's a railroad dick, all excited. I guess he gets paid by the head for guys he catches. He pulls his gun and we come down. He takes us to the police barracks. The other boy tells them about himself, but he doesn't know much about me, and I tell them nothing, only my name, afraid they'll take me back. They can't decide whether to put me in juvenile or county jail, but I look older, so it's jail, like real hard cons, guys in on murder raps and armed robbery. I'm there a week, and even though I have passes made at me, I act tough, and nobody really gives me any trouble. But the police get my name—my father must have put in a missing persons—and my brother-in-law, a Portuguese fellow named Manuel, a fireman, nice fellow, married to one of my step-sisters, he and her come down to pick me up. This time I'm in front of a judge, because a complaint has been filed. That judge puts me on probation, and he says if I run away again its reform school.

"I go home for another year. One day, it's after midnight, and my stepmother and dad are in bed, and she's still nagging, telling him what a bum I am. Finally, the poor guy gets up and takes his belt and lets me have it. He goes back to bed and I leave Boston five minutes later. I have a few bucks and I take the Greyhound to New York. I land on 42nd Street. For two days I'm going crazy looking for a job, anything, and the only guys I meet on the street are homosexuals. I wave them off. Somehow, I wander into what they call, "Hells Kitchen," around 39th and 11th Avenue, full of fruit stands and pushcarts. There's this stand owned by a Jewish man, name of Jack Goldberg, real nice guy, kind of eccentric, but real nice. We hit it off. He don't need anybody, but he puts me on anyway. I'm a good worker, and he pays me $15 a week. My food and room is $4 a week, so I'm OK. But the neighborhood: kids there who would kill for twenty bucks. They see me and wonder what the hell I'm doing there. Well, they rough me up for a while, and then I got no choice, its a showdown. The chief of the gang, a punk, maybe sixteen, me, I'm fifteen, anyway he used to carry this short chain. It was a show-off thing, like a cop on the beat twirling his club. He corners me in a doorway and he says, 'Ok, pal,' he used other words, but I say 'pal.' 'How will you have it?' Well, you fight or you run. He says, 'I'm gonna stick my two fingers right in your eyes.' Well, there's a spoke from a broken wheel on the ground and I grab it and I come down on him so hard he really should have died. Blood all over. The cops come and question everybody, and nobody knows nothing. It works. Now they accept me. I live with them, go out with them, shoot craps. Sometimes I'm the lookout for the cops, and sometimes they are lookout while I run the game.

"It's about this time that Congress makes this law that all aliens has to register, so now, even though I'm a minor, its run-ins with cops asking where I'm born. If I register, I tell my age, that means Dorchester, and me on probation. I stay six months with Goldberg, but Hell's Kitchen, which is lousy in summer, is, I mean, real lousy in winter. Goldberg and I get in to some disagreement over some small thing and, by mutual agreement, I quit.

"So, it's Sunday, the 7th of December. I go to see a movie from France, they don't have any dirty French movies then, just movies from France. It was on Times Square. I come out and there's hollering and the lights was flashing, and everybody says Japan has sunk our battleships. I go to a movie and everything's calm; I come out, and it's war.

"But for me things go better, jobs are easier. I go to another fruit stand, owned by an Italian, in Yorkville, mostly German. There I do better. I'm able to steal five-ten dollars a week—not that I like to steal—but I still got to go west. The way I did it, when I sell an order for fifty cents, I stick the money down in my apron, and I know the register is fifty cents off. Then when I sell an order, say $2.75, I ring $2.25, and at the end of the day the register is even.

"I must explain that right after we get into the war, Congress enacted that all enemy aliens has to be home before dark. Which was tough, because it was spring and I was going nuts. I have $200 saved up, maybe half from what I lifted and, somehow, the boss finds out how I got it. He don't want to fire me because workers are hard to get, but he's not happy. So he says, 'you can handle the produce, Joe, but you don't go near the cash register.' Well, I wanted to quit anyway. I go to Trailways and there a guy tells me about these car pools where people will carry riders for a few bucks. Well, I find a guy, but he's going only to Cleveland, and you wouldn't want to hear about how that guy tries to screw his passengers, but, finally, I make L.A.

"Well, its a big city, I'm barely sixteen, and I don't know nobody, and which way do you go? I'm wandering around and just by fate I go east and I come to 7th and Central, which is the produce market, so, naturally, that's my kind of work. I'm walking through and who do I meet by chance? Jack Goldberg again. He couldn't believe it. He'd left New York when he heard that all these Japs was being evacuated from California to internment camps. They're leaving their fruit markets and people can buy them cheap, even for nothing, so he comes and gets one.

"He takes me to his house any my worries are over. I find a room for three dollars a week in the house of a German-Jewish lady that Hitler had threw out of Germany. There's two other roomers there, a couple of guys from Germany that Hitler also run out. These two had to register for the Alien Act and be home before dark. They take it for granted that I'm native born, and they sure envy that.

"Well, to skip some, its 1942, and the war is on full-blast. I, being sixteen, don't have to be in until I'm eighteen. Even though I'm working for Goldberg, me and another guy start looking around for a market of our own, because these Japs are moving out fast. We find one we can get for nothing down. We were going to be partners, but I don't like partners because you can't make decisions. So I figure, since neither one of us is investing anything, I wasn't screwing him. I tell him I don't think the place will make it, and maybe he better take it. But next day he decides he don't want no part of it, either. So now I go to the owner, and he asks how old am I, and I say, 'twenty-two.' He don't believe it, but he makes me a lease anyway and I have a market.

"So things are smooth for a while, but then I see that I'll have to register for the draft; they're closing in fast. And what do you do with a market? I get an idea. I have a new Dodge convertible and I decide to go to Boston and maybe get my dad to run it, except I go to Tijuana first, for a little run at the race track. And I visit a brothel. It was godawful but, anyway, I take a girl. A week later halfway to Boston, I start to itch. I scratch everyplace, all the way to Boston, and I'm afraid to ask anybody what's wrong. I drive up to my father's market, and everybody's happy because they don't know if I'm alive. I stay a month, and all the time itching. So then we decide that my younger sister, Lena, and my father, come west and take the store. I stand it all the way to Bristol, Oklahoma, and there I'm going crazy so I find a doctor. He says, 'You got crabs.' I had got them in Mexico and now, after all this time, you can imagine how dug in they were. "Well, a couple of months later, fate takes me to Oklahoma again. I seem to be the marrying kind. I meet a girl, Susan was her name, and I take her off, and we marry in Georgia, and that lasts three years. About this time I'm running a little whiskey, and just before we enter Oklahoma we're crossing Arkansas where there is a heavy rain and the cops are slowing down the cars. They see my car is riding low and they phone ahead to Oklahoma, and when I cross the line, the sheriff is waiting. He makes me open the trunk. Those Oklahoma cops don't really care about locking me up, they want the whiskey. They was real friendly. They let me sleep in the courthouse. Next day they take me to a judge and they ask me if I'm willing to forfeit the whiskey and pay $150. It suits me because they could have taken the car. They get four cases of Schenley and I'm free.

"We head back to Los Angeles, and now I got to face it. There's no more dodging the army. I sign in and, finally, I'm in the war. Its been a lot of mileage since that day in Times Square.

"My wife stays in this apartment in Los Angeles, and I go to San Pedro, California, for induction and then Ft. Lewis, Washington, for basic training. But army life is lousy. You know, some two-bit corporal tells you to pick up a cigarette butt. I'm in maybe six weeks and I tell a corporal to go to hell, and that's a summary court-martial. But not too bad. There's no confinement, you do three hours shoveling sand on a mountain in Olympia. Its supposed to be for thirty days but I shovel a couple of days and I can't see it. Couple of days later I'm in town with a friend, and we see a car with keys in it. You know, we don't stop that car, except for gas, until we hit L.A. I go to the wife's apartment and they tell me she's gone to Oklahoma with her mother. Also, she's pregnant. So my friend, he stops in L.A., but I keep going. This car was a Ford, real bad tires, good motor, but real bad tires. I take off for Oklahoma, but I need tires, so on the way to the freeway there is this bowling alley on La Cienega Boulevard, and in back is a parking lot. That's where I pick up California plates because my car has Washington plates. I finally make Oklahoma, and you know, that woman has gone to New Orleans with a girl friend. I make New Orleans and she's gone back to Oklahoma. I'm going through Lousiana and there's a red light flashing behind me. It's the police and I figure this is it. Here I am, I'm AWOL, I'm an alien, and I'm driving a hot car. Well, they ask a hundred questions except is it my car. Finally, one of them says, 'OK, you can go, but fix that taillight, it's blinking.' How close can you get?

"Now it's tires. You can't buy them, you have to have a certificate from the War Stabilization something: no trouble with gas because the farmers, lots of them, have drums hidden in the barn and they sell it black market; but tires are harder. Anyway, I pull into a gas station and it kills me. I'm almost broke and I got to order four retreads. The guy says he's going off duty and will I pay for them now; his son will come out and put them on. So the son comes out: I watch him while he puts on four *new* tires, and I debate what to do all the time he's doing it, but I drive on.

"That's a lot of grief just to get to Oklahoma, but, finally, I find her, and boy, is she pregnant! I talk her into coming with me to Fort Lewis, her and her girl friend. We're going through Colorado and suddenly, no brakes. I'm going downhill and I step on the brakes. I go into a skid and plough into a ditch. My wife is so shook up I thought she would have a miscarriage. But she didn't, because if she did, my God, my daughter wouldn't be alive today.

"Well, in two days we're in Olympia. It's just breaking daylight when I pull up to where I took the car. I wipe off all fingerprints and I leave it, not ten feet from where I took it, only it's seventeen days later. The owner, when he gets up, he's got to see them four new tires. So now we're on foot again. We take the bus to Ft. Lewis and I find my wife a place to stay, and I check in with the brass. Naturally, it's court martial. But the commander is a good guy, and he only gives me ninety days.

"So now I draw the combat engineers. My wife's rooming house isn't so hot and I send her to L.A. But the engineers don't last and I get transferred to another company. Which was a break. There's these two guys in my company that were aliens, and they tell me they're thinking to become citizens. You see, during the war, any alien who's in the service can make citizen fast. All you do is go in front of a judge, swear allegiance for ten minutes, and it's over. Me and these two guys, we go in front of a judge and we raise our hands and we take the oath and we're citizens. Well, things go fast. They're going to ship us to the Pacific, but just before we get our orders, a regulation comes out—by that time our baby was born—that any fathers who were drafted and didn't volunteer can get out because the war is almost over. Germany is falling apart and Japan's not doing too good either. Well, I ain't no Patton and I don't see any Italian making general, so I say what the hell, I can't see where doing the Manual of Arms in California is going to bother Hitler any, and I grab it. All of a sudden you're in civilian clothes, and you're free. But right about the same time my wife decides she can't keep up with me, and it's divorce. So I'm out of the army, and single, and back in the store, except now it looks like a crummy way to live, selling apples, for God's sake. I'm nuts about gambling and I head for Reno. I have a system I figured out. Naturally, I go broke. But I meet this girl, she's standing right in front of the Riverside Hotel. She's sixteen, her name is Kay, and she's waiting for a bus. I try to pick her up, but she looks the other way. She has such beautiful legs, I make a U-turn and come back, and this time she gets in. She tells me her troubles. How she can't get along with her step-dad. So I say 'Why don't you come to Los Angeles and live with me?' She decided, bang! We pick up what stuff she has and we head for Los Angeles. We get married and with her I have two other children. One's twenty-four now and the other's twenty-two.

"But this is before the babies. I can't get cranked up, no education, no trade, always broke. I try jobs and, finally, her and I, we head for Salt Lake. Maybe I can get a fruit stand in the Mormon country, but no go. We're in a rooming house, and I collect the 52-20, that the government pays ex-GIs who are out of a job, and she gets a job in a lunch counter. One day, we're absolutely flat, and she gets laid off. There's this ad in the paper that says cherry picking, 25¢ an hour, and I figure it's a little better than nothing. I hock my watch and coat for four dollars, but I wait till next day, and next day, no dime for the bus. I start walking. I'm half-way there and there's this gas station and I stop for a drink, and who's sitting there at a goddam desk? An army recruiting sergeant. I hate the army and the last thing I want to do is enlist, but it's hot, and back in our room our food is one box of peanut brittle. He looks at me and he says, 'Buddy, you look just right.' I said, 'OK, let's go.'

"They give me money for my wife, and we're off to Ft. Ord.

Pretty soon, somehow, I make the military police. I'm working the stockade and I make friends with a captain and he makes me a corporal. I graduate from the MP Corps and I'm shipped to Guam, in the CID investigating division. Well, part of the job is to check venereal cases, the idea being we find what girls are spreading it and get them cured. So we interview these guys. Sometimes they say a local girl, and other times, you won't believe this, they say it's army nurses. What's more, they paid them fifty bucks: that's like two hundred today. These nurses have them by the balls, an island, few women, all men, and they're whoring on the side. I never forgot.

"Back in the states I'm on town patrol in Monterey, policing GIs. One day I'm in the Monterey police station and I start fooling around with my revolver and it goes off. You know what a gun sounds like indoors, you can't hear for half an hour. I barely miss my buddy but I make a hole in the floor. So for that they ship me to an infantry company, and the moral is you just can't tell when a kick in the ass is your big break. I'm never really broke since. All the rest of the time I'm in the army, it's gambling. I'm taking these poor farm recruits who don't know how to play. The game is blackjack, which is murder for a beginner, and I'm pulling the stuff that real gamblers would laugh at, switching the deck, turning the deck over. Every month I rack up four-five hundred. I make enough to buy a car, and the Reno fever gets worse. My C.O. won't give me a pass so I wait until he leaves, and I steal his book of forms and I write my own. I make it to Reno and my system holds up three-four days, and I'm broke again."

Joe endured the rest of his enlistment. When he was finally discharged, he decided to go to Oakland, California, for no reason he can name.

In Oakland Sicilians had formed a transplanted army, men who knew that their best chances lay in the janitor-laborer-dishwasher level of jobs. Joe got one where, he says, "you qualify if you're able to stand. I start driving a cab. That fleet owner, he checks me for two things—do I see good and do I drink while driving!" He built up a fast knowledge of the Bay Area, fighting the cab over streetcar tracks, steering through the jam of trucks of industrial Oakland, getting fares that went as far north as the

"Little Italy" of Pittsburgh and as far south as the Spanish mission country of San Jose. It was during this period that it came to him that the only way to make it big was girls. What men want, how they are, was pounded into him by his passengers.

Today, some twenty years later, Joe, who knows that some Nevadans think he is contemptible, that he figures in state gossip as a noisy, boastful procurer, shrugs it off. He has his secret count of the important Nevada men who have come to him for money, and gotten it. "They ain't modest," he explains softly, "When they hit you, it's for thousands." He is calmly cynical about this, and will tell you that if he nods, new generations of politicians will get in line, happy to add to the list of those beholden to him. He will ask, whimsically, why it is that the men in the "dirty" industries, that is, whoring and gambling, should be singled out to underwrite so much of the state's political costs. "Now they come to me," he says, "Some directly, some through their managers, some through relatives."

He shrugs off his critics on another count: he has decided that most men are conformists in public and unbelievably lascivious in private. When excited by this idea, he sees himself as a Galileo, alone in his own integrity, fighting for his own theories of human law. Now that his income has soared beyond the wildest dreams of his youth, now that Reno's banks figure his one-man operation at well above a million dollar annual gross, he wants vindication. He has lived some twenty years in the Reno area, and has been inside only a few of its distinguished homes.

But all this—the experience with man in the mass, his indenture into sexual service, his experience with the human Eros, the final cynicism—were still to come. In Oakland, starting his day at 4 P.M., when offices began to let out, he felt that all the servility, the bowing to the moods of any stranger who got into his cab, was a bunch of crap. "Hell, it had as much reward as washing latrines." He was twenty-six when he tried driving a taxi, and he thought that now was the time to go for the money. His second wife had found Joe too much to keep up with and had gotten a divorce. Joe turned in his cab to open his first whorehouse.

"There's some weird fate that keeps me involved with the law,"

Joe finds. "That first house is right across the street from the cops. Right across from City Hall. What I do is make a deal with the owner of this hotel: I take his best suite, it wasn't much, and I set up a central point, like a dispatcher. I tell the taxi drivers that I got girls, and any customers can call me at this number. When a customer calls, I agree on whatever hour he wants and I tell him the room number. Then I call the owner of the hotel and tell him which room is reserved and the customer will rent it from him. I get the girl there when the customer is there. That hotel owner, he made a fortune renting the same rooms over and over, and it's a full day's rent every time. I have five girls. Sometimes I keep them in rooms right in the hotel, some, they want to sleep in their own places, so they wait by the phone. The fees—remember this is back in the 50s—was ten dollars minimum which, by the way, also turns out to be maximum most of the time. The customer pays the hotel separate. Afterwards, the girl stops by my room and I take half.

"Well, that business is good and bad. I got five girls, two of them was knockouts, and they're turning three, five, ten tricks a day each, but there's the cops. The third week a cop rings the bell and he tells me they know all about it. But he's reasonable: if I want to keep going it's OK, but I take care of them. So we set up the payoff; the two-bit jerk is happy with fifty a week. I meet him after hours, when he's in civilian clothes, and I give him his envelope. But that location is just too much: customers was coming in and out, taxis pulling up and leaving, and maybe a thousand city employees right across the way. Some of their windows look right into mine. One day the cop comes in, and its bad news. He says he can't protect me any more. The fix is not up high enough and, naturally, I'm too small for the kind of money it would take for a real fix up high. He says that even though I'm small, I'm making waves. He says I got to fold, and I did.

"Now I try an idea. Instead of a hotel, I open a place of my own. I rent a little house and I start small, just three girls, and I serve Orientals only. I pass the word among Oriental taxi drivers and waiters that it's a speciality house, them only. My real reason they never guess. You see, in those times no police department has a single Oriental on the force. When the cops want to bust you, they send one of their cops in disguise to frame one of your girls. So I figure, if I serve Orientals only, there's no mathematical chance any customer will be a cop. It works, anyway for a while. The cops hear about my new operation, of course, and they see how I'm being cute, keeping out any stoolies, so one day they make a raid. And I mean raid. You seen these movies, Edward G. Robinson and Raft movies, where they come charging in with axes? You know, where the ax has a blade on one side and a fire hook on the other? Well, that's what they had. They make kindling out of the front door; they even took out the frame. They haul us to jail, me and the girls. So I'm in front of another judge, and he says he's got nothing against the girls, but it's me. So the deal is, I pay a fine and they let the girls go. And that was the end of that. My first go in California don't work because, basically, when you're against the law, you can't make it. I close the house, and this is when I make the decision. I say goodbye to California, and I decide to go to Nevada, because there it's legal."

5

Joe, His Wars

ONCE AGAIN Conforte took the beautiful drive through the Sierras to Reno, a man seeking new lands and under the impression that prostitution was legal in Nevada. Today, so many years later, Joe can still get a bit tangled by the law's complications, and it is wonderful to watch the face of his attorney, Stanley Brown, when Joe takes over and decides to clarify the whole thing—statute, ordinance, decision, and common law. In Reno, Joe roamed around for months testing the climate. He got cozy with bartenders and cab drivers; he threw dice in what was then a small Harrah's, and he talked with the dealers. He discussed his idea with lawyers, tavern owners, police, always to find the answer the same, no way. "One lawyer, he tells me I stand a better chance of setting up a few beds in the Vatican." Quite probably, Joe could have set up in one of the small towns along 80, but that was peanuts. Joe wanted the coitus of one of America's two gambling cities, a city that was starved for girls, outlawed since Pearl Harbor.

It took only days to discover that Washoe was hostile, in fact, almost phobic in its determination to block any return of the famous three, the Alamo, Green Lantern, and Mohawk. The man who spoke for the town was the District Attorney, Dyer Jensen, a man Joe remembers as "A nice guy, and pure rock." At one point,

Joe asked several people whether Jensen might be holding out for an offer, and was told not to try it. Joe brooded over Jensen's stubbornness for some months, then one day he decided to meet the problem head on, face the lion in his den. Joe called on Dyer Jensen in his book-lined courthouse office. After a few friendly generalities, Joe asked him, courteously and man-to-man, how come such a liberal city should take such a hard attitude on so human a thing as fucking. Jensen explained gently that it was against the law and, more particularly, against the law as stated by Nevada's Supreme Court in the "Cunningham" case, about which Joe would learn so much later. He was so nice about it, so unpatronizing, that when Joe walked out he was filled with admiration. He was passing the Riverside Hotel when he saw the window display of the florist. He ducked in and told the clerk to send Jensen the enormous rubber plant in the window. The D.A. kept it alongside his American flag until he left office.

In refusing Joe, Jensen was skipping a lot of complex explaining, taking a conversational shortcut by simply saying that houses were against the law. Actually, it was the reasoning which has been policy in Reno and in Las Vegas for twenty-five years, and based on the policy which has had many names: the "Don't-Bait-Congress" policy, the "Don't-Rock-the-Boat" policy, the "Walk-with-Low-Profile" policy, the "Don't-Rub-Their-Noses-in-It" policy, and one—attributed to the late Benny Goffstein, colorful boss of Las Vegas' Riviera—the injunction, "Never-Piss-on-the-FBI." Later, writers took liberties with this, and one gave the quote as "Don't-Never-Piss-on-Congress." It is an interesting story of the thinking of the gambling bosses.

By the time Joe hit Nevada in 1955, the gambling owners, who have since taken control of the state, were already strong. In Las Vegas, that first money factory, Siegel's Flamingo, had now been duplicated eleven times, to give the state its own Kuwait, the boulevard known as the "Strip." In Reno, in the north, the gambling men had brought the first real money the north had ever known, and it has kept its people grateful ever since. Each year gambling income topped the record of the year before. With fewer people than Idaho, Nevada was soon earning the money of states with twice the population. Gambling brought jobs, allowed its people to skip an income tax, to have low taxes generally. And the people who brought the wealth—Harrah, Smith, Levinson, Dalitz, Riddle, Houssels, Webb—had the gratitude of everyone. Of course, there have always been a few souls who said gambling was a dirty and parasitic business, but it became seditious to say so. Money was pouring in, and this was the good part.

But there was still the terrible, enduring fear that Nevada's bliss could end. Ever since it was found that Siegel was a gangster, and that so many of the original Las Vegas owners had some sort of eastern hookup, the native Nevadan lived in dread of a Washington crackdown; the dread that Congress could close gambling and return Nevada to the poverty of its youth. Nevadans realized that the rest of the nation considered it a unique, dirty growth, and that the dangers that could flow from this revulsion were permanent. Ten years after Siegel, when gambling had rescued the state, it had also become the most villified business in America. Gambling, with its assumed gang ties, had revolted the nation's editors, and provoked the long attack which became known as the "18-Year Diatribe." (See Chapter 8.) No accusation was too dirty to direct at a state which was assumed to be one of the four or five centers of organized crime. In the legislature, worry became a way of life. Ten and fifteen years after Kefauver's investigation,[1] senators were still repeating his warning, that Nevada gambling must go. J. Edgar Hoover reacted by making his Nevada force one of the biggest in America.

Following the Kefauver disclosures, there were many attempts in Congress to write bills to end Nevada gambling. The bills were defeated in every case by Nevada Senator Pat McCarran, who argued that they were unconstitutional, that they violated states' rights. But the anti-gambling forces kept looking for a formula and, in 1951, they thought they had one—kill gambling by taxing it to death. A house bill was introduced that put a 10 percent tax

---

[1] The 1950 hearings of the U.S. Senate Committee, headed by Senator Estes Kefauver, which first announced that Nevada casinos were owned by the underworld.

on every "gambling transaction," nationwide. In Nevada the bill is still remembered as the document that could have wrecked the state.[2]

Nevada mounted a powerful overnight lobby, and managed to have Nevada exempted, but from then on, the owners lived with the knowledge that another such bill could be passed by any Congress that got sufficiently fed up with Nevada.

The federal anger held. Some years later, when Robert Kennedy had become Attorney General, Nevada learned that he represented a phobic form of the national dislike, and that his specific hatred of Nevada was as strong as his hatred of crime in the abstract.

As the press diatribe continued, the gambling bosses agreed on the policy of defense. The core idea was that Nevada, which had so many bad images—gambling, criminal ownership, skimming —must not taunt the nation with any more. Translated, this meant prohibiting many things. Nevada should avoid becoming a narcotics center. Its police should try to keep the state's drug traffic below comparable state averages. Nevada should try to keep all crime below comparable averages; it should try to avoid murder, rape, extortion, robbery. Nevada should bar the honky-tonk businesses that have shady hookups. The gambling bosses blocked three attempts to bring in dog racing, three to introduce horse racing, two attempts to have state or private lotteries, three attempts to legalize wire betting, and several to legalize massage parlors. One Las Vegas commissioner even wanted a freeze on pawnshops, arguing that they dramatize the destitution caused by gambling. The sleazy burlesque houses, that were standard in all big cities, were long discouraged in Nevada. As for legal prostitution, both gambling cities said "no."

---

[2] It would have ended Nevada gambling on the day the president signed it. No casino would have tried to see how it worked because its mathematics were so lethal. To take a case: a man sits down at a 21 game with $1000 and plays, as many men do, off and on during the day for a total of six hours' playing time. At moments, he may be hundreds or thousands ahead, and at others, playing on credit. Assume that his bets average $30 each, and that he makes sixty bets an hour (often the pace of 21) the IRS would take $3 per play, or $180 per hour. For the six hours, the IRS would take $1,080. No one even tried to figure what a "transaction" might be in slot machine play.

So on that summer morning in 1955, when Joe pulled into Reno in his green Kaiser, innocent in the assumption that a gambling state is an "anything-goes" state, he was bucking the decisions of strong men. The gambling owners had decided that open whorehouses in Reno or Las Vegas could be the last straw for those powerful Nevada-haters[3] in Washington. But no one explained the "walk softly" doctrine to Joe, who would have called it crap if anyone had.

Faced with Washoe's Maginot Line, Joe went to the maps. Like any general, he studied roads and boundaries. He was seeking a spot outside of Washoe, and as near as possible to Reno. Washoe's nearest neighbor counties are Storey and Lyon, both of which come together in the canyon of the Truckee River, near a forgotten village called Wadsworth. In this triangle, where three counties met, Joe got to know ranchers and county lines and riparian rights as no district attorney ever could. He would park his car and take hikes through the tree-filled riverbottom. He became one of the few men who could point to an abandoned Indian buggy and tell, within feet, how close it was to what line. Eventually, the choices had narrowed down to a patch of alfalfa pasture which had what he needed. It was just outside Washoe, in Storey, yet within four hundred yards of the great lifeline, 80.

The village of Wadsworth has never had much. Some three hundred people then, and fewer now, all in a sprawl of shacks, and so many of them empty that it had the feel of a ghost town. But to Joe its values were geographic; four peninsulas ended there: Washoe County has a tiny bulge that barely embraces Wadsworth. Storey County has a point that reaches within a quarter-mile of Wadsworth. A third county, Lyon, zigzags to a point about as close and, roughly coinciding with the Washoe boundaries, there is a federal peninsula, the Pyramid Indian Reservation, which also embraces Wadsworth. Joe figured that if he operated in this triangle of boundaries, it would take a survey party to determine where he was. A girl-house here, of course,

---

[3] It was quite a *Who's Who* of enemies, a list that seemed to be self-renewing through the years. The list began with Senator Kefauver, ran through the eras of Senator McClellan and Attorney General Bobby Kennedy, and, most recently, included President Nixon's Attorney General, Richard Kleindienst.

would be pretty far from Reno, but the cost to customers would be bearable. "I talk to Reno cab drivers and they figure most of them would settle on 15 bucks flat round trip, to include reasonable waiting time, of course." (Over the years, Joe would learn that after waiting twenty or thirty mind-boggling minutes, some drivers lose all character and go in themselves so that, at times, a passenger would have to wait for his driver.)

While Wadsworth itself offered several fall-down abandoned houses, they were in Washoe. In Storey, there were only two, both on desolate, starved little farms. Joe picked the better one, a four-room affair. He brought in carpenters and electricians, and on a warm afternoon in June, he moved in with his girls.

Within days, Joe had put up road signs with arrows that pointed to the "Triangle River Ranch."[4] He turned to promotion. Word spread through Nevada and neighboring states that the drought was over. Once again you could get naked young girls who did everything. Gossip added the usual embroidery, and there were stories that in Wadsworth[5] newspaper men got half-rates, and judges were served free.

Joe was operating five months when he met the woman who would become the stabilizing force in his life, the person who would fit into his plans, who would adjust to the contours of his personality in such a way as to complete what he needed to survive the years of his adversity. Sally was a handsome and practical woman. She had never been a prostitute but saw nothing wrong with women who were. She had operated a couple of small houses off and on in Nevada, but without the ego, the drive, and the flair that it needs to do it big. Sally called on Joe one day to ask for advice, and the idea hit both of them that if they got married they could pool their ideas as well as labor. For reasons they have forgotten, they postponed the ceremony for two years.

Sally entered into the arrangement which has endured, in

---

[4] There is disagreement in Nevada as to who first used "ranch" for a girl-house. At least ten houses use it today, but we may have to wait for some professor to exhume the records to see if Joe is right in his claim that it was he who started it.

[5] Joe was not really in Wadsworth—a half-mile beyond—but close enough so that in time the names Wadsworth and Joe's became almost interchangeable.

which she was really the manager—she runs things 95 percent of the time, but gives way to Joe in those fitful, irregular moments when he chooses to take over and, for the run of his mood, be acting czar. Sally found Joe's house woefully inadquate, and decided on a major alteration. But Joe had already begun to feel the shape of things to come, the fact that he might need more than one house in what could be a harassed and mobile business. He had noticed that, a quarter-mile away, there was a tumble-down little shack that was also in Storey. Joe bought it. Sally did a remodeling that almost demolished the second house. When the contractors were through, the Confortes had put $30,000 into a bungalow containing eight rooms and two baths. Later, when that part of Nevada had four of Joe's girl-plants, his first would become known as the "White House," and the second, the cele-brated "Green House."

When Sally teamed up with Joe she knew, of course, that her man had had many girls. Joe had also had several affairs that were serious. One was with a girl who had taken the name of Beverly, and whom Sally met simply as one of Joe's first workers. Beverly would survive the years, always standing by through Joe's convul-sive life. She was certainly the most loyal girl Joe had ever known, outside of Sally. Beverly started as a White House girl, but has since taken on many roles. She has become the kind of helper for which Joe has never really found a good name: the choices, "host-ess," "assistant madam," "supervisor," would be too much an inva-sion of Sally's authority. He finally settled on calling them "maids." Sally accepted Beverly as a good whore. For a long time she never knew the full extent of her involvement with Joe, nor that she and Joe had had a son.

Measured against Joe's compulsion to travel several thousand miles a month, his first three years at the Triangle were relatively quiet. He might have lived quite peacefully with his operations had he been modest, content to speak softly, be inconspicuous, and, as with the madams of Nevada, to walk with low profile. But Joe is not modest. Since he considers prostitution as honorable as any business in the phone book, he made the illogical jump to the idea that those who used his girls thought so too. Then, as now, he would get into syllogistic crises, like a troubled St. Thomas Aquinas, when he saw Nevada's eminent enter his house, devour his girls, and say "thanks" when told that it was on the house. Joe's judicial detachment was shot to hell by such episodes. Within a year of opening the Green House, he had seen so many Reno and Carson men use his beds, such a variety of city, county, and state officials that, adding two plus two, he got five, and felt that he was being accepted. Joe was never cynical enough to understand how there could be such back-slapping and cordiality wherever he went, that men should accept his campaign help, his charity money, his complimentary girls, and then, in their homes and clubs, joke about the colorful pimp. With innocent exuberance, Joe began making a bit of a show of his visits to Reno. Word would go through town; Joe was in Harrah's with two gorgeous babes, one on his left holding his chips, and one on his right holding his money. Joe would drive through town in an open convertible with laughing girls, redheads, blonds, brunettes. Some people thought it funny and some thought it shocking. District Attorney Jensen heard complaints: law and decency were being mocked. The man was using the sanctuary of another county to show open contempt. Jensen began to feel that he should find some way of checkmating Joe or hear talk of dereliction in office. Jensen tangled with Joe a few times and tried to have him arrested; once he set up a barricade on 80, stopping all cars in the hope that Joe would be in one of them. But Jensen never really made it a contest. For one thing, Jensen would soon decide to leave office, for another, he had a grudging fondness for Joe. Joe's real troubles started when Jensen's assistant D.A., William J. Raggio, went for the big job and won.

Young Bill Raggio had been an assistant D.A. since 1952. After Joe opened, he was in a good position to see the undeniable surge of the Triangle. He heard what everybody heard, that Joe was growing, that he had branched out, and his newest places were the Desert Inn and Montgomery Pass. Joe says that these two rather sorry places gave him a reputation for empire, which was nice but not deserved, because both did poorly in bad locations.

Joe was beginning to show some prosperity, which meant that all kinds of men were coming to him with deals. One man offered him a restaurant and bar, located in a magnificent part of the Sier-

ras, at the crest of a ridge where Highway 6 crosses into California, a dramatic Alpine region of pines, crags, meadows, and
streams. Joe bought it. He put in a manager who found that the
users of historic Montgomery Pass were few and that, more important, there was no surrounding community to serve. Inevitably,
Joe got to wondering whether a few girls might help. He set up a
cottage in back, put in three girls, and after a time got a little
trade. But the "Pass" taught him two axioms; one, that a whorehouse does fine wherever there are deer hunters, but, since the
deer season is so short, "Don't count on them." And "Don't count
on skiers." Come autumn, the Pass saw a great passage of Volkswagens with skis on top, whose drivers would come in for hamburgers. "But the skier," says Joe, "and this goes for the Dolomites
or Switzerland, is a boy who carries his chick with him. You
couldn't sell him a girl if you threw in a tankful of gas." Still, it
was Joe's private disappointment, while Reno whispered that Joe
was putting together a chain operation.

His reasons for opening the Desert Inn were more compelling.
The Triangle was on a section of 80 which had few turnoffs. For
the men who lived in the area of Carson and the gambling end of
Lake Tahoe, the Green House was a long drive and this was bad
for "sudden impulse" business. This was observed by a competitor, who managed to get clearance from Lyon County officials and
opened a house, the Starlight, just six miles away from Carson. Joe
tried to ignore the place but it was cutting into his business. So
Joe found land near the Starlight, put up a house, and named it
the Desert Inn. He felt sure that down in Las Vegas, the owners
of the celebrated DI would not mind. But both the DI and Montgomery Pass meant the kind of absentee management which put
so much mileage on cars. To run the four places, the White
House, the Green House, the Pass, and the Desert Inn, Joe had to
set up a rotation between his two trusted helpers, Beverly and
Brigette (more about her later); it meant commuting for Sally
and many tire-squealing drives for Joe himself. Still, the poorest of
the four, the Pass, made some money, while the Green House was
beginning to look like one of the best operations in all of Nevada.

William Raggio was determined to go far in life. Even as a boy he toyed with dreams of becoming governor or senator. But he could hardly do so as a banker, rancher, or military man; he would have to do it on the career rails he had chosen, as a D.A., and as a wrathful crusader against crime. It is possible that Raggio might not have felt so confronted if the Wadsworth house had been opened by a Schultz or a Sheridan or a Stein. But for the operator to be an Italian meant that Raggio might be accused of going easy on a co-national. Raggio also faced an odd little racial situation; he was descended from the Genovese, while Joe was Sicilian. As is well known, the entire Italian peninsula lives in something of a north-south cultural pecking order. The Piedmontese and Milanese of the north patronize the Tuscans, the Tuscans smile at Romans farther south, and most Romans tend to think everything south is slightly quaint. These little racial conceits travel well. They have even survived the Atlantic crossing. In a hundred Little Italys, on New York's lower East Side, and on Columbus Avenue in San Francisco, they have passed from father to son. As a result, a Milanese bootblack in Camden or a Tuscan janitor in Cleveland will patronize a New York Calabrian, even if he is a member of Congress. In Nevada, as well as California, the Genovese were entrenched; they were a hard-working people who had no indigents and quite a few millionaires. Like most of Italy's racial clans, they hated being lumped in with Sicilians as Italians.

When Joe arrived, the local Genovese groaned. And when the nation's newspapers began writing about the free-wheeling Nevada procurer whose name made him an Italian procurer, they would have been happy to raise a fund to have him deported. Years later, when Joe had frustrated a number of people who tried to get him out, and when his income put him in a class with Texans, people assumed that now the big bank, the First National, with its large Genovese staff, would take a kinder view of Joe. The assumption was wrong because, except for nominal sums in a checking account, Joe didn't use banks. Inevitably, Nevadans read the stories about the Mafia, of its love for prostitution, and the rumors that Lucky Luciano had run it all. Some people wondered whether this fellow, Conforte, just might have some dotted-line hookup with the syndicates, and the thought bothered the uptight Italians of Reno. Actually, state police soon decided that Joe was a loner, but this did not stop the occasional questions. Raggio felt that to express distaste for Conforte was smart on all counts.

The contrasts between Joe and his future Nemesis were great. Joe's education consisted of four grades in Dorchester, and he had read his first book in prison only because a departing con had left one behind. Raggio, on the other hand, had attended three universities, and had had his choice of fraternities. After receiving his law degree at the University of California, he received several offers for law partnerships, which fitted into the joke that the ideal law firm has four WASPs, one Jew, and one Italian. He moved fast. Within a year, at twenty-six, he became Assistant D.A. He soon fixed his image statewide. He was urbane, liked and resented. One judge said of him, "You had to like him because of his charm, but you couldn't have a drink with him without seeing the fantastic ambition, that poorly concealed wish to be president." As a D.A. he was hell on wheels, working hard and putting on tough courtroom performances. The Reno of his time could not give him the sensational cases, the showcase trials of the big cities, so he made do with what he had. He became a ferociously efficient prosecutor of any man who had the bad luck to stumble in Washoe.

Raggio began to think of Joe Conforte in something of the way J. Edgar Hoover used to think of Bobby Kennedy, that is, as a man born to drive him nuts. In their huge courthouse headquarters, Raggio and his deputies got feedback from everyone; taxi drivers, truckers, and countless Reno men who had tried the Triangle, all reporting that Joe was doing great. And, some would add, the business was mostly from Reno.

Raggio has always been gregarious. After work, as he left the courthouse, he would stop at the Mapes Bar. At that hour, the place could look like a private men's club. The town's professional and business men gathered there and the banter at the bar would be informed and sharp. Raggio, sipping his bourbon, came to believe that Reno's attorneys were sworn to a pact to invent some new Raggio-Conforte joke every week. There are men who have watched the Raggio-Conforte feud who are sure that it hardened because of the laughter. In the bars, men found it amusing that Joe should have set up only a few yards beyond Raggio's reach. Raggio, a law and order man, laughed without much humor.

The feud started almost as soon as Raggio had moved up as top man, though the two have different versions of the how and why. Joe says that Raggio was cordial at first, that they would kid in their encounters, and that at one time Raggio even solicited Joe's help in getting votes. Their first meeting, Joe says, occurred when Raggio was contemplating a small suit. Like all members of the D.A.'s staff, Raggio used his office for private practice, and he had been retained by a dentist to collect a bill. The amount, $350, was owed by one of Joe's girls. Raggio met with Joe to discuss the bill and Joe was delighted to accommodate such a powerhouse. He peeled off a $100 bill then and there and promised that the girl would pay in full.

But it was obvious that Raggio had decided he could not be friendly with Joe. The hostility was subtle at first. It became clear that terrible day when Raggio told Joe that he was not to use Washoe, not as his home, not for shopping, not for visits, not for recreation. At a meeting attended by Raggio's deputies, Joe was told that if he wanted to enter Washoe, he would have to ask permission each time. Joe found that he could now enter Reno in something of the way visitors enter Nevada's nuclear test site, with a permit issued at the gate, to be surrendered on leaving. Joe thought this was pure Hitlerism, and he took an oath he would never ask permission. He was determined to challenge Raggio, and the chance came the next day. Joe drove into Reno at noon to see a doctor about suspected ulcers, and ran into deputies who placed him under arrest. The law that Raggio used went back to Nevada's beginnings, the one that says that any man who habitually frequents the premises of prostitution shall be deemed a vagrant.

Joe seethed. "Vagrants are bums, and every year I'm giving as much to charities as Raggio earns." He posted bond, and swore, if necessary, to carry the fight all the way to the Supreme Court. Still, he was aware that change had come. There was no way of knowing how long he must live under bond. If Reno was to be off-limits, he might as well be banned from Nevada.

Joe has always had girls, uncountable, unremembered girls, who blur in memory as blonds, redheads, and jets. His coital count is a fact which Sally has had to accept. In that kind of union, where husband and wife preside jointly over rooms in which, year in and year out, men hit climax on an average of once every ten minutes, Sally found it hard to control a man who thinks girls are for screwing. Moreover, Sally was still some time away from marrying Joe, and not quite in a position to talk like a wife. In the year of his big trouble with Raggio, Joe was a man who might have had to go to the Middle East to find sexual peers, for only those sultans, emirs and sheiks, with real life harems, had anything like his own willing stable. But at that moment, Joe was not playing the field because he was taken with one, the one he remembers as having the ability to make him oblivious to other girls.

She was born Elsie Mae Hitson and, like so many of the girls, had what is variously called a nickname or "whorehouse" name: Elsie's was Carmen. She had driven up to the house one day, asked for a job, and gotten it, to become the girl he favored the most for several years. "Built like a Coca-Cola bottle," he says, "and never no moods. She looked a little Elizabeth Taylorish, but more gay. She liked everybody." Carmen worked for him and served her daily quota of men, at one time helping out at Montgomery Pass when he needed people who were dependable. But her hours in the back room made no difference in their feeling for each other. They still had that emotional something which they considered their separate love. Joe took her everywhere. Like so many men of northern Nevada, Joe had become a baseball fanatic when the New York Giants moved to San Francisco, just as so many Las Vegans developed instant love for the Brooklyn Dodgers when they moved to Los Angeles. (Joe's attorney says that if Reno people could ever understand Joe's terrible need to identify, to be a joiner, to share, to be accepted as a fellow booster, they could get Joe to build a new City Hall.) He and Carmen had fine weekends on the coast, staying in good hotels, dining at Fisherman's Wharf, and shouting at Candlestick Park. He would drive Carmen to visit her folks in Escondido, an amiable household, where the mother, divorced from Carmen's father and remarried, was not upset that Carmen should be at the Triangle, and happy that she was Joe's best girl.

One Sunday afternoon, Joe and Carmen took a drive down the Truckee Canyon and almost automatically fell to discussing what had become Joe's cross, the "No trespass" declared by Raggio. They saw it as a something that could wreck a career, and they drove in worried thought. Then Carmen was hit with an idea. "Joe honey," she said, "what if we get Jackie over here and sic her onto the son-of-a-bitch? Get him to buy her drinks. How about that, a D.A. buying drinks for a minor?" Joe's imagination took flight; he was airborne for days. Within minutes he was orchestrating a plot, taken with the lovely vision of that symbol of law and order, Raggio, buying drinks for a teenage girl.

"Jackie" was Carmen's younger sister, a girl whom he had met several times when they visited her family in Escondido, California. Jackie did not have her sister's beauty, but she was quiet and thoughtful, and pretty enough to know that boys stared. She was also acutely aware that she had huge breasts. She looked older than seventeen. Jackie was no longer at home: she did not get along with her stepfather and she was living with friends in a neighboring town. She had found a job as a carhop in a place called the Carhop. Early one morning, Carmen started the drive to California to get her, and as she drove Joe's white Ford pickup truck,[6] she started a considerable chain of events. As one result, Nevada would have one of the fascinating court trials of its history; as another, Raggio would bring in a grand jury indictment that would send Joe to jail.

Most of the events are told in two versions, Raggio's and Joe's. The most truthful version may be Joe's, since it is so candidly

---

[6] Thirteen years later, Joe Conforte, standing in front of Reno's First National Bank, passed out 31 thousand-dollar bills to a man who delivered a customized Lincoln Continental Mark IV, made for him in Los Angeles. This car became the stablemate of a long black Cadillac for which Joe paid $10,000, as a used car, which the seller said had been used by Patricia Nixon. But these were the cars of his affluence, and the vehicle used by Carmen to go for Jackie was the Triangle's two-year-old, all-purpose burden bearer.

self-incriminating. Carmen found Jackie at the Carhop and persuaded her to come to Wadsworth for the framing of Raggio. She
was given a room at the White House, as Joe worked on his script.

Here Joe showed a nice understanding of a situation peculiar to
Reno. For something like thirty years, ever since Nevada lowered
the divorce residency requirement to six weeks, Reno lawyers
have had the female pickings of stallions at stud. The women
arrived, first on the smoky trains of the Overland Limited, then on
the streamliner City of San Francisco, later, by plane, to add
thirty new faces a day, as the average over the years. Generally,
the lady had no knowledge of the town, no friends in it, and only
one contact, her lawyer, who often would be at the plane or train
to meet her. They were women who had left homes, condemned
to wait out their time in a hotel or guest house. For some reason,
buried in our ways, most of them were young. Now, facing the
trauma of divorce, they fell easily into a stereotype, into the
image of the "Reno divorcee," a woman who is lonely, broody,
restless, and, in her psychological mixup, what the boys called an
"easy lay." Since the only man she knew was her attorney, she
looked to him for introductions, to get her somehow through a
bearable exile. In Reno gossip it was a constant joke; the lawyers
who were clever had the pickings of movie directors. Those who
were bachelors, and those others who could mollify their wives
about meetings with their clients, fell into easy affairs. Ordinary
men built up such lifetime conquests as they could never have
managed in another environment. One celebrated Reno bachelor
(a president of the First National Bank, and not an attorney)
made it a twenty-year sub-career to meet each month's most beautiful arrivals. When Joe planned the undermining of Raggio, his
mind went to the custom in which it is so easy for a lady to step off
a plane in the morning and be on a first-name basis with her lawyer
that night.

Joe sought a complete script. Jackie became Mrs. Val Newton
(Joe happened to be eating Fig Newtons), a woman of twenty-
two who was in Reno for a divorce. Joe invented a husband, a
navy man, and a short, bleary marriage. Jackie had met "Val" and
had gone with him to Tijuana where they drank a lot. Afterward,

her sailor left, presumably to return to his ship. Joe knew that attorneys need detail and he tried to supply it. Raggio would want the name of the ship, and Jackie came up with the USS *Winnebago* which, though not a naval vessel, was the Coast Guard vessel on which Jackie's brother had served. Equipped with an identity and a past, Jackie called on Raggio.

It was on a late Friday afternoon, and she had no trouble getting him to accept her case. She acted her part beautifully, according to Joe, and suspiciously according to Raggio. She said she had no hotel room, and Raggio arranged to get her into the Riverside, into Room 610. That night she called Joe to report a hopeful start. Joe told her to keep pushing and to report when ready.

On Monday, Joe and Carmen picked Jackie up and took her for a drive. She told them that she had made an appointment with Raggio. They had met, gone to the Riverside bar and, in full sight of a number of friends who dropped by, and who even sat at the table, Raggio bought her drinks. She met a number of Raggio's friends, including the goodlooking attorney, John Squire Drendel. Jackie said that they bought so many rounds of drinks that she got drunk. She then went up to her room, was joined there by Raggio and one of his cronies; the two men had flipped a coin to see who would have her, then the loser left, and the winner, Raggio, spent some time with her in intercourse. Under questioning by Joe, she gave the mechanics and details.

Joe moved immediately. He drove Jackie and Carmen to the office of his attorney, Frank Petersen, and had Jackie tell her story. Joe told the astonished lawyer that he wanted a parley with the D.A. himself, and would Petersen set up the meeting. Petersen relayed the request to Raggio, who delayed three days before agreeing to meet with Joe. It was to have been a meeting of three: Petersen, Conforte, and Raggio, but on the appointed day, Petersen found he had to be in Winnemucca.

The two men met at the street doorway at nine in the evening. They exchanged guarded hellos and went upstairs; they searched each other and went into a half-joking, half-grim banter as to who was bugged. The meeting went two hours, a dialogue in which, unquestionably, Conforte tried to extort the D.A., and in which the D.A. showed matching guile, for the whole thing was being fed to recorders. They created what is still the second longest tape in the annals of Nevada trials. (The longest was made by the FBI when taping Ruby Kolod of the Las Vegas Desert Inn.) Raggio had used the three-day delay to bring in the well-known California detective, Harold Lipset, whose speciality was tapping, bugging, and recording. Raggio had gone to the owners of the building, Harrah's Club, and had asked the man who is now its president, Maurice Sheppard, for permission to get into the office above that of Petersen. The highly professional Lipset was given access and, knowing that tapes can have static or blanks, installed not only one machine but two. The conversational duel, caught by his recorders, was duly played to a jury, its sounds complete to grunts, explanations, argument, an occasional "shit" and "fuck" by Joe, and much hesitation by the D.A., who knew he was speaking for posterity. Joe hedged for a while and then came out with it: Jackie had told her mother about her intercourse with him in room 610, this quite apart from the other serious matter, giving drinks to a minor. The mother was mad and was threatening prosecution. Joe was sure that he could call her off. He told Raggio that he wanted a truce, a trade, actually; if Raggio stopped his war, Joe was sure he could persuade Jackie's mother to forget everything. At moments, the two men even seemed to enjoy the contest, the lobs, volleys, the scoring of points. At the end of two hours, Joe escalated; he asked Raggio for four things: (1) that he dismiss the vagrancy suit, (2) that he make an apology of sorts, some statement that the arrest was made in error, (3) that Raggio stop blocking him from coming to Reno, (4) and, almost as an afterthought, a favor for a friend, the doctor who made the weekly inspection of his girls, and who was then under indictment for the very act of which Joe accused Raggio, furnishing liquor to a minor. Joe suggested that Raggio quash that charge too. If Raggio did these things, or at least the main one, to lay off, Joe was sure he could persuade Mrs. Hitson to forget the violation of her daughter. When, around midnight, each man felt he had made his points many times, they parted, with Raggio making a vague promise to let him know.

The D.A. made Joe sweat for four days. Toward evening of the fourth day, Raggio put in a call to the White House, to be told that Joe was at the Desert Inn. He reached Joe there and told him he wanted a meeting, and suggested a picnic ground, Bowers Mansion, which was in Washoe County. Joe, nervous and worried, agreed to meet, but proposed Virginia City. He called his attorney to explain developments. Petersen's advice was to get out of the state, that night, that minute. Joe, for once inclined to listen to an attorney, began making plans. He was packing when the doorbell sounded to admit two Washoe deputies carrying a warrant. He was taken to Reno, booked, and charged with attempted extortion of a public official. Joe, accustomed to posting bail in the low 100s, now learned that, after discussion with Raggio, Reno's Judge Beemer had set bond at $50,000, a sum which ranked among the all-time highs. Joe called bondsmen, but they told him that they could not make that amount at that hour, and Joe finished the night in jail.

Next day, Joe switched attorneys. Petersen had become a reluctant advocate; he was not happy with the case and was worried about taking on Raggio. He suggested bowing out, and Joe agreed that a lawyer, whose office had been bugged, should. Joe now hired Gordon Rice, a man of whom he is still fond, but on whose drinking problem he blames his poor defense and his years in prison. Rice got bail reduced to $15,000, and Joe was free, free to begin a new phase of his life, the months of almost daily, frantic developments in the contest with Raggio, the fight to stay out of jail, and the fight to get Raggio identified as "the D.A. who preaches morality and fucks minors."

There was no quarter. One evening, Joe entered the Riverside for a session of cards in one of the hotel's private upstairs playing rooms, at a moment when Raggio was drinking in the Riverside's downstairs bar. Raggio knew of the visit within minutes and called the sheriff to arrest Joe. Joe posted bail and returned to his game, only to see the same arresting officer come in and say, "Joe, we go again." Joe posted a second bail, but on his return to the Riverside, he took a table in the bar itself, a few feet from Raggio's table. Again, Raggio called the sheriff, and again Joe posted bail. He would have gone back once more, if only to build up a case for his civil rights attorneys, but the arresting officer pleaded with Joe to call it a night.

From this point on, Joe's affairs could have used four ringmasters, because the war with Raggio had four fronts. One was financial; Joe had to keep in funds because, without money, any hope of avoiding prison was lost. He must make sure of the daily $300 to $400 the wars were costing. Second, somehow, one or two operations must keep going, this in the face of new abatements, new raids, new arrests of his girls. Four to eight girls must copulate through thick and thin. It meant fast physical moves of his business, because a moment would come when he would be bucking not only Raggio in Washoe, but a team-up of three D.A.s of three counties. On a third front, he must try to keep control of the Hitson sisters because if he lost them, he would lose the witnesses that could keep him out of prison. His fourth was the legal front, where he suffered defeats because his growing contempt for lawyers led him to act on his own, taking plunges on impulse that attorney Rice didn't know about. Joe had entered on his own frantic thousand days.

Now Raggio, who had made Reno off-limits, went farther. He got word to Reno's main gambling houses and restaurants that Joe should not be served. Word went to the two big gambling clubs, Harrah's and Harolds, to the four main hotels, the Golden, Mapes, Riverside, and Holiday, and to the two swank restaurants, Eugene's and Vario's, that Joe must not be accommodated. Reaction was typical of a small town. Some owners felt it was not smart to cross a D.A., and Joe got a reading on his popularity. The Holiday and Golden Hotels told him to stay away. Harrah's and Harolds told him he was welcome. Vario's told him to come in any time, while Eugene's took the same straddle as the Riverside; he could come, but they hoped he wouldn't. While Joe was trying to learn how many more places might be off-limits, Raggio moved again. He told the story to a Grand Jury and got an indictment. The accuser was now the state. As the year ended, Joe had to raise money by selling Montgomery Pass. A Joe Campo agreed to pay him $100,000, giving him $10,000 as a down payment.

Nineteen-sixty started and ended badly. Joe intended to go any length to reverse the vagrancy charge and he asked for a jury trial. In February the jury found him guilty and he was given thirty days and a $500 fine. Stubbornly, Joe would carry this case all the way to the U.S. Supreme Court, but at the moment he had lost twice; awaiting trial for extortion and awaiting appeal on vagrancy. The costs were staggering. Joe worked doggedly to keep his places going; to Joe it was simple economics, and to Raggio arrogant defiance.

Joe was never able to agree that the old law should make him, a proprietor, a "vagrant" and, in any case, he thought such a charge should be made, if at all, by Storey. But to Raggio, this nice point in jurisdiction did not change the fact that if Joe operated in Storey and lived in Washoe, he, Raggio, would be laughed at. He prevailed upon two men in Storey, Judge Hanna and District Attorney Robert Moore, to make common cause. Moore, left to his own ways, might have been inclined to live and let live, but Raggio convinced him that in giving Joe sanctuary he was exposing himself to criticism. Joe was making headlines, and the headlines were snide about what Joe might be paying Moore. Raggio kept urging Moore to crack down, to use the "Cunningham" case.

Nevada's girl industry was badly shaken in 1949, six years before Joe arrived. A Mrs. Mae Cunningham had opened a house in Reno, and been arrested. At her trial, the judge ruled that while Nevada had no statute barring prostitution, the common law did condemn nuisances. The judge itemized the many things that went on in a house, acts which were nuisances, and ruled that any house was a nuisance, per se. When reaffirmed by the Supreme Court, the decision became basic law.

Raggio convinced Moore that even though Storey had no laws against prostitution, "Cunningham" was all he needed. Moore agreed, and issued the judgment that declared Joe a nuisance. Joe went to lawyers but got no comfort. Angrily, he learned that he and Sally must close the Green House. Soon, Nevada newspapers reported that Joe was out of business. Actually, Joe had evacuated the Green House but had moved his girls the short distance to his White House in Lyon County, and he and Sally took up residence at the Desert Inn. Raggio was not content with the abatement of the Green House, for what was to stop Joe from moving back in? He worked on Moore to eliminate the house itself.

Toward sunset of a day in mid-March, some fifteen people converged on the Wadsworth pasture. In charge were District Attorneys Raggio and Moore, each attended by his own sheriff and deputies. Additionally, Raggio had persuaded the Sparks Fire Department to send its trucks along to avoid any spread of fire. The party was rounded out by reporters and photographers. They made sure that no room contained any human or pet and, after discovery of what they thought was some mysterious wiring, poured gasoline over everything.

"You know," says Joe, "most fires leave some damn thing standing, a chunk of wall, a chimney, a half-burned chair. But Raggio must have stayed there all night fanning it with his hat. It was ashes. Everything, the pipes even, they was bent down and covered with ashes." Joe has kept the newspaper that shows Raggio and Moore happily shaking hands against a background of flame!

There were men who cheered the fire-eating D.A. who was stamping out vice, and there were those who thought, considering Nevada's hundred-year history of whores, that Raggio was making quite a fuss over a single house. Lawyers still wonder whether a judge's order to abate covered doing it with gasoline. As one of the many moves in the long duel, Sally sued Raggio for damages, charging the D.A. with illegal burning, a case that would drag on and be settled through compromise, after Joe had been in prison some years.

There are many views on Conforte but no one questions his courage. It wells up from primordial glands, a courage based on his own angry logic, a courage so intense that it can look like paranoid conceit. Each defeat hardens his obsession and makes him a tougher crusader. He was now so committed to the girl business that he could not think of quitting. Simultaneously he was (1) out on bond awaiting trail for attempted extortion, (2) awaiting disposition of the vagrancy charge, and (3) facing a contempt charge for reopening the White House after it had been abated. Undaunted, with the White House locked, and his Green House a pile of ash, Joe went on to trailers. A fixed house was easy to find, but a trailer could be moved in the time between a friendly informer's phone call and more raids by a Raggio or a Moore. That May, the Confortes bought a sixty-foot "Detroiter," which they fitted with four compartments, plus dinette, kitchen, and bath. By June, Joe was again in the news. Reno heard that Joe was moving the trailer around the riverbottom so often that cab drivers had to check the location before accepting a fare. On various nights, the girls could be in Washoe, Storey, or Lyon.

Joe should have retained control of Jackie, who was scheduled to testify that the D.A. had bought her drinks, that he had had intercourse with her, that he thus joined the group of eligibles who might be charged with fatherhood in her ensuing pregnancy. But in the next months of razzle-dazzle, Joe lost Jackie. Jackie's travail began soon after Joe's arrest.

Here the story picks up a girl who used the name Scarlet O'Neil, and whose real name Joe never knew. She was a Green House girl. "Irish pretty," Joe remembers, "like that Maureen O'Hara, and full of laughs." Joe got to know her because she and Carmen were chums. Joe decided it would be best if Jackie were out of Nevada. He sent her off with Carmen and Scarlet to San Francisco where he thought, in an unplanned way, that Jackie could live quietly and be out of Raggio's reach. But Joe failed to reckon with the boredom that can hit girls accustomed to the intense life of the Triangle. The girls became unstable as mercury, seemingly unable to endure any one place. They had been in a San Francisco motel a week when Joe joined them, only to learn that Scarlet wanted to go to Seattle to see her boyfriend. Scarlet left, and within days, both Hitson sisters were so bored that Joe sent them to Seattle, by train, to join Scarlet.

As to Jackie's own sexual history, she had had five boys before Carmen picked her up. In Seattle, Jackie met a Jack Martin, and went with him to Vancouver. While Jackie was in Vancouver, Carmen returned to San Francisco and had hardly unpacked, when Scarlet was on the phone to tell her that Jackie was back in Seattle. Carmen flew back to Seattle to be with Jackie.

During March and April, Jackie had her longest stay in any one place. Joe placed her with Beverly in a small apartment. He was restless, and he took the girls for long drives; they went shopping and to the movies. One day Beverly told Joe that Jackie had confided that she was pregnant. Joe quizzed Jackie, but found her uncertain about the father. It was not a happy house. Raggio was doing everything to postpone the trial. He had a strong case: most definitely there had been an attempt to extort. But victory on that point alone was not sufficient. He had to kill the fornication story,

even though it was no part of the case. If it were established that
he had seduced a client of seventeen, his career would be seriously hurt. It was imperative that he reach Jackie and get her to
change Joe's version of the facts. But Jackie had been shipped off
by Joe. Again, Raggio called on Detective Harold Lipset.

Detective Lipset, working on fees paid by the state, was his
usually efficient self. He inquired among Joe's girls. They told him
that Jackie was in San Francisco, living in an apartment with Joe's
friend, Beverly. Lipset took an apartment across the street. From
its windows, his men watched Beverly, Jackie, and Joe go in and
out. Lipset then journeyed to Escondido to talk with Jackie's
mother. He convinced Mrs. Hitson that Jackie was on the wrong
side. She called Jackie and arranged a meeting with Lipset. The
friendly detective persuaded the girl that only grief lay ahead
with Joe, that she should come over to Raggio's side. In early
May, Jackie abandoned Joe. Lipset and his men waited until Beverly and Joe were out, slipped across the street, and took her off.
A day or so later, she met with Raggio in San Francisco. Joe says
it was brainwashing, with threats of prosecution, and Raggio says
he simply asked her to tell the truth. She was kept in California
and, as the trial neared, moved to the home of parents of Attorney
Taber, in Reno.

Joe thought Jackie's departure was tantamount to a kidnapping
by a D.A., and he said as much to a reporter for the *San Francisco
Call Bulletin*, which ran a headline, "Nevada D.A. Involved in
Kidnapping." Raggio eventually sued the paper for libel, and collected damages of $15,000.

With Jackie in the hands of his own people, Raggio moved for a
quick trial. It opened in late June. It didn't take long, five days,
and Joe's best moment may have come with the selection of
jurors, when a number of prospects disqualified themselves as
they admitted to some sympathy for Mr. Conforte because of the
burning of his house. Beyond that, it was a straight, legal chute to
Carson. Raggio was barred from the courtroom, except as a witness; a D.A. cannot prosecute a case in which he himself is the
central figure. The court appointed two Reno attorneys to handle
the prosecution, John Bartlett and Harold Taber.

When Joe realized he had lost Jackie to Raggio, he decided that

Carmen should testify, that she should tell the jury that she had gone up to room 610, hidden in a closet, and witnessed the sexual encounter. Carmen so testified. It must have sounded to the jury as what Joe said it was, "The part we made up." In any event, the issue, to judge and prosecutors, was not intercourse. The issue was Joe's attempt to work a deal, and it became terribly clear that he had tried. On top of that, the girl who was supposedly violated said there had been no sex, and that the whole frameup had been her sister's idea.

Jackie's pregnancy was a town topic that June, because all the candidates for fatherhood were so colorful; Nevada's own Raggio, its own Joe Conforte, and the hearsay pimp of Seattle, Jack Martin. While people were divided as to the father, and many doubted that Raggio got to her, it was obvious someone had. At the trial, the tense, worried girl had ballooned, and she wore maternity clothes. Joe, who would have been happy to establish that Raggio was the father, did not go so far as to make the charge. He makes a distinction between intercourse and insemination, and his own hunch was that Jackie had been fertilized in Seattle.

In windup, the prosecution made a strong, scathing summation, while the defense made none. The jury filed out, to return in four hours, with a "guilty" verdict. Two days later, Judge Bowen convened to pronounce sentence; he gave Joe a tongue-lashing, and a sentence of three to five years.

Joe, who is almost pathologically optimistic, finally knew depression. He applied for appeal bond, to find that bond is tougher after a conviction than after arrest. It was set at $50,000. His attorneys tried to have the amount reduced, but judge and prosecutors insisted that high bond was proper. Joe sat in his cell eleven days before bondsmen could arrange the amount, and he now paid the first of two $5,000 fees, as the yearly cost of liberty.

Normally, when Joe is in trouble, his wife, Sally, moves fast and efficiently to fill the gaps, to handle the crises, consult lawyers, and run the houses; she becomes Joe's alter ego. But two days after the conviction, and while Joe was in jail, the abstemious Sally was in a grinding smash-up with a drunken driver. She was in the hospital for two months with hip and spine injuries. Four operations would be necessary in the next fifteen years, leaving her crippled for life.

The month brought change in the life-styles of both. Joe would be free on bail for almost two years, a period in which, up to his last free hour, he fought for a new trial. In the long troubled time it never occurred to him to quit the business.

Now the Conforte girls became, if anything, even more mobile. While Raggio's costs were being borne by the state, Joe's were on Joe. No defeat must slow the business; a block on income meant an end to lawyers, made jail more certain. But to survive, Joe had to keep moving. The taxi drivers of Reno and the tourists of 80 now had to inquire in saloons whether Joe had his girls in the White House, the Desert Inn, or the trailer which could wander like a browsing deer.

There were days—when Joe had his girls in Storey—when he mounted the "sheriff's watch." The county seat of Storey is Virginia City, a town that is bisected by a single street whose ends make the only two approaches. Joe bought two old cars and hired a man to sit in them at different times and places to observe the sheriff's door. "In those times," Joe explains, "there was little reason for a sheriff to go much beyond the city limits, because Virginia City was all there was to the county. So if a patrol car moved out more than two miles, chances were it was headed my way. The lookout would phone and say, 'They've left.' Joe would move the girls. When the sheriff's cars were back at the courthouse, the lookout would call again, 'They're back,' and Joe would resume.

It was in this period, too, that Joe graduated from conflict with counties to conflict with the United States. Here it must be noted that in all states the legal problems of Indians fall to the state's U.S. attorney. In Nevada, this meant the Reno office of U.S. Attorney, Peter Rittenhouse, who had a staff of eleven assistants, and a deputy whose name was Stanley Brown. Brown was a young man who had only recently passed the bar, and who had a sentimental interest in Indian affairs. One night, Brown was at the Mapes Hotel bar, elbow-to-elbow in the usual jam of lawyers, when someone called out in a loud and stagy voice, "Hey Stan, did you know you've got a whorehouse on that reservation of yours?"

Brown did not really believe it, but next day he borrowed a jeep and drove to Wadsworth. He parked at the edge of the jungle of the river-bottom, and set out on foot. Brown is a pilot and familiar with maps. He studied several and, sure enough, in Joe's dodging to rotate jurisdictions, he had towed his girls onto Indian land. Back in town, Brown called his colleagues into his office and told them about the encroacher. Joe had a long trailer in the cottonwoods, and five assorted blonds, redheads, and Latin cuties who were pulling in ten and twenty cars per night, all inside the reservation by a quarter-mile. "And," said Brown, "if some drunk hits a tree or another car head-on, one party at interest would be the U.S.A." When the jokes died down, everyone agreed that while Conforte was not a national crisis, Nevada would be a national joke if Walter Winchell or Drew Pearson should hear about the new use of Indian land. Some senator might rise to address the chamber, and J. Edgar would not be amused. Everyone agreed that whatever was done should be done quietly so as not to alert *Life* magazine. Here began the long exchange of memos between Reno and Washington, in which a number of lawyers went into the matter of Indian treaties, Paiute sovereignty, and Joe. Eventually, Joe had them all frustrated. The Department of Justice wound up telling its Reno office to back off because Washington could find no applicable law prohibiting commercial love on the specific issue that the heavy breathing took place on Indian soil. Besides, Joe had moved.

There was a sort of all-county awareness of Joe that year, the worry of police that any empty house that suddenly showed lights might be the new Joe's. Reporters loved his tenacity, and there was admiration for the efficiency with which he could pack and be gone. Folks thought it a Nevada version of the contests in Tennessee between moonshiners and revenuers, except that moonshiners had it easier. All they had to do was find a new canyon, move still, barrels and jugs, and be careful not to show smoke. Joe's moves were more demanding. Apart from moving girls, their gear, beds, and bathroom paraphernalia, he had to live with the contradiction; be invisible to sheriffs and findable by taxis. Besides, Joe was never really happy doing things too quietly. But showmanship was out now, because Joe had run out of houses. The

Green House was not even ashes any more because the cinders
had blown off in the strong winds that came down from the
Sierras. The White House lay closed by abatement. Montgomery
Pass had reverted to what it was when he bought it, a bar and
lunch counter, and the Desert Inn was momentarily closed because Lyon officials had picked up some of Raggio's zeal and were
driving him crazy with raids. Joe was down to one shelter, the
"Detroiter." He had moved it around a lot that month, and his
latest idea had been to park it astraddle of the Storey-Lyon Line,
"thirty feet," he explains, "give or take a foot or two, in each
county."

All of which decided the D.A.s of his three host counties that
there was no point in chasing him from one to the other. They
met, fixed a date, and gave orders to their three sheriffs to mount
a raid with complete secrecy. There was to be no whispered leak
that would allow Joe to slip away. Unless Joe was in Utah, someone in the raiding party would have jurisdiction. The advance
scouts had no trouble locating Joe.

"It's a little after sunset when they come," he remembers,
"about thirty of them. They got unidentified cars, they got patrol
cars, they got trucks. They come charging in, and they're carrying
rifles, shotguns, and pistols: there wasn't that many closed in on
Bonnie and Clyde. They arrest the girls, three scared kids, and
pack them off. They don't arrest me (possibly, because actions
against Joe were already pending in all three counties, and pending before the state itself). They make me sit in a patrol car while
they hitch a truck to the trailer, and they tow it off. They tow it
behind the Storey Courthouse. It sits there two months. Got so
the tourists would visit the historic sites, the Sutro Tunnel, the
Opera House, and the rest, and then they want to go through the
trailer and see the beds. It takes me two months to bail it out."

Joe faced prison largely, he believed, because Raggio had got
hold of Jackie and brainwashed her, threatening her with conspiracy to extort. She had completely reversed her story about
sex in the Riverside. Now, out on bond and awaiting appeal, Joe
was obsessed with reaching Jackie, to make friends again and see
if he could get her to tell why she had switched.

Joe's life was a controlled frenzy, and he seldom had time to pursue one problem for long. It was some months before he could get to California and try to learn what had happened with Jackie.

After the trial, Jackie had assumed that Joe had no love for her, and she had kept out of his way. Joe had his troubles, but she also had hers, mainly where to have her baby. The advice she got from Raggio, her mother, and her friends was to enter the Florence Crittendon Home in Los Angeles. Her daughter, born in August, was placed in a foster home. Manipulated, courted, seldom feeling important and sometimes feeling suicidal, Jackie was especially depressed about having surrendered her baby. She did the inevitable—she looked for friendship, found a boy and got married. She told her husband everything, a story such as few husbands hear, and the two were young enough to think that they could put it all behind them.

But the persistent Joe sought them out. He assured Jackie that he was not angry, that he understood why she should have feared Raggio. He got to know Jackie's husband and argued that a D.A. was getting away with murder. Joe took them on a vacation to Mexico and in time won them over. He wanted a new trial. To get a new trial he thought that he should get Jackie, the key witness, to say that she had perjured herself.

In time, Jackie and her husband agreed that she would testify. Joe drove Jackie to the office of an attorney in Sacramento and had him prepare an affidavit, which Jackie signed, in which she reversed her story. Now she declared that she had perjured herself because Raggio had coerced her, telling her that if she did not give his version of events, she could go to prison. She declared that she had slept with him but had denied this, too, because of coercion. These were jolting statements but, not content, Joe had her add a massive lie—that Joe had had nothing to do with the entire plot.

Joe would now make two attempts to use the affidavit, but it would not be honored because the whopper about his nonparticipation killed the credibility of everything.

With the affidavit in his pocket, Joe returned to Reno, had attorney Rice file it with the Nevada Supreme Court, and sat back waiting for word that a new trial would be set. The court did not even reply. Joe was stunned. "It's not that they denied the request or said it had no merit—they just didn't even answer.' Seeking comfort from Rice, he got none. Rice told him that the Supreme Court did not have to answer at all.

To his list of defeats he now added two more, one that seemed slight and temporary and another that in effect closed the gates on Joe. It was now well after the trial and Joe was free because he was paying $400 a month to bondsmen. He had lost a dozen skirmishes to Raggio but was more than ever determined to tell the world his version of the Riverside copulation. Joe has always had a blind spot on this point because to him the central outrage was that a prosecutor should have possessed Jackie, made her deny it and then perjured himself. Paying no attention to lawyers, Joe reasoned that if he could get Jackie into another courtroom, to explain that she had perjured herself, a new trial would be automatic. Pursuing this strategy, he hit disaster.

Determined to get that affidavit to someone with the power to get Raggio, he decided that the man would be Nevada's Attorney General, Roger Foley. The affidavit was delivered to Foley's office by the Hitson sisters themselves. Next day both Carmen and Jackie were served with subpoenas and ordered to appear before the grand jury then in session. Carmen's subpoena was withdrawn almost immediately, but Jackie was ordered to testify. Again Joe went through his sequence of shock, anger, frustration and hope. "Fine," he said on recovering. "Now the story just got to come out."

Since proceedings of grand juries are secret, Joe's knowledge of what Jackie said came from Jackie. She told him later that she gave the jury the story they had planned. But this was another miscalculation. Following the grand jury session, Jackie was arrested and jailed, charged with perjury—not for what she had said at the trial, but for her new story.

Again Joe went from shock to gloom to anger and, finally, to hope. "They can't convict her without a trial," he said. "This ain't Russia. There has to be a trial, and Jackie will tell that story." Her bond was set at $15,000, a sum Joe found hard to raise.

In the meantime, Jackie's luck held. In jail she suddenly began suffering pains and was rushed to a hospital. Doctors found that she had a tubal pregnancy, which had to be terminated surgically.

Next day, when Jackie came out of anesthesia, she found that one of her feet was in manacles attached to the bed. This enraged her husband, who put in some hot calls to the sheriff's office, only to be told that if he didn't cool down he would be escorted out of town. It was some days before her bail was reduced to $5,000 and Joe could have her released.

Joe now went to John Squire Drendel, the attorney who had been on the edge of the affair ever since he had met Jackie at the Riverside. Drendel had testified at the trial and was almost as close to the feud as Raggio or Conforte. He agreed to handle Jackie's defense, but he told Joe, "I want ten grand." Joe thinks they eventually settled for half that amount. Joe set the conditions: "No deal, no dismissal, no probation. We want a trial. We don't need you for a dismissal because Raggio would give her one today if she let up on him." Then, as an afterthought, Joe asked Drendel to see if he could manage somehow to get a judge other than Bowen.

Over the years, Joe had begun to think that there was some evil coincidence in the way he was walking into walls. "It's getting to be one hell of a list of low pitches," he said, "and so many, come to think of it, where the judge, whether he's presiding or issuing writs or motions, seems to be Grant Bowen." Joe had heard about courthouse cliques, city hall cousins, fraternity-brother deals, and he knew that there was strong admiration between Raggio and Bowen. "So I tell Squire, Make sure you get another fuckin' judge. Drendel gives me the impression he will try."

But Joe's moves were still under the wrong stars. "Couple days before the trial, Drendel calls me. He says there's a subpoena out for me to testify and that this ain't good, and why don't I take a trip? I pick up Carmen, and we take off for Ellay. We're out of contact for a few days and we get back the day after the trial. I call Drendel and he's out of town. We call Jackie's house and she's gone to Escondido. I call her mother and that's when I got it. Jesus Christ almighty! Jackie's pleaded guilty! She's confessed to perjury! They let her off with a year's probation."

In shock, Joe heard that there had been a meeting in the chambers of "guess who?—yep, Judge Bowen," a meeting attended

by four men and a girl. "There she was," says Joe, "a kid, she's
under arrest, she's out on bail, she's facing, far as she knows, two
to fourteen years. She's fresh out of the hospital where she's had
this operation—with those manacles to the bed, remember—and
not long out of this other hospital where they took her when she
tried to commit suicide. Me and her sister are away and not by
her side, and now she's in a room with three big-shot lawyers—
Drendel, Raggio, one of his assistant D.A.s—and Judge Bowen.
Jesus, she's too scared to breathe; she just can't see standing them
off. They tell her it can be prison if she goes to trial, and they
tell her it's probation if she pleads guilty. So she pleads guilty.
I didn't even look up Drendel; I was afraid I'd kill him."

When Joe talks about the vicissitudes—the years with all their
false starts and mistaken entries, the little things—a stop at a gas
station or a drink with a sheriff—can take on the importance of a
moon landing. Joe, hungering in his way for form, searching for
the big cohesion, some sign of structure, can take an hour over an
event which only he sees as supporting some principle, some evidence of order in the cosmos. Remembering the last throes, the
days when he had run out of moves, when he knew it would be
prison, he recalls a run of events that came a little earlier and
whose moral may lie in his stricture, "You know, don't ever relax
so much that you piss into the wind."

Back when Joe was visiting Jackie's folks in Escondido, the
fates made him miss one of the great events of the year, the
World Series between the Yankees and the Pittsburgh Pirates.
Not even Raggio's shadow could make him forget his passion for
baseball. Joe used Mrs. Hitson's phone to call a Reno bookie, and
then had the obedient Sally deliver $15,000 for a bet, even money,
on the Pirates. It turned into a seven-game cliffhanger, and Joe
remembers its stolen bases and strikeouts and infield flies, and the
Series' last Wagnerian moment. "It's the seventh game, and
they're playing in Pittsburgh at Forbes Field, and it's all tied up,
three games to three. It's the last half of the ninth and the Yankees
are ahead, ten to nine. Pittsburgh's up for the last time. So the
Yanks get them down to two outs, and one more out, and its over,
and people are beginning to leave. Then somebody hits one to

Tony (Kubek) at shortstop. Ordinarily, Tony would put it in his pocket and walk off the field. But the ball takes a bad hop, and it hits him in the neck. So now Pittsburgh's got a man on base. Next guy up is Bill Maseroski, and he hits a homer. I sit there, watchin' that radio, I'm fifteen grand ahead, and I'm still so sorry for Kubek I want to send him a case of whiskey."

A few days later, Joe returned to Reno to pick up his $30,000. He learned that in Washington, Justice William O. Douglas had wanted to review Joe's vagrancy case, but the court majority had not. Joe had reached the end of the line; there was nothing left to do to avoid serving the thirty days on his contempt conviction. That very day, the pickup order went out and Joe met some more of those apologetic deputies. "Look, Joe, we got to do it, it's our job." They drove him to the Virginia City jail where he would serve twenty-five days, preliminary to his time in Carson. Joe was on the best of terms with the jailer, who assured him he would make things as pleasant as possible. Within two days, they were going out to dinner, having girls set up from Joe's place, and Joe was using the office for his interminable phone calls. Joe was not searched, which was good, because in his money belt he had the $30,000. "Well, there's no security problem in the jail because there's only one other guy in it, a poor jerk who's in for exposure. Lord, can you imagine that? Me, with maybe a thousand girls I've had, and this poor guy, he just shows it?" But they became friends, and Joe used him for errands.

Now the problem was the calendar. For some months Joe had been following the campaign battle of Nixon and Kennedy and had felt that Kennedy would win. With the $30,000 belt chafing his skin, he wanted to make a bet, but the Reno bookies were not handling much election money. "I get out of jail November eighth and the election is next day. I pick up two girls, Cathie and Beverly—Beverly was pregnant now, carrying my baby—and we head for Las Vegas. I got two things to do, one is get a bet on Kennedy, and one is get some Las Vegas votes for Ernest Brown. You see, Supreme Court Judge, Frank MacNamee, was up for re-election and Brown is running against him. I hate the son-of-a-bitch because he makes it so plain he hates me. I figure if Brown wins, I got a better chance on my appeal. We pick up a few hundred Brown campaign cards, and the minute we hit Vegas, I put the girls to talking it up in the Negro district. I know it's going to be close, and maybe two hundred-three hundred more votes in Las Vegas would give me a new judge. We register in the Fremont, and it's just hours before the country starts voting. I got trouble finding a bet; the odds has changed, and everybody figures it's close. But the grapevine works, and two club owners come over to visit me. They'll take Nixon, but they want two-to-one. We come to an even bet, and me and them, we put $60,000 in the safe of the Fremont Hotel. The returns start coming in around eight. For a while, I'm winning on Ernie Brown and losing on Kennedy. By midnight, it's over. I win on Kennedy and I lose the Supreme Court. But that Las Vegas has style; they hand me the sixty thousand like it's an old magazine. Next day, me and the girls get ready to drive back. I send the girls ahead while I stop by the cashier's cage. In the middle of the casino there's this dealer knows me, and he calls out, 'Hey, Joe, how about some action?' I stop at his table for a few plays and, well, you can guess. It took six hours. I blew the 60,000, and before I'm through I sign a marker for fourteen more. We head for Reno where it's probably going to be more bad news, and I'm thinking all the attorneys that sixty grand would have paid for. Later, I call Eddie Levinson, the boss over at the Fremont, and I tell him, 'that marker, you know what to do with it?' Eddie laughs and says, 'OK, Joe, we'll wash it out.'"

As the Christmas holidays approached, Joe knew that he must accept the fact of prison. With fading hope he listened to a politician who told him not to despair, that his jail time would be short; the man would talk to Governor Sawyer, and would swing a pardon before Joe had been in a year. Joe wanted to believe him. Incurably curious about everything new, he found himself thinking that prison, particularly for a short time, might not be too bad, might even hold some fun. On New Year's Eve he took a party to Harrah's, at Lake Tahoe, to see the Louis Prima show, and was pleased to read next day that a columnist called him "jaunty." It was the last newspaper mention until January 10th, a snowy afternoon, when two sheriff's deputies drove him to Carson.

Joe's passage through the Carson prison produced stories that lifers still talk about, one of them about filet mignons. Joe's new friend, Cleary, who was in for life, had risen to Chief of Commissary, a job that put him in charge of ordering, warehousing, and cooking for some four hundred men. Joe's admiration was mixed. "Here's a guy who's smart enough to be running a hotel, and he don't know about filets." So Joe told him. He explained that every cow has two, and to look for one in each loin. "Jim has some con cutting down the meat, some lost soul who thinks there's only two cuts of beef, pot roast and stew." Joe told Cleary that as each carcass came in, he should grab the filets before they could be lost to the great cauldrons of Mulligan. One should be delivered to the mansion of Governor Sawyer, where the servants were prison trusties. The other was to be held back for the little prison club, a revolving group that included the captain, guards, trusties, Jim, and Joe. The dinners ended when Joe left.

But before he left, Joe had turned campaign manager. While Joe was in Carson, Raggio's term was running out, and Washoe county was preparing for an election. A Reno attorney, Harry Anderson, an obscure man who was not rated as a legal luminary, decided to trun against Raggio. Anderson had been the defense attorney in a hard-fought trial, had lost to Raggio, and had come out of it with a dislike for the powerhouse D.A. He decided to run against him. He knew that his chances were poor but, in any case, a campaign would give him the platform for blasting Raggio. But Anderson needed campaign helpers who also hated the D.A., and where better to find them than in a penitentiary? Anderson called on Joe and found him bursting with campaign ideas. Anderson became a frequent visitor to the prison. It became another of Warden Fogliani's problems to ignore the laughter of the cons, while providing Joe with a conference room. "One morning," Cleary remembers, "we been up all night, we're still writing copy for TV, when a guard tells us Anderson's outside waiting for his script." Anderson lost.

Warden Fogliani did not object too much to Joe's publicity because it meant a break in the grimness of prison life. The casino caused worldwide talk, and brought a writer-photographer team from the *London Times*. They wrote a story which may have intrigued the British, but which brought a little trouble at home. "The Reno IRS got flack on that one," Cleary said, "because these Englishmen imply there's tax evasion right in the cells. So IRS gives us an audit. It had the cons rolling on the floor. Still, it turns out funny. I never thought I'd ever say those IRS guys are nice, but they were. They give us the audit, the bankroll, which we keep in the warden's safe, our bookkeeping and payouts, and they decide that what we're doing is peanuts, and on the up and up. The agents are sympathetic, and one of 'em says that if we get any more flack to let him know and he'll give us a good Dun and Bradstreet."

But this was not the same IRS team that caused Joe to shift prisons. Long before his takeover of the casino, Joe had begun to interest the Treasury. His Triangle traffic had been under scrutiny, and per-car estimates were being made. After Joe was sent up, the IRS decided it had the evidence it needed. It brought an action charging tax evasion. Faced with his new problem Joe remembered the attorney, Stanley Brown, who had been so nice the time Joe had strayed onto Indian land. Brown had now left government and gone into private practice. He was developing a name as a tax man. So Joe hired Stanley Brown to start what would become the long, love-hate relationship of Brown and Conforte. It was, in fact, about sixteen years later that a Reno attorney called Brown on the phone. "Stan," he asked, "do you still represent Joe?"

Brown was momentarily stuck. "Take your time," said the caller, "I understand."

But Brown had decided. "Yes," he said, "I would say I do. Joe was in just yesterday to pay his bill, and he seldom lets a week go by without calling, if only to gossip. Of course, I understand he has other lawyers. But, yes, I would say I'm still in the corral."

But on that grim day when Joe had to use the warden's office to shape his tax defense, there was no question of his need for Brown. Joe became a commuter, leaving the Carson prison to spend hours each day in Carson's federal court.

The U.S. Attorney had charged Joe with evasion on three counts, and turned the case over to a young assistant, Tom "Spike" Wilson, who had just passed the bar. Young Wilson did his best. But it was a frustrating case because its arithmetic was so impossible. Brown assembled a staff of tax men for the job of compiling figures, and found he was as baffled as the prosecutor as to how to measure sex volume. "If you can concede," says Brown, "that a trial can be funny, that one was. Joe had no accurate idea of what his income was, and neither did the IRS. The prosecutor was trying to establish some basics for whorehouse income, but where in America could you find any business to compare it to? And where on earth a man with Joe's odd expenses? The defendant had not kept books. If he had, he might have claimed as deduction what he gave to fifty charities, to governors, mayors, and maybe a quarter of the legislature. He's obsessed with being called generous, and he could never remember what the hell he gave to whom. No questions he understand his taxes, but as to how much, you'd need some astral computer to keep up with him." The jurors retired, and after two days, said they could not agree. Conforte and Brown felt they had at least a half-victory.

Both sides now saw the gamble. Another trial would have to be fought with the same figures and the same guesswork, so they began to talk compromise. Wilson and Brown asked the judge whether he would consider a lesser plea, and the judge said he would listen. Brown and Wilson came to an agreement; Joe would plead guilty to one count, and Wilson would dismiss the other two. Joe says he also got the impression that he would get no more imprisonment than was already left of his Nevada time, which would amount to probation for any new time. The assumption was wrong. The judge who had presided, and who knew about the compromise, was replaced by a judge who had no part in, or sympathy with, plea-bargaining. When the case reached him as a plea of guilty, he jolted everyone by giving Joe three years, the time to run concurrently with his Nevada time, and the remainder to be served in a federal penitentiary. Nevada's parole board, which is always troubled about the crowding in its prison, welcomes any chance to reduce the jam. On learning that another prison wanted Joe, it commuted his term to the time served. Joe left for Terminal Island, near San Pedro, California, and then moved to McNeil.

Back in Wadsworth, Sally, Beverly, and Brigette, another of

Joe's "maids," had started the bad years. On the job Joe works as
hard at promoting sales as General Motors. He has the sense of
publicity of a Bob Hope, a Johnny Carson, or a Nelson Rockefeller, and his news file has thousands of stories, splashes spaced
out over the years, of his new ideas, his fights, his charities: "Joe
offers Reno free bus service" . . . "Joe teams with Sammy Davis,
Jr., for Heart Fund" . . . "Joe denies senate ambitions" . . . "Joe
honors energy crisis, puts girls in pants suits," most of them good
for a front page. But with Joe gone, publicity stopped and business
sagged. Thousands of men went through Reno without knowing
that girls could be had at prices starting at ten dollars. With Joe
gone, Sally was not as harassed as Joe had been; Raggio's angei
was with Joe, not Sally. But she still had troubles, for it was the
kind of business that brings complaints. Sally herself moved the
trailer several times after Joe left. But the big blow was the
appearance of a competitor. For now a man appeared who set up
a rival house, also in Storey, and so close to Reno as to make Wadsworth seem as distant as Newfoundland.

With Joe away, it was widely assumed that he was through,
that when his time was up he would emerge, beaten and cowed.
Anyone who manages to be a two-time loser in twenty months is
assumed to be slow about re-entering a dangerous business. (Sally
tried to persuade Joe to quit, and in her visits to Carson and then
to McNeil, she tried to make him plan a different life. She even
made a down payment on some land near Wadsworth on which
they might build a motel.) With Joe gone, a number of men
looked to the attractions of Storey County. District Attorney
Moore had retired, and some men had begun to wonder if they
couldn't replace Joe. Of these, the first to move was a Richard
Bennet. Bennet had far less pioneering to do than Conforte, for
Joe had broken trail and cleared the land. Bennet had only to fill a
vacuum, to persuade the Storey commissioners that Joe was a
legal cripple. The Storey commissioners, whose tolerance and
understanding had already been widened by Joe, went along.
They told Bennet that he could set up a house if he could find a
location. Bennet already had, and here he showed himself to be
even a better geographer than Joe. Seeking that Route to Cathay,
that Northwest Passage, the spot which would be outside the

realm of Raggio, but near the Mecca of hungry men, Reno, he found it on the Perri ranch.

Storey has a point which reaches within eight miles of Reno, twenty-seven miles closer than the Triangle, on the ranch of the two wealthy Perri brothers. When Joe first scouted Storey, he had looked at this ranch but had assumed that the owners would not be interested in renting for the girl trade. But Bennet talked to the Perris, and found them agreeable. Imitating Joe, he bought trailers—four as against Joe's one—and linked them into a compound. Ten months after Joe had entered McNeil, Bennet spread word in Reno that twelve new girls were available, much closer to town, in a place that would be known as "Mustang."

On Sally's visits to McNeil, she saw that Joe seemed to wobble between depression and anger. The federal prison was no Carson, and gave no leeway to organizers. Sally told her husband how business had sagged. She was having trouble with even small bills because the legal battles had used up about everything. She gave him what gossip she could about Bennet; that he was getting all the business from Reno. As Joe neared the end of his time, his assets were down to Sally and a stubborn hope. Then, four months before his release, Joe got the first break in a long run of woe, a windfall that went back to the day they burned the Green House.

That Nevada spectacle, a brothel owner taking on a D.A., was funny, but no funnier than a D.A., fuming with Old Testament anger and forming a raiding party for the kind of burning that went out with Salem. There were many views. Of the Nevada men who read about the burning, it would be hard to say whether twenty percent or eighty percent had slept with a brothel girl. To those who had, the burning was a farce, and Raggio a Don Quixote charging windmills. Reno lawyers would chide Raggio, "Hey, Bill, my client, St. Mary's Hospital, sometimes spills trash in the alley, hope you're not thinking of burning it down?" Joe's insurance company, which eventually paid Joe $16,000, got a letter suggesting it could recover from Raggio because the D.A. had failed to get a burning permit. The story made hundreds of papers, and such was the delighted coverage that one writer exposed himself to libel and had to pay. He was one of the nation's most sophisticated columnists, the enormously popular Herb Caen of the *San Francisco Chronicle*. Caen, then as now, was the most widely read columnist of the west, a witty commentator on the ways of California's eminent. But he got into trouble when he got whimsical about the burning.

When the Raggio-Moore party went through the Green House before pouring the gasoline, someone spotted a loudspeaker in the room which Sally used as her office and bedroom. A loudspeaker in a whorehouse is fascinating, so they delayed the burning long enough to trace out the wiring. A half-hour of ax work exposed wires that led from the loudspeaker to each of the bedrooms, and in each bedroom the wires led to a microphone, no larger than a walnut, discreetly hidden, whether behind a vase, lamp, or headboard.

In a San Francisco courtroom, long after the burning, Sally explained that the hookup had been designed by the Confortes because of what they knew of the sexual quirks of the human male. There are times, she told the judge, when a girl needs help, and the loudspeaker was there to bring it fast. The Confortes had learned that a girl can find herself in a room with a man whose pleasure is to mutilate. Some men like to kill the girl they have loved, while others like to kill prostitutes. There is always the little percentage whose ways are as bizarre as those listed by Dr. Krafft-Ebing in his volume on sex deviations: as examples, the man who demands that a girl urinate or defecate on him, the man whose "French" is not ecstatic until his penis shows blood. In most cases the girl can rush out and scream, but sometimes she can't reach the door. To guard against the excessively sick, the Confortes had put in the loudspeaker hookup. Every girl was told that in case of trouble, she should press the button on the microphone and scream, "Help!" (The Confortes say that in the years in Wadsworth, girls used the microphone only two or three times.)

But to the men of the burning party the microphones raised intriguing questions: how many prominent men had had their sexual whisperings recorded on tape? It made the raiders even more eager to light the matches. It was some months later that someone gave the microphone story to the celebrated Caen. Joe thinks it was Raggio, and Raggio has long since stopped bothering to deny anything said by Joe. The pixyish Caen, noting that many of Joe's customers were Californians, wondered how many might be sweating out how many years wondering who owned what tapes. Millions laughed, but the Confortes fumed. They said that in all their years, no customer had ever been discussed, much less photographed or recorded. Joe, who has heard all kinds of sexual invective, thought this the worst, the implied blackmailing of customers. With his extortion trial grinding on, and while he was free on bail, he heard Reno's new "microphone" jokes. Friends told him that if the story were false, he could sue. Joe showed the column to a lawyer who suggested that Joe see a San Francisco lawyer, a Charles Morgan, who had been involved in litigation with the *Chronicle* before. Morgan questioned the Confortes, the girls, the maid, and the installing electrician, and give as his opinion that Joe had a case. Confortes entered suit against Caen and the *San Francisco Chronicle*.

But in Joe's frenetic life, the crises of January are dwarfed by those of March. Lawsuits drag on and are almost forgotten. Joe went on to other battles. The *Chronicle* suit, however, was nursed by Morgan. When Joe was serving his last months at McNeil, and looking forward to release, he got a phone call. He was playing bridge in the yard when the rectangle echoed to a sound that cons love, the sound that can mean a pleasant break, your name on the loudspeaker. The big horn told convict Joseph Conforte to report to the office. Inside, a caseworker pointed to a phone. It was Morgan in San Francisco: "Joe, my boy, we won the suit."

For a moment, Joe remembers he went blank. He asked, "What suit?"

"Against Caen and the *Chronicle*! We won! It will go to appeal, of course, but I think we'll win there too. It's an interesting decision," said the attorney. "The judge gives you ten thousand and one dollars."

"Jesus that is interesting," said Joe.

"No, I mean the reasoning," said Morgan. "The court awards you one dollar for damage to your reputation, and $10,000 as punitive damage against Caen."

"Jesus, one buck for my good name." But the slur was balanced out by the money, and Joe's hopes began to rise. Morgan thought it best to clinch things. The case could go to appeal and stretch out for years. To assure earlier payment, it was settled at $6,000. When Joe walked out of McNeil, the first costs of his comeback had been provided by the distinguished *San Francisco Chronicle*.

Joe came out of McNeil one overcast day with four months cut off for good behavior, and promptly confounded everyone who had assumed that he was through. He came out breathing fire. He had entered prison thinking he would be gone a year at most. He could hardly know that his Carson time would be followed by McNeil time. He assumed that he would be out soon, and that the Storey men with whom he had made his deals would hold to them. Now, eons later, he felt the OK to Bennet had been a doublecross. It was with this situation that he started that phase of his life which he describes as the "comeback." He plotted it with the detail of a Nixon, after his defeat by Kennedy; he showed the persistence of a de Gaulle.

As to the moves of that time, they cannot be told in too much detail, because they still interest too many authorities. While Joe lives with a compulsion to tell all, he is cautious here. He sees nothing too bad about the small thefts of his youth, and thinks it hypocritical to deny them. He sees nothing unusual about payments to officials, and thinks it ridiculous to say there were none. He says it's a public duty to explain bribery, because people will then understand government better. But as to the moves of the comeback, he becomes evasive. He promises to tell it all when more time has passed, when the statute of limitations more clearly shields more men and events, when the men involved are out of reach of public outrage. But even when told in generalities, without names or amounts, without the details of the showdowns, it is clear that the comeback was rough, a mini-version of those territory fights which, on a bigger scale, in Detroit or Cleveland, produced the movies on gang wars. "Not big," he laughs, "and no real rough stuff, God knows, but you get the message across that you are coming back, and you let everybody know Joe's got balls."

The comeback took two years, that is, to achieve peace and a clear understanding as to who would operate in Storey. But he took over control of Mustang in ten months, in a sale which, technically, was voluntary.

Joe met Bennet. They entered into a period of rough negotiations. They would meet to argue equities and such practicalities as whether the new group should sell out or be pushed out. Joe would shout that he had an exclusive, a monopoly right, only to be told, with matching obscenities, that he was now just another licensee. Joe argued that there was room for only one and that, as pioneer, it should be he. The Bennet group told him that the Storey commissioners had written him off as dead. Finally, Joe and Bennet agreed on a price—which Joe will not disclose—in a five-year payoff.

But persuading Bennet to sell was only first base. To run a business without dread of writs and summonses, you should be in a county where the officials like you, a county where the interpretation of the law of nuisance lies with men—commissioners, sheriff, and D.A.—who think you're great. Joe had converted one set of politicians, but he realized that he should replace certain perfidious men with other, right-minded men, for office. He must go to the voters.

In January of 1969, when Richard Nixon took his first oath as president, Joe set about creating what must be the tiniest political machine in America. It was a mini-version of the machines of cities, complete to the housewives and merchants who rose up in meetings to explain the advantages of having Joe. To clinch things, he enlarged a town. He bought land in a canyon, a little west of Mustang, in Storey, of course, in the settlement of Lockwood. He added trailers and filled them with tenants who were acutely aware of the low rents. Typically, the settlement is plain, a sprawl of aluminum vehicles propped up on blocks, with no paving, curbs, or sidewalks. But it has water and septic tanks, and in it his people are happy enough. What with the bargain housing and other favors, they see nothing wrong with voting Joe's way.

Joe began an intense time, a high whine period, with some of the elements of such larger political classics as Lyndon Johnson's capture of Austin, or Bobby Kennedy's capture of New York. For Joe had begun to see how things are done. While he could probably buy his way through commissions for the rest of time, life would be better if he were legal. He needed a law for Mustang. He tested the idea on lawyers, D.A.s, and members of the legislature, and remembers their reaction as a long, collective shudder. No state, no city, no county had ever legalized whores. "So what?" said Joe—a little jab at American jurisprudence did not upset him. Joe became a one-man movement, working for the ordinance that would bring the blessed legality. The Storey men were nervous. Legalize? They groaned. Joe's dream was some years in the selling. In the meantime, to give Storey peace of mind, he told the boys it might be best if he paid an official license fee, say, $1,000 a month. The commissioners were delighted. Later, when Joe's famous county ordinance had been written, it sailed through like a resolution honoring Mother's Day. It was emphatically an American first: it legalized prostitution. Joe saw, of course, that such a law would bring blasts at the commissioners and at the county. He realized that Storey folks would need good arguments to defend it, so he told the boys that the law itself should set a license fee so impressive as to be a good defense. The respectful commissioners asked Joe what he had in mind. Joe suggested that $18,000 a year should be about right. He started payments as the law went into effect. Oddly, this tribute produced two views, one—probably the majority view—that there was nothing chintzy about Joe, and a minority view that $18,000 was little enough for what was the nation's only girl franchise, and one that would make him a millionaire. Joe continued the quarterly payments until the day when the commissioners asked if they might have a parley. The county was in trouble, they began, and the sheriff's office alone was eating heavily into the budget, and . . . Joe saw it coming. "Let's get to the bottom line," he said. "You fellows be happier if we make it $25,000?" It remains the levy today.

In capturing Storey, Joe hardly produced any new rules. Where Joe is innovative is in his tendency to spit when explaining these things, a temptation which is also strong with the owners in Las Vegas, but which they control better.

In time, the sovereigns of Reno agreed to let up on Joe and to concede him all freedoms. For times had changed. One came from a Supreme Court decision that Storey had the right to legalize girls; a development that made it awkward for Reno to hound a man who was legal, just eight miles away. Another was the new permissiveness, which made all moralizing sound odd. But the biggest factor probably was the reluctance of Reno men to scold after they themselves had accepted Joe, whether by sneaking into his Mustang rooms, or by sitting, with several hundred others, at Reno's smokers. For Reno loves the big stag evening, and the entertainment chairmen called on Joe for many of them. After such gatherings, where one of Joe's girls might present a judge with a dildo, they felt they had forfeited all right to judge.

6

Joe's English is the plus and minus of his views on society. He hates hypocrisy and avoids words he thinks affected. Thus "hypocrisy" itself becomes "bullshit." On the other hand, he will use "vagina" even with taxi drivers, because he feels that its many synonyms are show-off, he-man vulgarity. Again, he prefers "fucking" to "intercourse." In referring to his place on the river he used to have problems. To call it the "Mustang," was the same formal crap as referring to a wife as "Mrs. Conforte." To call it the "whorehouse" was to be too pointedly masochistic, and to say "the place" was indirection. He felt he had it right when he began calling it "the joint."

Joe, His Joint Today

NEVADA IS HUGE and small. People are few. In Reno or Las Vegas or Ely, men speak of "Grant," and assume you understand they mean former Governor Grant Sawyer. They say, "Paul," knowing you understand it is his successor, Paul Laxalt, or "Mike," who followed Laxalt. In Reno's gambling row they talk of Sid, of whom there is only one, the huge, amiable Sidney Wyman, casino boss of the Las Vegas Dunes. Starting at the southern tip, where Nevada is literally a point, a sliver of the Mojave desert shoved between the identical Mojave deserts of California and Arizona, a driver goes north, around Las Vegas, Tonopah, and Reno and, with some six hundred miles on the odometer, crosses into Idaho where he sees only wilderness, and possibly two hundred people all the way.

The world of the prostitutes is clubby. Joe discovered how much so when he found how many of the girls of one town had worked in the others. Girls in the bars of 80 talk with a certain fondness of Jay Sarno, boss of the Las Vegas Circus Circus (himself a man with Joe Conforte's casual attitude on sex), girls who did well there, but who could not stand the fear of arrest in Las Vegas and who came north. Girls in Elko gossip about Las Vegas, and speak knowingly of the Sands, Tropicana or the Dunes. Along 80 are girls who know how the security men run girls in the

149

Hughes hotels. Everywhere they speak of the prices a girl can get in Las Vegas. In the world's loneliest house, Bobby's, a trailer hook-up, perched on a windy slope outside of Tonopah, there are girls who talk of "Lamb's boys," meaning the deputies of that mystic figure, the sheriff of Clark County. And everywhere they talk of Joe, his crazy ways, his wonderful food, and the money you can make there.

When Margaret drove up to the Mustang gate to ask for a job, she was spotted getting out of her car by Brigette, the lady who manages, despite all her other jobs, to hover near the window that commands the approach to Joe's. Brigette does everything but go with customers, and is the most quietly efficient girl Joe has ever known. When she answers the phone which, though unlisted, rings many times per hour, she is as cryptic as a TV detective, for she assumes that all voices on Mustang phones must go on tape. Whether she is paying the girls their daily earnings, or giving money to Matt, the handyman, for groceries, she is softly, pleasantly terse. She is still good-looking, as Joe demonstrates when he grabs her by the neck and forces her to hold still.

"Ain't she beautiful?" Joe will ask, while Brigette stands, eyes lowered and expressionless, trying to be patient. "You know how long she's been at it? I mean in the business? Not that she is now, she hasn't worked at it for years now, but anyway, Brigette, honey, how old are you?"

"You know very well," she says gravely, anxious to break away.

"Well, say it anyway."

Almost inaudibly she murmurs, "Thirty-eight."

"And how many years in the business, I mean active?"

"Twenty-two."

"She started at sixteen," Joe says beaming. Joe thinks that anyone who can survive that much battering is admirable, but there is more: the business can't be that bad if a girl can show such health and well-being after the years Brigette has known. She has tawny skin, and the healthy verve of a gym instructor. Joe has many reasons for his affection; one is that she is as compulsively active as he is. If Brigette finds herself, in a rare moment, with nothing to do, no buzzer or phone to answer, no towels to gather, no girl asking for a conference, she reaches for a dusting cloth. Over the years, she has seen more bedroom invention than Masters and Johnson, and she has no interest in discussing any of it.

Management in Mustang rotates casually. When Joe is in, for short visits, generally at night, he becomes boss in residence. Even Jeannie, the cook, will ask if she should use frozen vegetables instead of fresh. Joe thunders no. But Joe has become a man of large affairs. He may look in only briefly, and can be gone for weeks. In which case, the second in command is Sally. But Sally, too, gets weary of the business and may leave things to the maids. With both Joe and Sally away, authority shifts to Brigette, and so completely that no one thinks of questioning her rulings. It is Brigette who knows that while the place may be vibrating under a full quota of thirty-eight girls, two have secret plans to quit, that another is having boyfriend trouble and might leave, that another is reacting badly to penicillin, and that another, who plans a week's vacation, is so fey that she cannot be counted on to return. It is Brigette who knows that even with thirty-eight girls in action she should be lining up four reserves. Brigette, slim, pretty, wise, grateful for a job that has made her independent, would take the rack rather than discuss Joe. She knows she is dealing with a man you take as is. You don't challenge Joe, or even advise him much. You serve him with the obeisance, the vast understanding that Richelieu gave Louis XIII, and you are grateful for the bonuses that you invest in real estate. In her quiet way, Brigette has also learned to work with Joe's other women. For years she has watched Joe pick a girl at random and take off. She knows that Joe's marriage to Sally is a strange affair, that Joe honors his relationship, in the sense that he stays married, but his constant slips make Sally's life one long sigh. How classify a husband who feels it almost a personal challenge to sample possibly half the girls who pass through his doors? Sally's understanding is strengthened by the fact that in Mustang she sees the transgressions of the gentlemen of Reno, of Carson, of Nevada, of eminent Californians. Transgressions of lawyers, officials, merchants who, in some cases, repeat many times a year as they find a particular girl they like to come back to. Infidelity, to Sally, is part of woman's bargain. Brigette knows that, and she has learned to work with tactful acknowledgment of the dual sovereignty of Sally and Joe. Finally, Brigette has learned to work with Beverly.

Beverly is all kindness. She went prostitute at seventeen for reasons which, typically, are too complicated to analyze. She drifted, working the bottom rungs of the body trade until she wound up in the little seraglio near Wadsworth. She was a pretty girl, humble, practical, and realistic. After a trick she was happy to get into the kitchen to help with supper. Honest and thoughtful of others, complacent about a world where so many girls earn a living this way, she will help any one of them. From the first days in the Green House there was a special something between her and Joe. Even with Sally in hourly watchfulness, they managed an affair. When Beverly became pregnant, Joe agreed to Beverly's desire to have the baby. The boy has become Beverly's life and Joe's financial charge.

When Margaret Grey went to work at the Mustang, she adjusted fast. She had reached Mustang over a twisted road. She was starting her second year in Mabel's when she met the man who kept coming back, and who finally took her away. They left for the Oregon town where he ran a small roofing business. They bought a house and made a try for conformity. They agreed to a story that gave her a background in the middle west. They spoke of having children and even felt a certain virtue in agreeing to have them only when they were sure about money for their education. They were fiercely determined to salvage the rest of their lives. Her man (she has chosen to call him Bill) had assured her of complete understanding—that it was a tough world, one that is even tougher for women, that he was making no judgments, that the past was dead. He had promised too much. Things happened which would be meaningless to others but which meant misery to a former prostitute. Bill developed an anxiety when, at a party, men told dirty jokes. He would glance at Margaret to see if her laughter was louder than others'. Movies were bad; the rising buttocks of a man over a woman put him in mind of her marathons in Ely. Lovemaking had its complexes; if he were slow reaching his moment, he might joke nastily about all the men she had known who were faster. But his worst problem was the dread that somewhere, in a store, a bar, a gas station, some man would go into the sudden stare that meant he remembered her. For a while she tried reason. "Look, you were willing to share me those times when you took me out, and then took me back to Mabel's: you knew what I would be doing that very night, hell, in a half-hour." It was logical, but Bill found no help in logic. She realized that she was dealing with the old thing, sexual jealousy, too strong for Bill to overcome. They finally separated, and Margaret lost a second man who could not adjust to her sexual history.

After her divorce, she saw that America was changing, that the X-rated movies of one June were ho-hum next June, that movie stars spoke of their illegitimate children, that thousands of teenagers had seen intercourse on film. The sex revolution was on and, for whatever reason, she could not make a living. After three years of straight life, Margaret knew the addresses of all the relief offices in Sacramento and Denver. She decided that sex was still her answer, and following the winds of rumor, she took the trail to Joe's.

When she got out of her car and stood there, staring at Joe's place, she was as startled as the thousands of men who have seen it for the first time. Joe's was not fancy. The famous house was trailers behind a tall fence. The gate had a sign, "Please ring bell and push."

Brigette had seen her, the slim, Spanish type in the skin-tight pants. She had the feeling that this one was professional without showing it. She hired Margaret within ten minutes. Brigette, who has hired hundreds of girls, thinks it unnecessary to give them the grand tour, silly to try to tell them everything when they will learn so much from the other girls. She explained Joe's pricing.

"You want to start now?"

"Well, I wasn't really sure I'd stay," Margaret said, "but why not, maybe I can take my car into town tomorrow."

As Brigette led Margaret to her room, they went through the parlor where several men sat on couches with girls. Margaret saw what she had heard about, that there was no bar, that the grim parlor was everything: it would be straight action in the little rooms, with no interludes where you talked over a drink. A couple

of girls looked up and smiled, but Margaret saw again that friend-
ships are guarded. She was shown to the room, recently vacated
by a girl named Cora. It was tight. The bed filled most of it, leaving a two-foot corridor on each side. For some reason, Cora had
left her poster behind. It was a sheet of cardboard, 4 x 5 feet, and
divided into twenty squares; each square showed a version of sex.
Some squares were so acrobatic that Margaret thought only a Jap-
anese gymnast could manage them.

"Jeannie is the cook," Brigette explained. "She has dinner on
what I mean is, she puts everything out, like buffet style, by five.
You eat anytime you want, with anybody you want. Now if you're
ever in here too long, and we get to wondering, we knock and ask
if everything's OK. You be sure to answer. If you don't answer, we
come in. None of the doors has locks. OK, you make the lineup
anytime you want. You can sit around and talk or start right in.
It'll be easy in a couple of days."

Out in the kitchen it was getting near the good hour when
Jeannie, the cook, was about through with the bustling that had
started at eight that morning. Jeannie is a non-talkative Negro
who has been in the Mustang since it opened. She is happy in her
job. The Mustang girls give her such uncomplicated acceptance as
she has never known before. Joe, Sally, Brigette, and Beverly let
her do what she wants. At one time, Joe, cheerfully authoritative
in everything, tried to give Jeannie some coaching in food; mostly,
that the food should be the best and no skimping. She found that
she had to plan several days ahead, to do all the ordering, and to
get it on the table. She fell into easy harmony with Matt, the
handyman. Jeannie, planning Thursday meals on Monday, gives
Matt a shopping list that can run two pages. The bulk of the food
for Mustang is provided by a wholesaler. Joe has set the policy
that any girl may ask for anything that suits her whim. Once an
incredulous reporter asked if this would cover ten girls who might
ask for filet mignon every day. Joe said, "Why not? They'd get
sick of it in a week." When the wholesaler cannot locate the raisin
cookies for Sue, or the strawberry yogurt for Mae, the item goes
on Matt's list. Matt has been known to irritate Sally by doggedly
trying ten stores in pursuit of diet chocolate ice cream.

Matt will study his list with practiced eye and estimate it

should run $150. He will tell Brigette, who goes into the cash box and takes out ten twenties. Matt is off in his pick-up. If you ride with him, he will manage to tell you that Joe is a great guy. "He don't look down your throat to check if you come back with the right change; lets you do your job."

Jeannie goes a little remote around ten each morning. She cooks slowly and without shortcuts. If the recipe for coleslaw says to soak the cabbage in ice water three hours, she has it on before noon. By mid-afternoon everyone knows that Jeannie has some nice surprise. As the girls run in and out of the kitchen to jot their entries on the chart, they may peek into a pot and sigh, "Oh, boy, curry." Around six, Jeannie passes the word, "Please tell everybody it's on." Her barricading table has it all. A customer was once shown the kitchen and said, "Man, what lovely stew." Jeannie corrected him. "It's not stew, it's pot au feu."

Mustang's kitchen has developed a certain fame of its own. It contains Jeannie's bay, the alcove with the huge floriated stove, the ovens and the sinks, the alcove which, towards evening, can suffuse the whole area with odors of rosemary and cinnamon. Jeannie's bay is walled off by a counter which becomes the buffet. Six feet away is the dining table, a glistening formica plane where everyone takes meals, girls, maids, guards, and handymen. Another wall has a third table across which moves, from one January to the next, well over a million dollars. Every few minutes girls approach the table with bills in hand, the advance payments of men who are momentarily alone in back rooms. Whoever is on duty presses the bills into a small wooden box on the table. In another business an owner with Joe's volume would use a cash register for the unending deposits and occasional withdrawals, but Joe thinks a cash register is too obvious. On the table, too, is the chart, the first document of Mustang, on which every girl makes the entries as to what she did that day and what she collected. The table also has two phones which may not be used by the girls, which are for management.

Above this table is the window that commands the approach to Mustang. It has been called the "command post." Since Joe's never closes, the window must be manned at all times. Men are observed as they approach. Only the rare drunk is barred. Inside, whoever presses the button works two circuits, one that releases a catch on the outside gate and one that sounds a buzzer in the parlor. The button may be in the hands of Sally, or Brigette, or Beverly or, in slack moments, Jeannie, the cook. When traffic is very heavy, as on Saturday and Sunday nights, it is the full-time job of a security guard.

By six, there may be one or ten girls at table. They know they can go there any time before nine, but not later, because that is when Jeannie clears things off, although the desserts will remain all night—strawberry shortcake or banana cream pie—to be cleared off when she returns at seven next morning.

Margaret took her plate to the table. She saw that the girls didn't talk much, that even here they keep to the arm's length distance which is their way, the noncommittal friendliness in which they never really tell much. A girl may cause a swirl of talk with a remark about corn, some sudden vision of a time on an Ohio farm, and for a few minutes they might chatter like housewives, but the talk doesn't last. They eat, mostly in silent thought, and whether they are thinking of childhood kitchens, or Thanksgivings, or double-crossing pimps is hard to say. As they stare at their plates they are only twenty feet from the window that shows more men coming in. Men, like the thousands who have come before, most of them to be there less than a half-hour before they go back to their cars. As long as the girls are at table they will miss the lineup, knowing that the men will go to whatever girls are on shift. The girls don't linger. Some will take time for a dish of Jeannie's Jell-O, but others skip it to hurry back to the lineup.

On her first lineup, Margaret was in a line of eight. Two men came in to stand, uncertain, eyes flicking from girl to girl, from face to groin to shoes, pausing on the buxom Aggie at the extreme left, swinging to the skeletal Negro, Julie, and to other girls Margaret did not know. The men tried to be offhand: one lit a cigarette. He pointed to a girl whom Margaret had not met, a lovely, slim thing with the shy smile of a madonna. He said simply, "You." The girl smiled, put her arm in his and led him off.

When the lineup broke up the girls went back to the couches to wait for the next buzzer. They picked up a magazine, or talked, or stared into space. With business so fast, however, lineups came one a minute. Margaret was in her third or fourth when a maid signaled and called her into the corridor, "You want to go double with Jill?"

Jill was one of the few girls Margaret could not understand. Her beauty was so remarkable that Margaret thought that even without talent a girl that ethereal should be able to marry, or model, or do something to exploit her face. She had magazine-cover coloring, jet hair, Irish eyes, an almost anemic transparency. She was shy and soft-voiced, almost timid. Beverly had observed that Jill got a big share of each day's customers, but only as first-timers. Few customers picked her a second time. Beverly guessed that it was because in the final nakedness she was too passive, too withdrawn.

Jill said amiably, "Hello, dear, this is Phil." Phil smiled and said, "Hi." Jill was competent. "We'll have a nice time, Phil, but you know you pay now."

Apparently, Phil knew. He was not bothered by the money handling. He was about to have an interval of something still unknown to most men, a period with two girls, and he agreed immediately when Jill said it would be $50. He paid with three twenties. Jill, who seemed to be the one who would be most engaged, asked, "Would you book it, dear?" Margaret was only minutes in a quick run to the kitchen. She handed the bills to Beverly, leaned over to make the entry on the chart, and took the ten that Beverly handed back. While she was out, Phil had taken off his pants and put them over the back of a chair, his eyes on Jill as she slipped out of her things and lay down on the bed. When Margaret handed him his change, he reached for his pants and put it into a pocket.

Phil was one of the silent ones, going to his pleasure and trusting the girls to improvise. He was up on an elbow over Jill, and for a moment Margaret thought he would try what is forbidden, to kiss her on the mouth. But he moved from kissing her neck to sucking her breasts. In a few moves he had his face buried between her legs. He was accustomed to this, stroking her deeply and expertly, so that if she were inclined to react at all, this would have done it. He held her lightly, his mouth leaving her only long enough to catch his breath. Margaret saw that Phil had a special sensuality. She fell to massaging him. After a time, and still without words, Phil switched girls, continuing his private orgy now with Margaret. It went on for ten minutes before Jill's voice came from another planet. "I'm sorry, darling, but I've got to interrupt. We're taking a long time. If you want to go more, we have to have another twenty."

He was irritated. "My God, it's OK, but do I have to pay now? Can't it wait?"

Jill was tender. "'House rules, darling."

"OK," he said. "It's in my pants, take it."

"No, darling, we can't."

"Why not?"

"Rules. A girl can't touch your clothes; we'd be fired if we touched your wallet."

"Well, you're not rolling a drunk, it's OK."

"No," said Jill. "You've got to do it. Here, it will only take a second."

Phil reached for his clothes and pulled out some bills. Margaret remembered something her husband had once said. "Christ, if I had to handle money at that moment I believe I'd go as impotent as a guy on an operating table. My God! Don't they mind?" Margaret knew that they do mind, that some men will not go to a house for that reason; the frank dealing in money. But it was a procedure which had been settled upon all over the world; men pay first. Which was logical enough: the services could hardly be free, there had to be payment, so the best way was to get it over with. A "good whore" is supposed to get the man's mind away from money. It should cease to matter as soon as the girl gets close. Jill was a good whore. While Phil was absorbed with Margaret, Jill played with him in a way that centered his universe in the tiny room. Suddenly, it was over. The experienced girls knew the signs; they knew when it meant only a rest and when it was over. For most men nothing is so final, so divisive of time, as the last convulsive shudder of love.

Once, a reporter discussed pimps with Margaret. He asked her if she had known many.

"Yes," she said. "You get to know girls, you go out with them, and chances are they will introduce the boyfriend. That's when you meet the pimp."

"How many of the Mustang girls had them?"

"Oh, maybe a fourth."

"Are they mostly Negro?"

"No, that's Las Vegas, where they run to black. Up here it's white. They're mostly young—I don't know why. They all seem to be under thirty. There's a book about them, *Psychology of the Pimp*, or something, but I never read it. I don't need to."

"What's your idea?"

"Well, once in the business, you go deeper and deeper, you accept more and more. A girl gets used to the idea that whoring is all right. She loses all jealousy herself and she's willing to team up with a man who doesn't give a damn, either. A pimp is a man who can't see where a wife working as a whore is any different from a wife waiting table. This idea, that her vagina is strictly his, he thinks is silly. Whores get the same way. Actually, when a whore goes for a pimp, it's her own way of wanting to get married, have a protector. They still need love, you know."

"Do the girls really give them all their money?"

"Yes, it's a little hard to believe, but it's true. I'd never go near one, but the girls who have them give them their money. Take Sue. She has one, but not the kind of guy who has other girls. He has no stable, just Sue. Her guy works up at Lake Tahoe. He's a carpenter, real straight, get-up-at-five-in-the-morning carpenter. When Sue gets time off, she goes up there and they live together, like man and wife. But he manages her. If she should have a run-in with Joe and get fired, he'd get in his pickup and go talk to the other places. He knows the owners, in Winnemucca, Elko, even Las Vegas. So that's one kind, he's got only one girl. But most pimps have three, or four, or even ten; that gets harder to understand because each one of the girls is crazy about him, even knowing he's sort of a sheik or something. Maybe it's like those Mormon setups where the girl is willing to be one of several wives."

"Does the pimp really help, that is, get her out of jail, get bond, get her placed, sit with her in the hospital?"

"Not up here so much, because up north the girls don't have

much trouble, they don't need a trouble shooter. It's down in Las Vegas that the pimp really helps."

"Does Joe deal with them? Does he accept them as brokers?"

"No, they keep trying to promote Joe, but he's smart. You know, pimping is against the law, and so is dealing with them; he shoos them away. Besides, who needs brokers? There are at least a hundred girls a month show up asking for jobs."

When Joe and Sally decided to marry, they were following what in most lands is considered wise mating. In royal courts, as among peasants, experience has taught that it is better if both have the same background; in their case both had run houses. They would have earnest breakfast talks about problems peculiar to the trade: what to do about the little crises, what to allow in Mustang. A girl would come running out of a room shrieking for the police, or angrily demanding a knife to kill a son-of-a-bitch who wanted to urinate in her rectum. Sally would try to soothe girls still trembling from their experiences. A man, who wanted to suck on a breast, got so carried away that he offered his girl an extra one hundred to hold still until he got a little blood. Men wanted anal entry. The approximately two hundred cars per day brought men who made the reasonable assumption that women in a whorehouse would go along with anything. For a long time, Joe and Sally had troubled talks on what to allow. It didn't help to decide that the house should stick to the standard perversions because, with changing times, the customer kept enlarging on what was standard. You cannot operate a place a week without making decisions forced by homosexuals. "Hey, Sal? Why don't you put in some guys out there, make them bookkeepers or guards, so us guys can drop in?" For this the Confortes had a consistent "no," for that was sure to guarantee Nevada's outrage. Reno women would corner Joe and ask if they could sneak in for just a teeny minute, to be hidden some place and allowed to watch. Joe turned down many such requests before learning there was French word for them, which he now uses with some style, "them voyeurs." The Confortes had to decide what to do about the men who wanted to be tied up and whipped or, in gentler mode, to have only their genitals tied; what to do about men who wanted to whip the girl, or who wanted two girls to whip each other. Joe and Sally were scared of sadism, mild or wild, but in time, they did enlarge the curriculum; they made skittish adjustment to some thirty acts which would have been considered the foulest perversions ten or fifteen years earlier. But they did so with a nice feeling for what might be too avant-garde. The Confortes have to keep re-examining the cultural mainstream. Their interest has always been success, not innovation. It was only after Joe had been asked to provide his tenth or twentieth girl for the smokers of Reno's eminent that he OK'd porno film shorties. The films were not really Joe's idea.

His girls kept telling him that if they had small projectors and the right film, they could arouse their men more and hike the fees. In time, the famous kitchen acquired still one more table, a small one, on which repose five or six small movie projectors. They play silent films. Girls say that when they start them buzzing in the tiny rooms, throwing a fuzzy, black and white image the size of a *Ladies Home Journal* on a plaster wall that, bad focus and cracked plaster notwithstanding, men get excited.

To all but the repeat customer, the lineup can be startling. Some men walk in and gasp, some freeze. For possibly a hundred men every day it is the first experience, twenty girls lined up just for him. A Reno man once raked Joe over for this. "Joe, Goddamn it, you're making so much money you've got to find new rocks to hide it under. Why don't you put in a bar? So the customers can have a little time to shop around and not have to decide, bang, bang."

Joe, who drinks very little, answered, "Well, I've thought about it. But I'm superstitious. Up to now we never called the sheriff once. There's not been a police car come over that bridge since we opened. So I put in a bar and I get maybe three-four drunks a night, well, figure the percentages, fifteen or twenty girls drinking and a few drunk customers, and two security guards who know how to keep their tempers, and me who don't—not always anyway—it's better we have no bar."

So Joe settled on the flow line that has been followed by one hundred to six hundred men each day through the years. The customer climbs three steps outdoors, takes five steps inside, and finds himself center stage facing a line of girls in an instant staring match. Because of scheduling foulups or unexpected mass arrivals, the line may have as few as three girls (despite Joe's rule that it must always have five) or as many as forty. Toward evening and through the night, it may reach wall to wall, "the senior graduating class," as the girls call it, which requires about eighteen bodies thigh-to-thigh to block off the room. More than eighteen starts the formation of a U.

The number of girls at the Mustang varies. The most Joe ever had in residence at one time was forty-two, but his more constant figure is thirty-five. While all girls want the best shift—the hours, generally, from seven PM to three AM—the house must rotate them so that all get the lean shifts, the "dogwatch," roughly two to eleven AM weekdays. The maids keep a "shift chart" that assures that every girl gets good and bad shifts. This still allows flexibility. Mustang has nights when the demand makes the house shake; the evenings of holidays, and when Reno has conventions. Brigette may get worried when she sees that the parking lot is jammed, that men are pouring in, and that the lineup is skimpy because so many girls are on their backs. At such times, she may knock on the door of a girl who has just gone to bed, and ask if she cares to return to help with the mob. Generally, she will tell the men to wait; she enters the parlor and calls out, "Have a cigarette, boys, there'll be girls out in a few minutes."

The men, facing other men in chairs across the room, sit and stare. As they wait, they will see an almost nude girl hurry across the parlor without looking at anyone. They have no way of knowing that she is headed for the chart to make her entry.

Once, Joe thought to coach his girls on how they should stand, and with what expression. But the girls voted him down on this. They use their own rules, the guild ways of the profession. They are simple. In the presence of another girl you don't sell, don't ham it up, don't flirt, simper, or imply that your body is the ultimate heaven. In bar houses, of course, when a man has picked his drinking companion, a girl may promise any paradise in her whispered talk. But in the lineups they want no *femme fatale,* no seductress, and the rule is "Don't fuck the guy by telepathy." So serious are the girls about this, so determined not to be coy, that some go the other way. A man staring at a line of girls sees them

stare back with what can be amusement or challenge, and sometimes if the girl has a crotch made tender by onslaught, outright-
hostility. Beverly says that many men would feel more comfortable if the girls acted up more, but the girls won't risk the jibes of
their mates. Besides, they know that in the long shifts, business
evens out, that each girl will get her share. "So they stand," Beverly says, "some of them with as much come-on as if she's waiting
for a dryer at a laundromat." If a man stares too long, a voice may
materialize, "Look, mister, why don't you decide so we can sit
down, we're tired." Toni, a Negro, so thin that she had trouble
keeping up her bra, and one of the biggest earners in Mustang
history, would stand with legs apart and arms crossed over her
head as if under police search. If a man waited too long she
would call out, "Hey, look, I'm the ugliest, can I sit down?"

A Las Vegas reporter, Colin McKinlay, once visited Mustang to
do one of the first stories Joe ever allowed. McKinlay wrote that
Joe had some of the most beautiful girls in Nevada which, from a
Las Vegas reporter, was high acclaim. But another reporter, visiting Joe's later, found few beauties and several who, he said,
reminded him of Ukrainian peasants; heavy-bodied, thick-legged
girls who resembled girl wrestlers. Both reporters were right,
because Joe's girls vary enormously from season to season. The
women who hire for Mustang—Sally, Beverly, and Brigette—
know that a hefty, big-hearted, battle-weary mother type can
have as many entries on her chart as a Miss Pasadena. Says Beverly, "There's thousands of men who want what they've had
before. They get worked up over memories, what it was like with
some big, comfortable gal, and this type of guy doesn't turn on
particularly for Miss eat-more-peaches week."

For the men who leave Mustang, the release, the memory, and
any lingering traces of perfume are carried away in cars that are
lost on Highway 80. For the girls who line up for new men, who
know new nakedness, new penises, new body smells, new forms of
lust, the experience is too complex to explain. But certainly, one
reason for agreeing to accept the sperm of just about anyone who
enters—even when his "check" is questionable—is the chart.
The chart is the vindication.

It is the tally of what she earned that day, the proof of what she has coming, the monetary total. Joe's chart is a simple thing today but, as the product of a mathematical mind, it represents years of thinking on how to compensate the girls. Joe devised a disposable chart. To understand its virtues one must recall one line in the laws of Nevada; no man may share in the earnings of a prostitute. Thus, theoretically, it could happen that if thirty-five girls had fifteen affairs each and shared with management each time, Joe would violate the law five hundred twenty-five times in one day. Joe simply adopts the position taken in all Nevada houses, that he is a landlord and not an employer, and so does not share in the earnings of prostitutes. When girls ask for a job they get the meticulous explanation that the Mustang does not hire girls. When the Mustang does add one, she becomes a tenant. She is given a room and works in a place whose doors admit about one hundred thousand men a year. When chosen by one of them she must set her own prices and do her own money handling. She will take his money and turn it over to whoever is on duty at the table. But it remains her money. Since she may receive five to twenty payments a day, she must record each as received, that is, what she turns over for safekeeping. For this there is the great chart.

The chart is a sheet of paper 4 feet wide and 3 feet up and down. At the start of each day, someone prints the name of each girl across the top—Lola, Tina, Millie, Sue, Chloris, Jane, Pam, Livia, Harla, etc. Under every name are two narrow columns that reach to the bottom of the page, one column for time entries and one for money.

Assume that "Bonnie" has a man in her room who is planning about ten minutes of fellatio, five of "lingus," and certainly no more than that of regular. Bonnie will dimple up, pat him playfully on the groin and tell him that will be $25. In most cases he will not bargain; he will go to his wallet and give Bonnie the bills. Bonnie leaves him for a moment, goes to the kitchen and hands the money to whoever is on duty at the table. Bonnie then leans over the chart, picks up a ballpoint pen, and in her two columns logs her starting time, say 3:18 PM, and the figure $25. The time entry is important. If, after a while, someone senses that Bonnie has been behind a closed door for a suspiciously long time, a blackout that could mean that she is dead from strangulation or lost in pleasure—someone will check Bonnie's time column to see just how long she has been occupied. No door has locks in Mustang, and any maid is free to barge in on any affair, whether prompted by a thud, an imagined scream, or long silence. When Bonnie's man is pale and subdued, she returns to the chart and logs in time of completion to the minute. Joe demands that at any instant of any day the chart show which rooms are in action and which idle. If thirty-one girls are on shift, thirty-one columns go inching downward. The girls are constantly being told to be neat, to keep their figures small and under each other. The time columns may show that Sue is having quite a run of quicky $10 minimums, and that the beefy Tamaris, with only five jobs, was busy all day with men who were good for $40 to $100. All things end, and so does a shift which is flexible, and which a girl can stretch into twelve to sixteen hours. When her day is done, Bonnie will ask whoever is on duty to figure her total. Someone will draw a line under her last entry, add the column and print her total in large figures, sometimes with a gay swirl of underlining. Bonnie may learn that her total is $230 for the day. The total may be eighteen inches from the top. At the end of a shift, as they make their last entries, the girls linger to stare at a sheet crowded with many kinds of handwriting, at entries that convey fantastic hours, at totals that cause admiring, "My Gawds."

On the chenille beds there is such invention as makes pricing difficult. If a man wants the now standard "69," girls understand it is $20, but if he is lost in ecstasy and groans into a second half-hour, price must reflect time. "Straight" is $10, with the understanding that any man worth his salt should free his girl in ten minutes. Even dull men come up with permutations, say, four variants, three with rabbity speed, and a fourth stretched out in forgetfulness of the world.

Joe thought he had about all human inventiveness priced, only to find that innovators were coming up with combinations that had his girls muttering. He and Sally had to re-think price. With the years, they developed a fairly standard table. Some men still want only the old prone act that created the species, but in two or three reprises, with recuperation in between. The girls have many names for it, and its cost rises in ten-minute intervals. They have prices for every act named by the Romans, and those invented since. The "double" starts at $50, but as performers can surprise even themselves with what they can get into *à trois*, the girls put an amiable increase for each new wildness and in so doing give final proof to Joe's claim that they, and not he, set prices. Since each girl makes her own little modifications of the basic price guide, it can happen that in one day's pilgrimage of three hundred men, a computer would find that twenty-two men got almost identical ecstasy from virtually identical acts, and yet paid twenty-two slightly different fees. Joe can't help that.

As to the absorbing question—what goes to Joe and what to the Bonnies—few people know. Assume Bonnie's gross for her day was $230, which Mustang holds as custodian. Her net will be paid to her in cash within hours of adding the total. At moment of payment, the Mustang will deduct a charge for board and another for room. The room charge is what, in theory, it is worth to work there. The sorriest of girls is expected to gross $1,000 a week. If, in any shift, a girl fails to do $50 gross, she pays neither room nor board for that day, and her earnings are transferred as the starter for her column next day. Reno gossip says Joe's room charge is 50 percent. Joe's attorneys don't know and don't want to know. The IRS says the figure is not in the public domain and Joe agrees. As for the chart, it is burned at the end of each day. Someone takes it outside, crumples it into a ball, tosses it into a garbage can, touches a match to it, and stands by to make sure no vagrant breeze blows it, half consumed, to some hillside where it can be picked up by roaming kids. The destruction of the great sheet is too bad in a way, because Joe could probably auction off the one-day histories, with their thirty-five kinds of handwriting, to collectors. But since even his attorneys have never seen one, the sheets, like certain moths, have a life cycle of only twenty-four hours.

"Beverly?"

"Yes?"

"I've heard you use the words, 'a good whore' several times. Apparently, you mean something very specific?"

"Well, sure. To begin with, the good whore is a girl who solves your problems and don't create them. And this is a business where it's problems every hour. The good whore makes it easy for the management, which is why you don't see us hire what all you men seem to want, the teenage, virgin-looking cutie-pies. They may look wonderful on TV but they can be a pain here in a house. The Lolitas just don't make good whores."

"Why?"

"Well, for example, they keep putting their own feeling into it too much, their own pride. Suppose a man comes in and he's a little drunk and bragging. Well, a young girl will get irritated and show it. The older girl takes it as it comes, makes him feel like the president. Take some customer who gets in back and suddenly says, 'Hey, you Italian or Jewish or something, because I don't like either.' Well, the good whore rolls with it. Take the guy who comes in and what he wants really is an audience, somebody to hear him talk or boast, how big a job he's got, what a big shot he is. Or take the guy who just can't help insulting whores. Some girls get mad and tell him off. Some girls come charging out of a room and shout for me to call the cops. It sounds funny, but the good whore sort of likes people, like a good nurse. One problem, and we get it a lot, is the guy who makes his deal, pays his money, and then, for some reason, he can't make it. Take some bitchy kid, who gets sarcastic, 'Look, mister, if you can't get it up it's not my problem.' But the good whore makes a man feel it happens all the time—with football players and wrestlers, real he-men. She will try a lot of things; the good ones are intuitive as hell, until finally, he reacts and she knows she's got it. But only a smart girl will bother that much. Of course, there's times when nothing works, and we give the guy his money back. We don't give up easy, because it's always a hell of a humiliation for the guy. Generally, we ask him if he wants another try with another girl. The first one, the good whore, she won't mind."

"Are you saying that a man will accept money back?"

"Jesus, yes. Not only take it, ask for it. There's all kinds. Some of them let a girl try everything, and when he can't make it, he blames the girl. Some guys laugh and tell the girl to keep the money and buy some perfume. See what I mean? The good gal smooths things, butters them up, maybe winds up working him for a hundred bucks, where a kid would send him away, swearing."

"In other words, the good whore blots out her own ego?"

"Yeah, right."

Sally Conforte has days when she resents her attachment to her husband. She has been on the verge of divorcing him several times, times when his ego becomes overpowering, when his arrogance kills all discussion, days when he looks upon all the rest of mankind as moronic. Yet, she is attached to him. Mixed in with his ego are the many streaks of kindness which balance out his Caesar days. For the most part, she has learned to adjust to him. In some things Sally thinks Joe is a genius. She has seen him when he had to raise $10,000 to survive the month, and months later, handing out $1,000 packets to men in the legislature. She has seen him pull victories out of disaster. But she knows, too, that she has to accept his crushing ego, that Joe is forever on-stage. During the years when Joe was in Carson, Sally made the fifty-mile trip from Wadsworth every Tuesday, to collide with Joe's ego, even there. One day, when she was shown into the vistors' room, a guard came back with Joe's message that he was all tied up in a bridge game, and would she please wait until he had finished the hand. Sally laughs. "I almost turned around and left that time, but he likes bridge the way he likes sex, and he was in prison and I wasn't."

Sally even paid to see Joe: There were times when she wanted to see him more than the allowable once a week. She learned that she could get around the prison rule by taking along a lawyer, since there is no limit to visits between lawyer and client. Sally hit on the idea of paying an attorney a $250 fee to accompany her on the three-hour trip.

Years later, a reporter found this startling. "Joe, do you mean to say that an attorney will accept a fee just to sit in the room and smoke while a wife visits with her husband?" Joe went thoughtful. "Lawyers," he said in a measured voice, "most of them are whores. A lawyer will represent a whore and really be a pimp, because he will hit a whore for a higher fee than he would ask another girl; that makes him share in her fucking, doesn't it? Those lawyers who came with Sally?—by the way, I hadn't hired Brown yet—they would sit there, maybe twenty feet away, and read a magazine. Then they would ride back with her. Hell, they would have taken $500 if she paid it." Here something tells Joe that he has gone too far. "Well, make three exceptions. I've hired maybe thirty in my time, and there's three that's honest. There's Morgan in San Francisco, and Brown here, and Harry Claibourne in Las Vegas. The others?" Here Conforte studies you. "Could I possibly be telling you, a reporter, anything you don't already know?"

Stanley Brown was twenty-eight when he was retained by Joe. Joe had gone through several lawyers in his years, but he did not choose Brown until the time he needed co-counsel on his tax case. While that case was lost, Joe thought that Brown had done as much as any man could. When Joe was off and forgotten in McNeil, Sally would ask Brown to visit Joe, sometimes on business, sometimes just to cheer him up. Brown did, and the gesture, for a man who was broke and a poor prospect for business, was something Joe would remember. When Joe got out, he became involved in so many plots that, hitting on the theory of the CIA, he decided to divide his operations among several lawyers so no one would know too much about his affairs. But in time, Joe settled on Brown for almost everything.

Brown had a degree from the University of San Francisco Jesuit School, but on coitus and the law he had to start from scratch. There aren't that many men in the business," he explains, "and not too much law on the problems that come from girl handling." He had a difficult field and a client who was different. In the first days, Joe would get him on the phone and blurt out a problem before Brown could interrupt. "Joe, damn it," Brown would say, "You don't do things this way! You simply must come to the office. You can't do things by phone."

"Oh hell, this is simple. A guy claims he got the clap here and . . ."

"There's other reasons, Joe."

"Like what?"

"Well, for one, your line is tapped."

"Balls! How do you know?"

"An Assistant Department of Justice Attorney told me so."

"You mean we're tapped right now? You mean they're running a tape on us right this very fucking minute?"

"Every word!"

"Jesus," said Joe, "I better stop swearing."

Over the years, Brown was able to give Joe a lot of advice on law, and a lot which he hoped was common sense. But one problem was posed not by Joe but by a madam in Winnemucca.

"Look, Stan, suppose I hire a minor?"

"You're violating several laws right there," Brown told her. "But go on."

"OK. Suppose I tell the kid that if she refuses to go double she'll have to go. Is that coercion? Maybe white slavery?"

"Well, it's not white slavery," said Brown, and let it go.

Life is changing for Brown too. Over the years he developed an image as Joe's trouble-shooter, and this led to the assumption that he spent much time in Mustang. Actually, Brown has never been there. But he likes to drink with reporters who have, and he pumps them about the Doras and the Susies. In recent times he has been working less on Mustang, and almost full time on Joe's new ventures. An indication of Joe's changing status is the fact that a bank which once sniffed at Joe recently agreed to lend him $300,000 for a land deal. It was not a total moral endorsement because the nine-man loan committe split seven to two on the loan but, as Joe said, "It wasn't no kick in the stomach either."

Joe is becoming a Nevada power. This will be shouted down by those who resent the idea, but realists admit it. He has become rich and is hungry for status. He has found that he can get status of sorts by giving money to politicians and to charity. Where, in the beginning, it was he who approached the politicians, they now come to him. To politicians, there is nothing wrong with Joe's money, although they like it in cash and unrecorded. There is nothing illegal in Joe's handouts, since the entire American political system depends on private contributions—a fact of life known a century before Watergate. Like most sophisticated donors, Joe has not asked for much in return: he has called in few promissory notes. He has made few demands on the legislature, or on the bosses of neighboring counties and cities. What he had done, he hopes, is build reservoirs of gratitude against the day he needs something big.

It is taken for granted in Nevada that Joe has no outside connections. Since he is Sicilian, and certainly the world's most self-publicized girl-boss, some people have assumed that he must have Mafia ties. But Joe's file in Reno shows an assortment of federal angers but no worries about Mafia connections. For Joe any contact with other men of the trade has been a sleeve-brush affair. He met hardly any of importance in Sicily and certainly met no "consiglieri" in Boston or Oakland. All intelligence reports describe Joe the same way, as a loner who is too arrogantly independent to team up with anyone, even the Mafia.

A few years ago, Joe was having trouble with his landlords, the Perris, who thought they should be getting more rent. Joe reached a settlement with them, but began looking for an alternate spot to move to. His broker found a hidden riverbank ranch that had all the advantages of Mustang—that is, it was accessible to 80. Joe bought it for a song. At the closing, the broker asked whether he intended to sell the sand and gravel. Joe went blank. "What sand?" It developed he had bought one of the richest deposits of high-grade sand and gravel within a hundred miles of Reno. In booming Nevada, Joe could close Mustang, if he chose, and have a good construction business. On another hunch, he built a restaurant and bar near Virginia City, a place on a hilltop which he named Cabin in the Sky, a $200,000 investment which, six months after its opening, was getting a capacity house almost every weekend. In another deal, he paid a million and a half for a piece of land near Reno, which he is converting into a golf course and a housing development, a project which he will consider a bust if it does not return three hundred percent.

Reporters find Joe accessible. He will pontificate on anything within his orbit, the orbit of a man both worldly and semiliterate. But he has a short attention span and finds it hell to sit still for questioning. He will ask reporters to go with him. "Hey, let's talk in the car; I got to go to Virginia City to see a guy." Once at the wheel, Joe can be questioned, if the reporter ignores the tire-squealing of the heavy White House limousine taking turns like a sports car. It was on one such drive that Joe stopped to duck into the offices of Reno's Donrey Media Co. This company owns newspapers, TV and radio stations, and several hundred Nevada billboards.

Joe was inside ten minutes. The reporter wondered what Joe could be doing in an advertising office, because Nevada law still says that brothels may not advertise.

"I just bought forty billboards," he said when he returned. "What the hell for?"

"To give to the candidates." Seeing the reporter's face, he went on, "You see, these politicians can be pretty dumb. They come for help and, suppose you like them, so you give them five hundred or a thousand. They've been too broke to buy their billboards in time. Some of them take their money and go tearing off and find all the boards been sold for months. So now when I want to back a guy, sometimes I don't even wait for him to call, I call him. I tell him to go get his advertising ready and tell him how many billboards he's got."

Joe is now only nominally manager of Mustang. He is involved in large affairs; at election time, he orders more polls than many candidates; he grooms new candidates and advises the old. He is in real estate, and takes long trips (a girl with him) to play bridge. When in Reno, he visits Mustang because he is eternally fascinated to see how many new men have found his parlor. Also, there is always a danger that someone will try to frame him and plant a girl who will testify that she was recruited in California —a violation of a law so old that younger people may not even have heard of it—the Mann Act. For a time, there was danger of lawsuits by Negros who might claim that in being refused a girl they were denied their civil rights. Joe is so free of racial prejudice that he leans the other way—he is pro-Negro. But the problem was touchy for years because, in whorehouse snobbisms, white men will pick Negro girls, but white girls do not want black men. The Mustang settled this tactfully. Joe set up a separate room, actually a smaller parlor, for the use of Negro men. When a black is seen coming up the steps, a signal goes to all girls on duty. Those willing to line up for him should go to the smaller room. Evolution has been rapid here, too. Where, in 1968, only a few girls would serve the second parlor—and this mostly to help Joe—many now serve both, so that Joe may soon take the big step and consolidate, opening one parlor to all. The last holdouts, the girls who will not go with a Negro, are the Negro girls. Anyone who asks Joe or the Negro girls to explain this ethnic nicety gets the most involved psychiatric minestrone since the demise of Gracie Allen.

The Confortes had to learn what to do when someone died. Only two have died in Joe's years at Mustang, the first in circumstances that set the procedure for all that might follow. It was a middle-aged man with high blood pressure. He had been drinking before he came and had given his girl a lusty time, with little result. Suddenly, he went supine, complained of not feeling well. He turned over, motionless and pale. The girl rushed out screaming. When Joe, the maids, and a guard went in, they saw that the man was dead. Word went through the house. As it happened, the Mustang had an old customer in the parlor, a friend of Joe's and Sally's. He had a great admiration for Joe and he called him aside. "Look, friend," he said, "you got no problem. I'll make like I'm taking him to the hospital, but instead, I'll take him down the river and dump him over the bridge." The Confortes were touched by the offer, but they explained that Mustang was legal: all that was necessary was to call the sheriff who would call the coroner. An hour later, as the man was being carried out, his girl recovered enough to say, "Well, the old geezer never broke out of a trot, but he died in the saddle." Today, when a man enters whose stamina appears to be in doubt, a girl may warn Sally, "Now don't blame me if he dies on horseback."

A college teacher once worked for Joe, though so briefly that she doubts that he would remember her. She was a ten-day dropout from her world, and in an anti-everything mood that prompted her to try Mustang. She was soon back at her job, teaching English lit in a California junior college. On her second day in the parlor, Joe, spotting a new face, stopped in midstride. "Hey, hello," he said cordially. "I'm Joe, as if you don't know."

Somehow she got around to asking if he had ever read Freud.

"Look, honey," Joe said, "I hear about the guy but, well, you know I never read any books at all, not until I'm maybe thirty-five, when I'm in prison. It was *Captain from Castile*. This con is paroled and he leaves the book behind. I start reading and, so help me, I never knew books did this, I mean, stretch out a story that long. This fellow Pedro de Vargas . . ."

Joe can never recall the excitement of discovering books without plunging into the story of the conquistador. "Anyway, it was sort of late to start reading. No, I never read Freud. You really suppose the guy knew a hell of a lot more about women than I do?"

Mustang and Reno are now less on his mind than Las Vegas. Las Vegas publishes two papers, and Joe gets both. He senses what more sophisticated men sense, that Las Vegas, which seems to have a new renaissance every few years, is on the edge of another. Metro Goldwyn Mayer, which has just given the city the world's largest resort hotel, is already being shaded by the announcement that four corporations plan new giants, each in the MGM class. This has prompted the joke that Las Vegas will have more bedrooms than Ohio, focusing eyes more intently than ever on the dizzying girl potentials.

While the Raggio-Conforte feud continues, the two men keep things to a low simmer, and they wave when they meet. Raggio ran for the state senate and won, and one of his first moves was to push for a law that would ban brothels within fifty miles of any large city, a law that would have closed Mustang. But Joe has friends in Carson, and the bill died in committee. Joe has developed a new confidence, a brashness, and a need for vindication which can seem paranoic. His need takes many shapes, and one is the determination to invade Las Vegas, which would mean a turn in Nevada's direction and a fight with the big owners who still say no.

To Joe, Las Vegas is an affront. Its prostitution, he believes, must be fifty times that of the Mustangs, Elkos, Winnemuccas, and Elys combined. He thinks it absurd that the celebrated Las Vegas bosses should get by with hundreds of times his coital volume without being called procurers. Joe, whom some call brave and some schizoid, knows that Las Vegas sees him as a man who is rocking a big, prosperous boat. He knows that he is opposed by those suave millionaires who still own some hotels, and by the corporations that own the others. He knows that the powers do not want to legalize prostitution, and that if it were legalized, it should not be run by a man with Joe's Barnum flair. But Joe continues his maneuvers to invade.

While Joe can be called eccentric, no one has called him stupid. He sees signs that in time, Las Vegas will legalize prostitution. His figures for the whores in the city sound like those for New York, and his estimate for specific hotels is so high that the owners could find them flattering. "Hell, Caesars Palace, the Dunes, the Sands, they're the most beautiful whorehouses on earth; they hide their volume behind gambling, but the Strip does the business of two hundred Mustangs."

He likes Las Vegas. In Caesars Palace, when word spreads that he is in, he is besieged—by girls who want to work for him, hit him for a loan, or be his date, and by pimps, salesmen, con men. He meets Las Vegas owners who smile and tell him to cool it, that his idea is OK but too far ahead of its time.

Whatever the inflation in his figures, they have an intriguing base. In the years since he first started recruiting for his White House, he has hired, he thinks, about two thousand six hundred whores. Of these, possibly five hundred came from Las Vegas, and these have been his CIA. Joe befriends his girls; he advances them money, lends them plane fare to see a child or a relative in a hospital. He senses when a girl wants time off to go to the post office or Western Union to send money. He is good at making them talk. He sits on the chenille beds in easy gossip with defeated creatures who, only weeks before, were call girls on the list of a Sahara pit boss, or who doubled as cocktail waitresses at the Tropicana or Caesars. In 1955, he was quizzing girls who had worked the Sahara of Milton Prell and, years later, patting the fannies of girls who could be their daughters, who had worked the Sahara of Del Webb. He has taken girls on laughing trips to Los Angeles, San Francisco, Palm Springs, Denmark, Sweden, Mexico, and Sicily. He quizzes them with the soft persistence of a friendly attorney. There is no question that he understands Las Vegas, its sexual market, and the speed of change in that market: he says that thousands of men stand ready to buy into the sex business as soon as law is liberalized a bit more, that investors are ready to go into whorehouses, or into the stocks of conglomerates that include them, just as Del Webb stockholders now invest in gambling.

But Joe's size-up of Las Vegas as the new Alaskan oil field, the new growth industry, is beside the point. On legal prostitution, Las Vegas bosses still say no. The individual owners, the corporations, the banks, and the sheriff have raised a Maginot Line. They want things as they are. The amount of prostitution in Las Vegas is, safely, that of Paris or Amsterdam, but its mechanics, its subdivisions, its management in the hotels, has been so beautifully distorted by so many writers, that, in the opinion of Ray Gubser, Deputy Chief of Metro police, few men really know the picture. The business is complicated and, to understand it, one must go back to see how much was started by accident and how much by design by that pioneer, the late Benjamin Siegel.

7

"They were really all Cecil De Milles, all in the same search for the fabulous."

Grant Sawyer, former
Governor of Nevada

"I suppose you could call it a fight for style in sex."

Eugene Murphy, former Public Relations
Director, Desert Inn and Stardust

Las Vegas:
The Troubled Adolescence

PROSTITUTION IN Las Vegas was big when the room count was small, and surged as Las Vegas became the city with the most hotel rooms of any city on earth. But in what can only be called managerial brilliance, the traffic was so well handled that, as of 1966, even that great biographer of Las Vegas, the *New York Times'* Wallace Turner—a man whose distaste for Las Vegas was second only to that of the late Bobby Kennedy—said that there really wasn't too much of it, that the woman-offering was largely illusion, implying that the owners rook the customer even in this.

It would be taking a cheap shot at the men of gambling—Dalitz, Goffstein, Prell, Houssels, Wells, and more recently, Hughes and Benedict—to say that they planned such vast sex. Rather, they adjusted. As, over the years, each new wing went out, as they added towers, and as new buildings became the thirty million or seventy million dollar "latest," the owners seemed to have anticipated the Yale University researchers. For the finding of the scholars was that the American male has some form of sex thought, conventional to orgiastic, about once every four hours each day. Without benefit of Yale, the owners seemed to know that the throb of reverie grows when the male enters their lobbies

179

and sees more bosoms, groins, and sex suggestions than Paris ever dreamed up. As they built the Las Vegas skyline, the owners adapted, amiable about taking man as he is.

It would have been good to know Benjamin Siegel. It is more than a quarter of a century since he was found in his girl's house, sprawled on a couch in a *Godfather* setting of oozing bullet holes. Generally, legend takes longer to develop, but Siegel moves fast even in death, and his legend gets gaudier with the years. There are many in today's Las Vegas who knew Siegel, but even with them memory has been subtly distorted.

In legend he was the first to buy up Las Vegas' part-time county commissioners, the first to buy up the boys in Nevada's legislature (false because Nevada had no controls then, so there was no need to pay anyone to go easy on controls). He was the first to stand off the mighty Kefauver committee (Kefauver didn't hit Nevada until Siegel had been dead three years). In legend he was the first gambling owner to induce celebrities to drink with hoods; partly true, though his guests were not as impressive as those in the stories. For the tales have John Kennedy, the Duke of Windsor, and Joan Crawford throwing dice with Jake the Barber, Horse-Face Licavoli, and Mo Mo Adamo. Still, his Flamingo did manage quite a social mix.

What is true is that Siegel pioneered the great sex exchange of Las Vegas. He was ahead of his time in believing that every man should have as much coitus as he can stand, twenty-five years ahead of the people who say it on talk shows today. It was his grand design that has made Las Vegas the most acutely pelvis-conscious city on earth. The inheritance was direct.

Siegel was a man of the rackets who has not yet received such biographical study as have Costello and Capone. He had moved his base to California, close enough to make him see the possibilities of Nevada. Looking eastward, Siegel saw the whole sensual fun package in a single flash—gambling, shows, excitement, girls. Men were impelled to gamble. It was visible everywhere, from the crowds in villages being taken at carnivals, to the office buildings with their numbers men. At one level, the gambling on sports, and at another, the gambling on the stock exchange, to say nothing of crap games in alleys and in private clubs. People would talk for months about a trip to Monte Carlo. Gambling pervaded America. Siegel envisioned a place where people could gamble not only in legal tranquility but in luxury. His idea was an old thing in Europe, of course, as for example, the Spa, whose basic idea is space. So he planned one for Nevada. Its first complete resort, with everything in one compound, something with the spaciousness of a Buckingham Palace. It should have everything; restaurants, not one, but three or four, and several bars, each in its own mood. The center would be the casino, but it should not dominate. There should be other wonders, inclusive of the magic hour, when the theatre curtain would go up on something to match anything done by Ziegfeld, or Earl Carrol, or De Mille. It should be a place where people would live in country club style, with sheriff, district attorney, and governor strolling by and smiling. And there should be girls, girls everywhere. Siegel was a year building his Flamingo, and his opening night is still remembered. People wandered through the carpeted rooms and stared at the quasi-distinction. They observed the chandeliers and what local editor Al Cahlan described as "pastrami under glass." Ben's Flamingo was no Claridges of London, no Ritz of Paris, and was not even finished, but it gave men a vision of lovely horizons. If Ben could do this with a lousy 6 million, what could you do with real money? Ben showed that Nevada gambling could be anything the mind could conceive. Nevada was as open as they said. You could mount a gambling operation at 2 million or 50 million; you could create a city of girls.

In 1946, when Siegel opened, America was still quite conservative. There was a continuing war between the men who ran hotels and men who wanted to get girls into them. In New York, the Waldorf, the Sherry Netherlands, the Pierre had grim, grey-haired ladies at desks facing elevators, ladies there ostensibly for security, but really to stop the wantons. Hotels still had that Mack Sennet figure, the house detective, who rapped on doors demanding to know if there was a woman in there. But Siegel's Flamingo went out in wings, and a man and his girl had the privacy they would have had in a tent in Alberta. The wings went out so far from the lobby that a man arriving with his "friend" need never show her. He could have a call girl every night who would never go near a main entrance.

The Flamingo was brash and gaudy, but a resort in the sense that its gardens covered acres and its rooms were far from the scrutiny of management. Word spread; the rich and medium rich came to try it. In the next twenty-five years, virtually every Las Vegas hotel copied Siegel's architecture. Starting with Siegel, the resort hotel became a new industry, where Nevada would become a new state, seeing its real birth after eighty years of gestation. Siegel was shot down in Beverly Hills for reasons unknown by associates unknown, six months after his opening. But Nevada doesn't mourn long. As one owner put it, "Nevada manages to screw those who try to screw it, and when Ben died everybody thought it was good riddance of a jerk who, however, left Nevada bequeathed of a lovely idea."

In less than ten years after Ben was laid away, groups of men from Miami, Chicago, Detroit, Cleveland, New York, had put together the money for bigger, grander hotels. By 1958, Las Vegas had ten places, the Flamingo, Thunderbird, Desert Inn, Sahara, Sands, Riviera, Dunes, Tropicana, Stardust, and Fremont—with gambling, theatre, restaurants, bars, and girls. As Nevada brought forth new names, crime writers kept pace, all adding to the image of an outlaw state, and all goading J. Edgar Hoover and Congress.

After the Flamingo came the Thunderbird, whose unhappy lot was that, consistently, through all the years when Las Vegas was trying for glamour, it was called the ugliest. It was a sprawling affair, at once nondescript and garish. It was built on Las Vegas Boulevard, before the "Strip" came into being, a mile north of Siegel's Flamingo. Las Vegas was a vastness of empty land then, and the Thunderbird was surrounded by the prevailing plant, a sparse prickly grey bush, usually festooned with windblown Kleenex. A New York writer wrote that it is hard to find a road outside Las Vegas that does not have a trash pile every quarter-mile. The Thunderbird was described as "Warehouse modern with Navajo decals, some beginning to peel." It was small, with no grounds to speak of and a showroom that was meager by Las Vegas standards. But it was the place that first brought the name "Lansky" to Nevada, in this case, Meyer's brother, Jake.

Part of the Nevada story is the thirty-year fight by legislatures and governors to pass control laws. It was first provoked by the

Thunderbird. In a history that was so often seamy, Nevada's first real notoriety started with the hearings of the Senate Kefauver Committee. This was the investigation that started the nation talking about gang take-over of an American state. Because of the long run of invective that followed those hearings, people have assumed that many hotels were offenders where, in fact, only three of the hotels were then in existence. As regards the Thunderbird, they were particularly fascinated that a hidden owner should be Jake Lansky, along with an owner of record, the Lieutenant Governor of Nevada.

In the life cycles of most hotels, the original owners—the suspect names—would be replaced by approved men who would preside as managers or presidents for ten or twenty years, in some cases to become institutions. The Thunderbird produced one such, the well known Joe Wells, a two hundred fifty pound, jovial extrovert. Wells was a movie-type westerner, the successful operator of a trucking company, "Wells Cargo," a man given to western hats and large, silver belt buckles. Wells would get the trade of the Nevadans, the ranchers, businessmen, the assemblymen of the distant Elys and Winnemuccas.

In terms of calendar, the Flamingo and the Thunderbird came first, but neither was typical of what would become the Las Vegas style. Siegel was tumult, a shooting star that burned out in a single flash. He was chaos in motion and he had the Flamingo bankrupt in months. His backers, tough and direct men, sent in replacements who gave the impression that the Flamingo was the property of the mob. (It was not until the arrival of Morris Lansburgh, himself a pretty rough diamond, that the Flamingo would show some style. As to the Thunderbird, it never pretended to style and so was untypical.)

The real pioneer, the man who set the methods, the style, the swank of Las Vegas, was Moe Dalitz, who came in 1949 to open the Desert Inn.[1] Even as a youth in Detroit he had a glandular

---

[1] The words "Desert Inn" would be set in type in what has been estimated as fifty thousand to fifteen million times a year. In books, magazines, and newspapers, it recurred as many times as the name of the current president. This held for twenty-three years, from 1948 to 1971, the year when Howard Hughes, the Desert Inn's last owner, left the hotel.

compulsion to be active. He got into illegal gambling in the east and was the catalyst for the group that came with investment money to take over the Desert Inn and, later, the Stardust. Dalitz became a journalistic fad. Over the years he generated as much printed matter as Mayor La Guardia, Dean Acheson, or Edward Kennedy. Legend soon had him representing sinister eastern interests, and this has created an interesting argument. Nevada has three ex-governors who say that they do not believe that Moe was ever in anything more sinister than bootlegging: the Governors are Russell, Sawyer, and Laxalt. Agreeing with them is a considerable establishment of Nevada bankers and lawyers, and a group that has received little publicity, the Las Vegas colony of retired FBI agents.

It makes for an interesting stand-off, a point destined to be moot, because the men who could settle it are either mute or dead. J. Edgar Hoover is gone. Dean Elson, Nevada's FBI chief for many years, lives by the bureau code that says FBI men do not write memoirs. Still, Elson did something eloquent. On retiring, he accepted a job as an executive in the Hughes hotels, a post that made him an office co-worker and colleague of other Hughes advisors, and the colleague of another advisor, Moe Dalitz. Elson's willingness to be an office team-mate of Dalitz was all the endorsement Moe needed.

So stands Moe, the man who set the patterns, the rules for the succession of investors who made Nevada richer every year, the pattern whereby each house tries to outdo the others in volume, in swank, and in theatre. A quarter-century after the Desert Inn opened, when MGM opened the largest gambling house in the world, it chose two men to head the operation: Al Benedict was made President, and Bernard Rothkopf, Executive Vice President, both men trained in Moe's Desert Inn.

Now and then an owner will take what is known as the "owner's stroll," an impulse that can come at two in the morning to take a walk through his place. Since the Desert Inn is typical, we might take a walk with Moe, say, on an evening in February 1966, which is a month before he will sell it to Howard Hughes and give Nevada's destiny still one more twist.

By now, his Desert Inn has something of the fame of New

York's Waldorf Astoria. The lobby appears modest enough, but few people really see it because what hits is the casino. There, a few feet to the right, begins the vista which millions still find hard to believe, a room the length of a football field, jammed with tables and surging with crowds, its dice, 21, and roulette islands so deep in people that they hide the dealers. Parallel with the casino, and as long, living in its own obscure half-light, is the vast "lounge," a bar so long that it needs six bartenders. Back of the bartenders is the elevated stage which, beginning at noon, has the first of four to six revolving shows that go on till dawn. In his stroll, Moe passes the lounge and will glance in on the restaurant, and passing that, and rounding the curve, is the cashier's cage. Here behind the iron grillework is a room that has its own litera-ture, its own mystique. This cage, in legend, does almost the busi-ness of the Chase Bank. Twenty feet beyond this is the entrance to one of the beautiful showrooms of the nation, the Crystal Room, the haunt of Jimmy Durante, Debbie Reynolds, Phil Harris, Bobby Gentry. Circling, Moe now comes to an alcove, pos-sibly one-hundredth the size of the Crystal Room, the set-back for the Baccarat table, the game which novelists call the game of dukes and kings.

Moving on, Moe sees his Monte Carlo Room, the dazzling res-taurant in red and white which he thought up on a trip to Paris, a room where a little paté, followed by quail, crêpes, and Dom Per-ignon for two, is, properly, $100 flat. Some twenty yards beyond are the first of three lesser restaurants in a row. Stepping outdoors, Moe will walk past the swimming pool and, beyond that, to the Desert Inn Country Club. This is three hundred acres of trees and turf, a green island in the center of Las Vegas, surrounded by a rim of houses which, from the first, has been called, seriously or sarcastically, the center of Las Vegas' society. It is a green enclave whose last two vacant lots were bought by Hughes for the house he built for Bob Maheu. Moe's country club is avoided by the men from Elko, Ely, and Winnemucca as being too effete. Moe himself, craggy of face, slim, middle height, walking through the club house, could be Dean Martin or Toots Shore, because every-one seems to stop him for a word. The Desert Inn group created swank. For years, until today's big new corporate owners came and lowered the standards, no one would think of appearing in its casino or showroom without coat and tie. As to the girl business, we will speak of this later.

The next investors to follow the Desert Inn were, oddly, rather obscure. The founders of the Sahara—today synonymous with Del Webb, Johnny Carson, Buddy Hackett—were small-time Oregon gamblers. They gave Las Vegas its first tall building, the original tower of fourteen stories, but they added no picturesque owners. Still, the writers, reluctant to give anyone careless carte blanche, did suggest that, with thirty-three names on the Sahara license, there must be some hidden criminals. After the usual chaos of reorganization, the many sales of shares, so complicated that tracing title is like tracing Balkan history, there emerged the respectable figure of President Milton Prell. He was a tall, vinegary man, uncommunicative, and so free of taint that when J. Edgar Hoover sneaked into town, it was to stay in Prell's own tower suite. The image of a staid, clean Sahara hung on. When Del Webb bought it, it had become the "cleanest," the hotel chosen for the visits of what few presidents would set foot in Nevada. But for glamour, nothing hit with quite so much lovely, murky mystery as the Sands.

To deal with its criminal aura first, one writer went so far as to say that the Sands had the biggest turnover of gangster owners of any hotel in America. Twenty years would pass without an indictment and without an arrest, but this never stopped the stories. The Sands added to Nevada's split personality in the sense that it brought new millions of money-heavy tourists, while adding to Nevada's dread. The writers tossed around such names as Joseph "Doc" Stacher and Meyer Lansky. Again Nevadans were reluctant to believe the writers, and Nevada's governors and gaming commissioners called the stories nonsense.

The Sands brought theatre in new dimensions. That story centers on Jack Entratter who had once been the manager of New York's famous Copacabana Club. It was a time when a number of obscure entertainers were fighting for New York recognition, and Entratter helped them. He signed them for the Copa, gave them loans, and urged other clubs to hire them. When Entratter came to Las Vegas as part of the Sands group, about ten of his former

actors had become national celebrities. They remembered him
with gratitude and agreed to work for the Sands only. They would
become known as "Entratter's Stable of Stars," a list that included
Danny Thomas, Red Skelton, Dean Martin, Jerry Lewis, Frank
Sinatra, Sammy Davis, Patti Page, Peter Lawford.

The Sands casino also acquired a rich-player prestige greater
than that of the Desert Inn. Its casino credit card holders were a
Who's Who. Carl Cohen became a Nevada name and then, like
several casino bosses, a world name. His day meant talks with the
world's money men, the Texas oil man, the New York industrialist,
the European playboy, the Hollywood actor. Cohen was the man
to whom even the Agha Kahn went for an OK on credit. When,
later, Hughes took over seven casinos, including the Sands,
Hughes' manager, Robert Maheu, hired Cohen, saying that there
was no casino boss on earth with Cohen's easy authority. When
MGM decided to open the world's largest casino, Cohen was the
automatic choice for casino boss.

The Sands was an entity, a pleasure house whose gourmet restaurant, the Regency Room, had the tone of Schlinder's 21, or
the Stork. Fine food in rooms filled with celebrities. Las Vegas'
glamour total was growing.

A new splash of color came with a man who was not of the
Strip. As visitors know, Las Vegas gambling grew up on two
streets some four miles apart. One is the "Strip," outside the city,
in Clark County. A three-mile stretch of glittering hotels, from
the Hacienda, at the southern end, to the Sahara, at the north, it is
a world of its own. But the city itself also has a "Strip," a downtown stretch on Fremont Street that is vastly different. Most casinos on Fremont Street have no hotel. With or without hotel, they
are compact, jammed together, without grounds, gardens, or
swimming pools. Fremont encompasses four blocks. Writers called
it "shirt sleeve" and "Coney Island." The four blocks have the
garish hoopla of New York's West 42nd Street. Tourists wander
around in the gingham and sports shirts of unpretentious America.
Inside, the play is in cheaper chips; signs read of 98¢ breakfasts,
contests, raffles, prizes. It is the street of the noisy huckster. The
biggest of its hotels was the fourteen-story Fremont, run by
Edward Levinson. Levinson, for some reason, built up the animos-

ity of the FBI. He was a soft-spoken, taciturn man who neither
drank nor smoked, and who put in an hour of exercise daily in the
YMCA. He was one of the first of the owners to come to Nevada,
and his name has thousands of mentions in the Diatribe, always
because of his friends, deemed to be crime-connected. One should
record that nothing was ever proved about Levinson, but the writers love him. To local people he was a self-effacing man who
ducked public appearances and who sent big checks to every
charity. On a balance sheet, as seen by Nevada governors, Levinson's Fremont alone might account for a Nevada revenue of 50
million, in taxes and trade, for he was one of the ten or twelve
who made the city seem delightfully sinister.

The desert city was intriguing millions of men who had a secret
yen to invest in Las Vegas, for the profits, as well as the casual
conversational throw-off in the country club, "I just bought two
points in the Desert Inn." In 1955, three groups brought in three
more famous names, the Dunes, Riviera, and the Royal Nevada,
which later made way for the Stardust.

With the Riviera opening, a nation that loved sinister glamour
got it. To begin with, it cost ten million dollars, which was big
money for a small hotel. Here was no floor plan done by the niece
of a partner, but interiors created by great architects. Its beauty
even drew praise from the *New York Times'* Wallace Turner. It
opened in March 1955 and had immediate money troubles. Its
manager, Gus Greenbaum, had already built up a lurid reputation
from his time in the Flamingo turbulence. It was almost as if a
drunken writer had done a script designed to shock. Greenbaum,
a disciple of Siegel, and a fabulous, rough, noisy charmer, hired as
his show director the celebrated Willie Bioff. Bioff left his breakfast table one morning in Phoenix, got into his car, stepped on the
starter, and was dismembered by dynamite.

Bioff's death was so unsettling to Greenbaum that he took to
narcotics, became a whoremonger, and began cheating the
owners. Greenbaum was found one day, almost decapitated, lying
next to his wife who had had her throat cut. All this to owners of
a place that had the style of New York's Plaza. However, the
Riviera soon acquired more distinguished owners and became one
of the swank hotels of America.

All new groups obeyed the Las Vegas law. As explained by Johnny Drew of the Stardust, "You start fast and keep it on the floorboard all the way. Your place must be so beautiful, the shows so fantastic, that you convert the columnists the first month." This was the thinking of the group that built the Dunes. Its casino was big and swank and was soon accepted as a "big player" prestige room. Such was the popularity of casino manager Sidney Wyman that he had a following within months. The Dunes had the huge theatre that would put on the Casino de Paris.

It was in 1957 that two events occurred that meant tens of millions of new money for the state. One was the opening of the Tropicana and the other a shooting in New York. In Manhattan, Frank Costello was crossing the lobby of his apartment house when a man fired a revolver at his head. The wound was slight and Costello was taken to a hospital. When detectives searched his clothes, they found a note in the handwriting of a man who was later identified as the comptroller of the newly opened Tropicana. The note was cryptic, a summary of gross win, some $650,-000 for the first three weeks of Tropicana operation. That note must take its place with the Treaty of Guadalupe Hidalgo as a Nevada asset. Thereafter, no writer could resist the charge that Las Vegas' most beautiful hotel was built by the mob. Again, historians will be stumped because FBI men have never been able to decide whether Costello was an owner or whether he was getting the hard sell to become one. But the note was delightfully scary and added to the pull on Americans to visit the strange city. The Tropicana was beautiful; many thought it topped the Sands and Riviera—a *Saturday Evening Post* writer called it the "Tiffany of the Strip." Eventually, the Tropicana would have the usual reorganization, but it would operate in that fog of doubt; the shuddery idea that some of its owners were still from Murder, Inc. At the time, Las Vegas hotels had some of the shrewdest public relations men in America. When questioned about "hood" stockholders, they would put on an expression of helpless concern, indicating they were not sure, that it just might be true. Thus they fanned the mystery. They knew that on whatever day the hotels were assumed to be clean, some of the romance would go. The Tropicana added glamour in big chunks, a huge casino, several restaurants, and the showroom that would become famous for the *Folies Bergere*. Like the other hotels, it went through its reorganizations and, in time, brought in its "new respectables," the father-son team of J. Kell Houssels, Sr. and Jr., both showcase names, both endorsed by the FBI.

The Tropicana also added a questionable new asset to Nevada, the first big hotel to be considered non-Jewish. In Las Vegas, virtually all the owners who had brought in the wealth and notoriety were Jews. Nevada was like so much of the west; its majority establishments were Nordic, Protestant whites. As recently as 1940, the fraternities of the Reno campus barred Jews. Nevada's small towns had few of them, and the combination of envy and resentment of Las Vegas made for casual, anti-Semitic slurs.

But the Tropicana's new bosses, the Houssels, were Dutch, the general manager, Robert Cannon, was Irish, and a major stockholder, W. D. Harrigan, was an Irishman from Alabama. Word spread that Las Vegas' newest place was not only gorgeous but straight WASP. This appealed to Texans, with the result that the Tropicana developed a big-player loyalty that was heavily Aryan from Houston, Dallas, and Fort Worth. This was a joke within a joke to Nevada governors who knew that half the stockholders were still Jewish, but it was hardly a subject for cocktail hour clarification.

It was ten years after the opening of the Desert Inn that a comedy of errors produced the vast Stardust. The idea man here was Tony Cornero Stralla, a man whose life was a montage of Errol Flynn adventures, though at sleazier levels. Variously known as Cornero or Stralla, he was never in anything sinister, yet, for a short moment, was the most flamboyant man in Las Vegas. He was an in-and-out visitor when he got the idea to build the biggest gambling spread on earth. In typical razzle-dazzle, Stralla put out a stock issue that raised some 3 million dollars before it was outlawed. His Royal Nevada, later to be called the Stardust, was three-quarters finished when he died of a heart attack. The Stardust was picked up by "Jake the Barber" Factor, a man with enough controversial friends to net several hundred mentions in the Diatribe. He was rich and did not need financing schemes.

He paid off lien-holders, finished the hotel, and then hit trouble. Nevada refused to give him a license. It was here that the Desert Inn people saw an opportunity. The Stardust was huge and shirt-sleeve. It had been designed for those of whom God has made so many, the modest people. The Desert Inn group leased it, did some altering, and soon had two more firsts: they had the largest casino in the world, and they had the showroom that would produce the *Lido de Paris*, a show which each year would have (and has at this hour) the world's largest audience.

At this point, the Las Vegas story takes still another twist. The twenty-four major places of Las Vegas fall into two blood lines. Virtually all hotels built up to this point, that is, before 1960, carried accusations of gang financing. All those built after 1960, in effect, those built after the Stardust, escaped this calumny. The Stardust was followed by a construction time gap, a demarcation that would separate the "good guys" and the "bad guys." The explanation is that Nevada gambling law had become so tough that no man with any kind of police record dared apply. The state, which had lived with fear since Kefauver, had developed controls so rigid that some lawyers today think them unconstitutional. As a result, there was investor hesitation that lasted some five years with an accompanying construction lag. To the Stardust's credits could be added the fact that it was the last to have suspect owners.

There are several dividing points in the city's tumultuous history. One such was the event that started the change in the name of the proprietors. From the beginning, the men of the casinos—the proprietors—had been called "the gamblers." Somehow, the name took hold in Reno well before Siegel came to Nevada. Reno had several small gambling operations before its legalization in 1931, and their operators were appreciated, if not always admired. Locals referred to them in gently sarcastic putdown, as "the gamblers." The name was picked up by writers, and it became the national designation when used by *Reader's Digest*, *The Saturday Evening Post*, *Collier's*, and the *New York Times*. But to many it was confusing. In a state where most owners will not pull a slot handle, the gamblers were the customers and not the proprietors. Then came the event that started the change in name.

In November 1963, a group of fight promoters came to Las

Vegas to try to promote a Cassius Clay-Sonny Liston fight. The owners had had experience with big fights and knew that the good ones bring big spenders. In this case the promoters wanted a $400,000 guarantee to stage it in Las Vegas. Las Vegas owners have never had any illusions about getting help from the rest of the city, from banks, utilities, or supermarkets. They knew that if they wanted an attraction they paid for it. Joe Wells, then President of the Thunderbird, and Charlie Rich, Vice President of the Dunes, were strong for the fight and decided that ten or twelve hotels could unite to make the guarantee. Wells called a few owners, found them receptive, and asked for a meeting of the Association. He suggested that it would be tactful to invite a few non-members, smaller operators who might want to share in the prestige of underwriting. The meeting was held in the Dunes.

It got out of hand. Somehow word got out that the meeting was open, and when the owners arrived, some two hundred men were already there, men whose role seemed to be to shout, cheer, and urge the hotels to grab the fight. Lost in the throng, conspicuous for their good clothes and badly-hidden irritation, were fifteen hotel executives. The promoters made their pitch: they explained details, the TV coverage, and how they would "scale the house," that is, price the tickets. It could have gone on indefinitely, with unknown men rising to cheer, when Allard Roen, a partner in the Desert Inn, whispered to the Director, "Look, get this circus over with, call the vote, and ask for $50,000 each. If we get more than eight commitments, we'll reduce the shares." It went around, and by the third "yes" it was clear that the room would produce the $400,000. With the last "yes," the owners headed for the doors. Moments later, a group of them were on the sidewalk waiting for their cars as reporters hovered nearby. The Director joined them and Roen turned on him. "You put on another carnival like that and I'm not attending any more meetings. I thought it was clear who should attend." The remark was overheard by Colin Mac-Kinlay, an editor of the Las Vegas *Review-Journal*.

He asked, "Who should attend, Mr. Roen?"

"The owners," said Roen impatiently. "They are the only ones who can say yes or no to $50,000 without going to a phone." The phrase had been used before, of course, but after MacKinlay wrote the story, it took hold generally. The term "the owners" now designates those men whose word can bind a hotel to any commitment.[2]

A husband and wife team from New York, Mr. and Mrs. Edward Lowe, noticed that all Las Vegas hotels were designed as an obstacle course, that to reach any restaurant, bar, newsstand, elevator, or toilet, you had to go past the casino. The Lowes got the idea that among the millions who came to Las Vegas there must be some people who would want something quiet, a hotel without the mobs of the casinos. They backed their idea with several million dollars and in 1963, gave Las Vegas the Tally Ho. What emerged was an English Christmas card, a reproduction of a sprawling Tudor country house that could have rightly belonged to a squire in Essex. Mrs. Lowe did the decorating, even furnishing some suites with antiques. It was one of the handsomest hotels in Nevada and it folded in a few months, the verdict, "Too much sleepy distinction." It alternately closed or limped along for some years before it was taken over by a group that did a massive remodeling job to create today's Aladdin, an affair as gaudy as the Tally Ho was distinguished. The Aladdin faltered. As a result of its wobbly economics, it made desperate readjustments; it went semi-burlesque, one of the first hotels to bring carney stuff to the Strip.

The next hotel after the Tally Ho was thought by some to be the most spectacular in the world, a structure that has been called everything; wonderful, vulgar, unbelievable, splendid, gauche, absurd: this was Caesars Palace. It was the brain child of two men, both shouting eccentrics; the diminutive, explosive, tan-

---

[2] By the way of epilogue, Las Vegas declined the fight later the same night. The Tropicana had not been represented at the meeting because its chairman, Kell Houssels, Sr., was in Los Angeles where he had horses running. Roen thought that even though the guarantee had been met, it would be courteous to ask Houssels if he cared to participate. He was reached in the clubhouse and surprised everyone with his strong objections. The fight, he said, would be a farce and would put the casinos in the position of staging it knowingly. Such was Houssel's stature that every owner agreed to drop it. The fight went to Miami where it is remembered as the disaster in which Liston took defeat while sitting on a stool in his corner at the end of the sixth round.

trum-prone Nate Jacobsen, and his obese, coarse, imaginative, dynamic partner, Jay Sarno. Caesars was different. Its builders wanted a De Mille spectacle, and they gave Las Vegas their idea of a Roman palace. It was huge and dead white, with Roman statues, and columns set back on a plaza with an enormous display of fountains. It was well financed. Within two years, Jacobsen would disclose that the bastardized version of the *Gianiculum* had repaid each of the original investors ten times his investment. Because of the explosive ways of Nate and Jay, it was generally expected that the Palace would not pull in the big players, but it confounded everyone. Jacobsen was a colorful player who could drop $50,000 in one evening and as much the next trying to recoup. He understood gambling. The Palace acquired the experienced Ash Resnick as the casino boss. From the beginning it offered the top names of theatre, Juliette Prowse, Steve Lawrence, Andy Williams, Tom Jones. Grudgingly, Las Vegas admitted that the raucous team was a success. Caesars Palace, too, would have its reorganization. After noisy boardroom battles, Jacobsen and Sarno would leave and stockholders would go to the other extreme, selecting as president, the quiet, decorative, Wall Street type, William Weinberger. The Palace has never had a bad quarter. After the arrival of Hughes, it inherited many of the big players who were chilled by the stuffiness of the Hughes management. And, though we will speak of it later, it had nights when a sheriff's deputy might count fifty wandering cuties between midnight and dawn.

Another twist in the odd history comes now. In 1966, when Las Vegas became airborne, the problems that had menaced Nevada since the days of Kefauver disappeared. Howard Hughes had arrived and started buying. The Hughes take-over of the celebrated places was like the absolution of a Pope. The lecherous old fraud, who later would be shown to have the principles of a Capone, with little of the rectitude of the Dalitzes and Cohens, came in with the aura of the Bank of England, and the reputation of being a brilliant, shrewd business man who was also politically honest. When he bought out the two hotels, the Desert Inn and the Sands, and as it became known that he was dickering for many more, his moves were taken as a signal all over America that investment money could be placed in Nevada gambling. Nothing short of a purchase by the Brookings Institution could have wrought the miracle worked by Hughes. Dozens of corporations that had been eyeing Nevada, but were afraid of its dirtiness, became serious.

Hughes came, bought six Las Vegas casinos, and one in Reno, and built nothing. Investors decided that Nevada had been purged, that gambling was clean, disinfected, respectable. Hughes started the turnover years that saw sales of most of the hotels and the formation of groups that would build others. Of the changes in gambling history, this was the biggest; it was the year of the miracle, of absolution, of rebirth.[3]

The Hughes absolution came at a moment when the nation itself was on a toboggan of permissiveness, when disclosures of vast corruption in business and government got shrugs, when political corruption left people numb, when many were too weary for more moral indignation. A time had come when the statement that Meyer Lansky might still own a piece of the Flamingo brought yawns. By now, some eighty million Americans had crossed the carpets of the Flamingo, Thunderbird, Desert Inn, Sands, Fremont, Sahara, Dunes, Riviera, and Tropicana. Gambling shares went on the stock exchange. Nevada now saw the buying splurge in which prominent corporations would buy out virtually every hotel not already owned by Hughes.

Nevada, a state which seems unable to go two years without something seismic, now got the Circus Circus. From the first, the big owners had agreed that, whatever the attacks on gambling, they would not swerve from the idea of keeping it swank. In this, such men as Moe Dalitz, Harvey Silbert, Sid Wyman, Carl Cohen, the Housells, and Del Webb were agreed: the Strip should go in for distinction. They were fairly successful. The Silver Slipper, of course, was always considered a castoff, a colorful Western saloon a bit out of place as a neighbor of the Riviera and Sands. Still, the

---

[3] With good timely coincidence, Nevada passed the "corporate licensing act" in 1968, the law that eased the entry of America's corporations into Nevada.

biggest descent from style came in 1968 when the Strip was jolted by Jay Sarno. Sarno had an idea that made many shudder. He built the first truly expensive circus, literally, a concrete circus tent, filled with all the gimmicks, stalls, concessions, trapezes, nets, and stands of a circus. In front, to be consistent, he put in formal water fountains. In another setting they would have been handsome, but at the Circus Circus the miniature Villa d'Este threw its mist on a merry-go-round. Still, no one thought of stopping Sarno who had every right to give the Strip its ultimate travesty. Many suspected that, garish or not, there would be people who would love it. These were vindicated when, five years after his opening, Sarno had done so well that he added an 8 million dollar annex. Sarno, as aggressive, belligerent, and outspoken as Conforte, is scornful of pretense, as he defines it. He has simple views of man's sexual needs and, as we will see, his Circus shows it.

Any group that puts together 10 or 100 million to build a hotel throws off stories—the pasts of the men themselves, their theories on entertainment, their ideas as to what level of customer to shoot for. The groups now strung out along the Strip were as different as European nationalities. But they had this in common; whether geared to customers who arrive on motorcycle or those who take suites, virtually every hotel made money at its own level.[4]

New groups now built on a new street, Paradise Road, which parallels the Strip. One group built the Landmark and sold it to Hughes, another built the huge International and sold it to Hilton. On the Strip itself, the Dunes added a twenty-four story tower that dwarfed its original structure.

Gambling earnings are announced quarterly, and every quarter Nevada people read that the quarter just passed had topped the one of the year before. Profits seemed almost guaranteed. The expansion, many believed, had just begun. The Dunes, huge, luxurious, and booming, was taken over by a New York company, Continental Connectors, which is controlled by two veteran Las Vegas bankers, Parry Thomas and Jerome Mack. Caesars Palace

---

[4] Four smaller hotels had spotty profit histories—the Hacienda, the Landmark, Castaways, and Thunderbird.

was showing such profits that it brought 60 million when sold to Lums. As for the Stardust, it added another chapter to its troubled history. As the state's most profitable spread, it gave Howard Hughes a neurotic obsession to own it. Moe was happy to sell to Hughes but was determined to get top dollar for it. Negotiations were difficult. Hughes kept Maheu laboring for five months of bickering before Dalitz and Maheu shook hands on 31 million. Everyone was exhausted and happy, when the Department of Justice moved in to block the sale. The U.S. Attorney General, fearing that Hughes was making a private ranch out of an American state, told him that he had bought enough. To Hughes it was a blow which, coupled with several to come, made him decide to leave Nevada. A disappointed Moe, determined to get out of gambling completely, made a hurried sale to Parvin Dohrmann and got 10 million more than had been agreed upon by Hughes.

The Aladdin, still wobbly, was also picked up by Parvin. This company, which now owned the Stardust, Aladdin, and Mint, got into such trouble with the American Stock Exchange that it decided to change its name and operate as Recrion Corp. As for the hoodooed Thunderbird, it was still swinging between break-even and loss when it was picked up by Del E. Webb, but not even his managers could make it go. Acknowledging defeat, Webb sold it to a little group of hopefuls at a low price. A little later, Webb had it back through repossession. Its best hour may have come recently when the Caesars Palace group bought it with the intent of razing part of it to make room for the proposed mega-sized, super-vast, two-thousand-room Marc Antony.

This, then, is the fast run of the growth years, a quarter of a century since Siegel, and a glance at the men who built the city that has such a huge side-line in women. But to understand the girl part it is necessary to see two other situations: one, the "Diatribe," the other, the "Whore Law" of Nevada.

8

"There is no parallel for it, no state to compare it to, because no other state was ever blasted as a state. Our history shows attacks on individual men —Benedict Arnold, Al Capone, Huey Long, Joe McCarthy—the nation's individual bastards, but not states. For eighteen years, Nevada was raked in a continuing diatribe. The country's best reporters worked the dictionary of invective; they called it everything, gang-controlled, venal, corrupt, vile, immoral, whore-ridden, crime-ridden, rotten. It ran from Kefauver, who started it in 1950, and it stopped with Hughes around 1968: that's eighteen years."

Ed Olsen, former AP Bureau
Chief for Nevada, and former
Chairman of the Gaming
Control Board.

The Diatribe:
Washington vs. Nevada

JACK DONNELLEY was attorney and advisor, for twenty-eight years, to the Desert Inn group. Well over six feet, with a handsome, stern head, and the aloof, slightly bored expression of a high court judge dealing with law clerks, he had a suavity envied by Nevada's governors. He lived in an expensive cottage (later used by Maheu) which was hidden in the shrubbery of the Desert Inn Country Club.

Every morning, on his way to his office, he would pass the newsstand, catching the headlines without breaking his stride. There on the floor, in tall stacks, lay the *New York Times*, the *Wall Street Journal*, the *Chicago Tribune*, the *Los Angeles Times* with their screaming headlines: LAS VEGAS OWNERS BEFORE GRAND JURY . . . IRS SUSPECTS THEFT OF MILLION A DAY . . . LAS VEGAS OWNER SLAIN . . . .

Donnelley was a sardonic man. He shared with Nevada's governors, its bankers, its senators, its businessmen the knowledge that Americans considered them all a bit depraved, men willing to live off the dirty gambling industry. Jack had learned to live with a diatribe that had lasted eighteen years.

It had begun with Siegel. Siegel had run his Flamingo six months before he was murdered. The headlines seemed unreal; Siegel, they said, had committed twenty to thirty murders, was a director of Murder, Inc., and had an arrest record like a village phone book. In Northern Nevada, on the shores of Lake Tahoe, a group had opened a casino whose top man, too, was killed. It was just another murder until police learned that the killer was a name in the newsrooms, the colorful Louis (Russian Louie) Strauss, whose composite story, whether myth or fact, ran through the familiar murder, rape, prostitution, narcotics, extortion, and larceny.

By 1950, American newspapers were running standard shock stories about rising crime. It reached such a point that Congress created an investigating committee to see how big it was. It was headed by Senator Estes Kefauver. Kefauver's report disclosed that a new cancer had hit America, crime was huge and organized, and part of its fascination came from its Nevada section. Nevada's gambling places, he said, were largely the property of the underworld. The report became a manual for American editors. For twenty-five years there was no shaking the nation's assumption that Las Vegas had big syndicate investment.

Las Vegas picked up more coats of grime when the noted reporter, Dan Fowler, blasted it in *Look* Magazine. Fowler called the business "legalized banditry."

After Fowler, the blasts took on rhythm. The next came in *Life* Magazine when the veteran reporter, Ernest Havemann, called Reno "Paradise Lost." Havemann did not go into the familiar crime index but spoke instead of the tawdriness of casinos and their mechanized voracity.

In 1955, the Thunderbird was closed by the state. The governor conferred with advisors for days, wondering how to soften the blow, and could find no way. He announced that the Thunderbird had been financed with undisclosed loans and that the lender was Jake Lansky, a brother of Meyer Lansky, the man who is in an all-time tie with Capone and Siegel as the most publicized hood of America.

Students of Nevada's cold war often wonder which of the blows did the most to identify Nevada as corrupt. Certainly, one was the article in *Reader's Digest* in 1959. The *Digest's* story was titled, "Las Vegas, the Underworld's Secret Jackpot," and the opening line was, "Legal gambling in Nevada is pouring a vast underground river of gold into the underworlds of our big cities . . . big name gangsters are entrenched in the . . . gambling casinos . . . mob discipline is administered away from Las Vegas . . . their names are . . . a Who's Who of Crime." It concluded, "Gold pouring into the pockets of the underworld is doing more to increase our big cities' crime potential for evil than anything since prohibition." The Nevada estimate was that it was read by twenty million people and echoed in hundreds of editorials.

The casinos produced men whose lifestyles could produce ten thousand clippings a month. One such was Ruby Kolod, colorful casino boss of the Desert Inn. The crime writers had let Ruby off lightly, saying only that in his native Cleveland he had been in illegal gambling and liquor. Ruby became a national story when it was disclosed that he had entered into an oil investment with a Denver attorney, Robert Sunshine, a man who would eventually be convicted of embezzlement. From the day of the deal, every month produced a Damon Runyon sequel.

Sunshine said Kolod got the $68,000 investment money by walking into the Desert Inn cage and picking it up, an act which would be "skim," and a felony, per se. The oil project failed and Sunshine went to the FBI charging that Kolod had sent two hoods to Denver to tell him to return the money or be liquidated. The FBI arrested Ruby on a charge of attempted extortion.

Kolod, who was fifty-five and terminally ill, fought to stay free. In desperation he shaped a defense that, incredible as it may sound, meant taking on the FBI, and the possible imprisonment of one of its top agents. Ruby knew that Nevada's FBI boss, Dean Elson, had tapped the Desert Inn phones, so he demanded that J. Edgar Hoover produce the tapes, arguing that they would prove he had not extorted. It was a sensation. In those days the FBI did not admit to tapping—which was a violation of federal law and Nevada law. To force the admission meant that Elson himself could go to jail. Elson, furious and worried, told people openly that the FBI could not permit Kolod to be the instrument that could send him, Elson, to jail. If Ruby persisted, Nevada would wish it had never been born. While Ruby was taking on the FBI, the ground shook again.

In 1963, Nevada was hit by the book that would start the

change in its gambling, its laws, and its history. This was *Green Felt Jungle*, written by two former Las Vegas reporters, Ed Reid and Ovid Demaris. It remains the greatest excoriation of an American state in the English language. It was lively, smooth, and authoritative. Jack Donnelley called it the greatest collection of deliberate distortions he had ever read. The book caused Dean Elson to lose his temper: when asked whether he or J. Edgar Hoover had been a source, Elson slammed his fist on a table and shouted that neither he nor Hoover had even met the authors. He called it wildly inaccurate.

But it became a world-wide best seller, read in the Philippines as in Denmark, and it sold heavily in Nevada. It, too, became a desk manual for American editors. *Green Felt* was a long, angry charge that . . . outside hoods owned most of Nevada gambling . . . that most Nevada owners were their partners or employees . . . that gamblers are by nature amoral, with few compunctions about murder, extortion, pimping, theft, blackmail, prostitution, usury, etc. It charged mob ownership with such detail that, ten years after publication, *Green Felt* was still generating hundreds of newspaper stories. It started the change. It produced a political movement in Nevada to tax gambling out of existence. It caused five Desert Inn partners to decide to sell whenever a serious buyer should appear. The same decision went for the owners of the Sands, Flamingo, and Riviera. It started the long drive to pass the "corporate licensing act," the law which would make it possible for outside corporations to come in and buy out the old timers. It caused the start of the reform movement to change the money handling in casinos, the sweeping reform that became known as "Regulation 6."

It was a time when Las Vegas people, stepping out on their lawns for the newspaper, saw headlines that made them hesitate to pick it up. While *Green Felt* was selling heavily, reporter, Wallace Turner, came out with a series in the *New York Times* which was syndicated all over the nation. Turner's recurring point was shock that a state should so far lose control. He expanded his series into the book *Gamblers' Money* which, with *Green Felt Jungle*, became a text on Las Vegas.

Owners now cringed under a new blow that caused a long run

of publicity and which, they believed, was clearly the worst. This was the blast of Professor Thorp in *Life* Magazine. Edward O. Thorp, a professor of mathematics at New Mexico State University, held the theory that by doing a computer study of the odds of the game of 21, the casinos could be licked. Thorp worked on his system, came to Nevada, gambled in dozens of casinos, won and lost, and returned to write the best-selling book, *Beat the Dealer*. But what stunned Nevada most was Thorp's statement that he was treated as an enemy in Nevada, that some places barred him, and that others brought in "mechanics," house experts who take over to cheat a player when he shows signs of winning. Thorp said that virtually every major casino does this.

Up to that hour it was assumed that anyone could say anything about any owner and no one would fight. This had been expressed with wonder by Melvin Belli when speaking to Jack Donnelley. He said, "Remarkable, you gentlemen never sue."

Actually, suits had been considered. There had been a meeting of the Association to consider whether to sue the authors and publishers of *Green Felt Jungle*. But the attorneys said "no."

They had two reasons; one was that innocence is hard to prove, but the bigger objection was the Pandora's box you open when you charge libel. In libel, the plaintiff exposes himself to the most complete examination that bears on rectitude. It allows the defendant to question, challenge, and explore any aspect of a plaintiff's world. For Nevada casinos to charge libel was to be prepared to testify on their operating secrets. It would be putting on such a courtroom spectacular as the nation had seldom seen. Whenever an owner was angered over some insult, his attorneys would go into "operation pacify"—that is, persuade him that he could not win, and that "This too shall pass." But with Thorp, this policy changed.

Every casino reported the same reaction. Casino bosses were getting phone calls from all over. Faithful players were asking if this could be true. Had they been playing against crooked dealers? Old, wealthy clients put the question to Moe Dalitz, to Houssels, to Wyman, to Riddle. Other players showed their hostility by taunting dealers, quitting a table after a few plays with a sarcastic mention of Thorp. Thorp had affected the public as no other attack had. Here was no silly tabloid feature but a claim by a respected man in a respected magazine. To hold to the traditional silence was to allow millions to think it was true. The owners decided they had no choice. Whatever the consequences of a court fight, the need to challenge Thorp became an absolute. At a meeting of the Association, five hotels agreed to sue *Life*, Thorp, and certain newspapers. They agreed to secrecy until the suits could be filed. Then, ten days later, it happened.

The Nevada Gaming Control Board had been getting secret reports that the Las Vegas casino, Silver Slipper, was cheating players. Nevada's gaming czar, Edward Olsen, assigned a squad of undercover men to pose as players and had them gambling in the Slipper for a week.[1] Working in complete secrecy he arranged a raid. One afternoon, fifteen agents gathered in the Slipper, moved in on all the tables, confiscated cards and dice, and herded some two hundred customers out of the doors and locked them up. Next day, the attorneys who were preparing to sue *Life* Magazine and Thorp exchanged phone calls. They agreed that this was not the time to defend casino honor.

Now the headlines returned to Kolod. The Denver jury found Kolod guilty of attempted extortion, so that papers reported that a Desert Inn owner was headed for jail. To Ruby's headlines, Nevada's governor added more.

Governor Grant Sawyer had become desperate, an embattled man who could be driven to blunders. He had been described as the governor who could stomach anything, a man who defended a mob-ridden industry. Sawyer's angry reply was that Nevada had no mob holdings, that Hoover did a lot of talking but never proved anything, that Washington had never made an arrest, never brought an indictment, never a conviction. Sawyer said that if one or fifty owners could be found guilty of anything, he would expel them. Now that the Department of Justice had brought in a conviction, Sawyer moved.

When Sawyer first took office, and in an attempt to show that

---

[1] As a comment on the times, half his agents were Negroes. It was a time when managers were still reluctant to hire Negro dealers and would hardly assume that Olsen would use them as detectives.

he had tough gambling police, Sawyer named a former FBI agent, Ray Abbaticchio, to head the Gaming Control Board.

In one of Abbaticchio's first inspection trips (in which state police are supposed to walk up to a table, stop the play, and examine dice or cards) the men stormed in with drawn guns. Another of his ideas was the "Black Book." It was a black cardboard binder of the sort school children use for themes. Inside, he put the mimeographed rap sheets of eleven of America's hoods. Ray distributed one hundred copies to Nevada casinos. Owners were told that none of the eleven could set foot in any house; to give any one a room, or even permission to sit in a lobby, would mean that the hotel could be closed down.

The reaction was shock that Sawyer should allow anything so juvenile. Any listing of U.S. hoods could produce not eleven but fifty to five hundred names, depending on one's viewpoint. Why eleven, and why these? Several of them had no conceivable Nevada connection. Abbaticchio had simply spun a wheel for faces for his book. Sawyer soon found that Abbaticchio was adding comedy to Nevada's image and replaced him with the highly competent Edward Olsen. The Black Book disappeared from circulation. It was considered a political boner that was best forgotten. Outside Nevada, the "book" took on added mystery as writers, unable to get one, spoke of "Nevada's Bible of Infamy."

The book was in a legal attic when Sawyer, desperate to prove that he can get tough when a felony is proved, decided to make every newspaper in the land. He made Kolod the twelfth name in the book. The headlines were everything he could have asked. Kolod would now be barred not only from entering his own Desert Inn, but from any of 2,000 casinos or chili joints that had a slot machine. Kolod's entry into the Black Book added thousands of stories to the Diatribe. The act cost Sawyer the governorship. Most owners, whatever their views on Kolod, thought Sawyer could have lifted his license without Black Book dramatics. Sawyer antagonized many owners, and in the next election, which was close, they made the difference.

In the press of the world, the attacks now became a stereotype. Despite all the excoriating attacks, no one, not Hoover, not Congress, not the press, had closed one hotel or forced out one owner.

To the contrary, the owners were approaching their first billion-dollar year.

But the showdown was near. For eighteen years, in mounting crescendo, the press had shown outrage over the state, an attack that was really a reprimand to J. Edgar Hoover and the Department of Justice. Hoover saw the disclosures as a reflection on the FBI. Congress, in awe of the great oligarch, did not critize him openly, but recognized his humiliation. Still Nevada did nothing, and the owners found no buyers despite the fact that virtually the entire Strip was for sale. Now came the blasts of 1966, which Nevada saw as the Washington decision for a showdown. The bombardment became known as the "Year of Stalingrad."

One of the attacks was the series in the *Chicago Sun Times*. This was nothing like the attacks of *Gamblers' Money or Green Felt Jungle*. Here there was no caution, no apparent concern for libel; it was the most graphic indictment of specific men, hotels, and alleged gangster ties in the entire Diatribe. The charges were repeated by papers all over the nation. It was hard to believe that any owner, any hotel, governor, or legislature could survive it. The attack caused Governor Sawyer to mount a state investigation to see if any of it could possibly be true. The hearing attracted some of the country's leading reporters. At the end, Sawyer said he could find no criminality, and the newspapers guffawed.

It was the year of the CBS television documentary. This exposé made charges that were totally new. CBS showed a map of the United States with a highway overlay, the highway showing the flow of Nevada "skim money" to cities of the midwest, the south, and the east.

The media had converted the nation into a grand jury and now, finally, the Nevada establishment knew that something had to be done. People prayed that certain owners would sell out, or that they would be hit by coronaries or embolisms. But nature abstained and the owners, who could find no buyers, held no fire sales. At this point a state election brought a moratorium.

Nevada's Lieutenant Governor, Paul Laxalt, decided to run for governor on the issue that Nevada must make peace with Washington. Laxalt, long a figure in gambling, was the attorney for the Sparks Nugget and Harvey's Wagon Wheel. He campaigned on the issue that Sawyer was baiting, challenging, and alienating Washington, which meant state suicide. Laxalt pledged to get along with Hoover. This added more whimsy to the Nevada story, because what Hoover wanted was to get rid of some twenty of the major owners, men who happened to be among the ranking owners of the state. Since Laxalt was going to every one of them for huge campaign contributions, the question was—whom would Laxalt banish if he won? Still, Laxalt got support from quite a few people and his campaign got $200,000 from the ailing Ruby Kolod, who wanted to destroy Sawyer before he died. (Ruby died shortly after Laxalt took office.)

Laxalt won, and Nevada had another bizarre situation. The question was—what would he do to appease Congress, Hoover, and the Department of Justice in view of the fact that (1) so many of the detested owners had financed him, (2) his biggest hotel contributor was the Desert Inn, and (3) his single biggest individual contributor was Ruby Kolod?

But Laxalt, whose term could have been a disaster, was rescued a month after his election by that great eccentric, Howard Hughes. In his first year, Hughes bought out the three hotels that had angered the FBI the most. At about the same time, the Nevada legislature moved: it succumbed to the lobbying of the Las Vegas owners who had been pushing for the "corporate licensing act," and passed the law which would allow public corporations to buy hotels in Nevada.

In the summer of the Hughes miracle, the Diatribe ended. New owners had come in, and the hood story passed into history. Three years after Hughes, Las Vegas groaned with pleasure over the opening of its Parthenon, the MGM Grand Hotel, which, inexplicably, *Time* magazine found a "monument to brashness and vulgarity."

9

Nevada Changes Course

IN THAT PILE-UP of abuse, known as "the" Diatribe," there was the further charge that the gamblers had also arranged Nevada's easy laws on prostitution. Writers accepted this, and the beleaguered owners, who had long stopped denying anything, did not bother to explain that they were innocent, that Nevada's so-called "legality" was really a swamp of vague law and that, in any event, it had been written by Nevada men long before Siegel or Hughes.

When Siegel arrived, the laws of Nevada's legislatures were no problem and, if inclined, he could have added a whore wing to his Flamingo. Siegel had entered a state whose legislators had been dancing around the subject for a hundred years. They had outlawed many whore-related acts, had frowned and scolded, but never come around to saying "no" to commercial coitus itself.

Starting in the days when they rode mules and buckboards to reach their capitol, the men came from villages that were about as sparse as the trading posts of Canada. Nevada had only one real cluster, Virginia City, which had the whore population of San Francisco. By the era of Hughes and Conforte, men had met in some fifty legislatures, and every so often they got mad at something and added a law. Somewhere, a madam must have opened up next to a schoolhouse because the legislature passed the law, still in effect, that says that brothels may not operate within three

hundred yards of school or church. (In Beatty, a mining town a
little east of Death Valley, townspeople complied and moved the
school.) Another law said that you may not force a girl into prostitution because of debt. Like all states, Nevada decided to outlaw
the pimp and Carson passed the law that says that no man may
accept the money which a girl earns from prostitution. In time,
there came the law that says that houses may not advertise, not
with signs, billboards, newspapers, pamphlets, or the slide projec-
tor movie ads of early times. No one could have forseen the day
when Joe would appear on nationwide TV in what is as candid
advertising as Linda Lovelace plugging *Deep Throat*. Some unrecorded madam inspired the law that says no one may operate on a
main street, and still another law came when it was found that
men were finding the places a home-away-from-home. This law
provided that any male who hangs around such places habitually,
whatever his connection, can be deemed a vagrant. (This was the
law used by Raggio to cite Joe for vagrancy.)

It took a century for some forty-five such niceties. During that
century, possibly two hundred madams worked Nevada towns.
Women opened up in Dayton, Belmont, and Manhattan, in the
era after Lincoln, and in Lovelock, Ely, and Las Vegas, in the
years after Taft. In every new decade, lawyers reached the same
conclusion—that Carson had certainly passed a lot of laws on the
dirty stuff but nowhere did the fine print *bar* prostitution. The
counties were on their own, free to close the "Ellies," tolerate
them or license them.

With Pearl Harbor, as we know, most counties closed down for
a while. But with the end of war, things got complicated. Nevada's counties now decided to go different ways. The two big
gambling counties (Reno and Las Vegas), obedient to the newly
arrived gamblers, decided to bar houses permanently.

In 1949 came the event that put a cloud on every house of the
fifteen open counties. In Reno, a Mrs. Mae Cunningham decided
to test the winds of tolerance and see whether the city had really
gone moral. She opened a house on Reno's "Commercial Row," a
seedy section fronting the railroad. Her place was described as
"One of those sad bungalows you find in any slum of any city."
Mae tried to operate quietly, which was difficult because you

can't be quiet with eleven girls. She worried the Reno establishment which was already committed to the "Don't-Bait-Congress" policy, and she upset police even more when they learned she was planning to add a wing for five more girls. People brought pressure, and District Attorney, Harold O. Taber, closed her down. Taber fell back on the old law that says, in the absence of state or local law, the common law prevails. And, Taber added, common law is clear and holds that prostitution is a nuisance. Taber argued this so well that the court upheld the abatement of Mrs. Cunningham. Mae went to the State Supreme Court, but the judges agreed with the Taber reasoning. An astonished state now heard that all its joints (about twenty-eight houses in fifteen counties) were nuisances and should be closed. This brought a rush to the law books as D.A.s wanted another look at what the law said about nuisances. But soon they were exchanging happy phone calls, relieved to discover that "Cunningham" need not be fatal. They found that it still lay with in the power of each D.A. to decide whether he should so label his own; nuisance is a nuisance only when a D.A. calls it that, and a judge agrees. In fifteen counties, D.A.s took the "take-it-easy" view and did nothing. Theirs became known as the "open counties."

So, as of Joe's arrival in 1955, this was the lineup: Washoe banned houses with total finality. In Las Vegas, houses were barred by the two ordinances of 1952 and 1955. In the fifteen open counties, D.A.s could see no nuisances. When Joe opened in Storey, an open county, his green and white houses were nuisances and subject to closure when any Storey D.A. should so decide.

No change came until 1965, when the powers in Reno got to worrying and thought they should build the anti-Joe wall a little higher. This was augmented when they saw that Joe, now out of McNeil, was making a strong comeback. They knew of his dream of moving to Reno, and that he was resourceful. Even though Raggio was still D.A., the powers decided to take no chances and passed an ordinance which bans every aspect of prostitution. Reno's walls were now high.

It was in 1971 that Joe caused Nevada to make legal history. He was now safe enough in Storey, where no one would dream of killing the golden goose by outlawing its biggest taxpayer, but he was vulnerable to the charge that he had everyone fixed. Joe wanted legality in large print. He was flexing muscles now, feeling a new power, well past the troubles with Raggio, and beginning to feel he was destiny's man. Hardly bothering with velvet-glove nonsense, he persuaded his Storey commissioners to pass the celebrated "Ordinance No. 38," a law which says clearly that it is county policy to legalize prostitution and to license it. An American county had finally lifted brothels out of centuries of twilight.

Of course, there were bets about what the Supreme Court might say about a county that declares legal that which common law says is a nuisance. Whatever the doubts, they were ended when the Supreme Court spoke in another case. This came in 1973. Again, as in so much whore law, it involved Joe, and again the catalyst was a madam, this time, a Mrs. Irene York.

Mrs. York was a lady who had once run a small house in Fallon, Nevada. Now, idle, and on the outside, she was fascinated by the pioneering law of Storey County. She was struck by the fact that while the county had legalized girls, only one person had received a license. She applied for Storey's second license. Naturally, Joe's boys turned her down. Mrs. York sued. Her action was a demand to know why Storey should not be forced to give more than one license. She lost. The court reasoned that if you concede a county the sovereign power to legalize, you concede its power to set quotas. Unpersuaded, Mrs. York went to the Nevada Supreme Court, which reaffirmed the lower ruling. In denying her a license they settled the larger issue: a county does have the power to permit prostitution. A Supreme Court had finally said that a county may legalize girls.

What then is the answer to the question, "Is prostitution legal in Nevada?" Its two big counties—with 80 percent of the population—say "no," while the two tiniest say "yes." The other thirteen, which are almost uninhabited, say nothing, and continue a permissive quota system by which a few selected madams may operate under the tolerant watchfulness of D.A., sheriff, PTA, and church.

10

The Girls of Las Vegas

BILL "BONNER," writer for a news syndicate, came to Las Vegas to do a story on prostitutes and left, a confirmed Vegas hater. Bonner would rather not be identified because his parting judgment is savage—that only a Senate investigation of Las Vegas could extract any truth from any owner. Bonner wanted to interview whores on the assumption that they would give facts and not repeat the folklore which so many girls themselves believe. But he found that call-girls, showgirls, cocktail waitresses gave the same "Who me?" as did the owners, lawyers, and police. "It is a vast, smooth mendacity," he says, "a universal conspiracy to deny." He was also stung by the sarcasm of District Attorney, George Franklin.

"What you do is you take a five-mile drive in a cab, and the driver will have it explained in four. Of course, he may tell you that Nixon went to Dental College and that Agnew is Howard Hughes, but when were you reporters slowed down by crap?"

Someone suggested that he talk to an attorney, Tom Pursel, who at one time had represented many prostitutes. Most lawyers spurn the business, professing to see a difference between defending murderers and the girls, but Pursel does not. After some years of it—night phone calls to his house, 2 A.M. bail, and court appearance next day—he got tired of it. Today he represents

219

only a few. "Old clients," he says, "who have been at it fifteen years." Pursel agreed to help Bonner. He called him a few days later to say that he had a girl who was willing to talk. "Blunt as a judge," Pursel said. "She said to tell you it will be 100 bucks, same as a trick, and you can go fifteen minutes or an hour." Thus Bonner met Marion of the flaming hair. He took her for a drive in the desert and heard her casual frankness on some things and her bland evasion on others. But Marion did stumble into the economics of sex when telling about the man in the green jacket, a man Marion had met by appointment in the Riviera. A bellman had told her what to look for and they had that instant recognition of strangers looking for each other. They sat in the lounge and drank, but the man seemed troubled. "He didn't want to go through with it, and he seemed to think that if he didn't, I'd call a pimp or some hoods to beat him up. I told him, 'Look honey, you don't have to do a thing. Whatever's bothering you, cool it, you don't have to do anything.'"

"What about the bell captain? Won't he be mad?"

Marion laughed—"Don't be silly. Irritated, but that's it."

The man relaxed. "Miss, it's just that I don't make that much money. My wife works and we have kids, and even though I'd love to, well, the idea of me blowing $100, and my wife stalling the dentist, I'm no big shot." Marion liked him and almost made it free. She suggested that he try next year. "They're beginning to cut prices," she said.

When Bonner asked if this was rare, she said, "Well, yes and no. You seldom have a man back off that way, but still, it's common because most men never go near a bellman. I'd say one in ten will go $100." Bonner felt he had something. He had found that prostitution was not as flagrantly visible as he had thought.[1]

The city's bed reputation, of course, was fantastic. In 1963, when the writing team of Reid and Demaris fixed its image world-wide with the book, *Green Felt Jungle*, they announced, in the chapter, "Sex for Sale," that 10 percent of the population was engaged in procuring. There is no question that it is huge, but

---

[1] Bonner's visit came before the changes that brought the great whore invasions of 1973-74.

this is meaningless unless given in figures, and it is here that Marion's story was helpful. For cost is a block. The great majority of men think $100 for one time is insane. Bonner talked to sheriffs' men who made the same point. "We have cruisers out there on 15 day and night." (15 is the freeway that feeds into Las Vegas from a hundred California towns.) "And weekends it's like the San Diego Freeway. But for every Lincoln Continental there's fifty jalopies, cars with two, three, five guys who might have been picking fruit in the orchards. There's Volkswagens with students from Pomona. Can you imagine these types going $100 or $5? When, by today's rules, the guys have a different chick every week? There's thousands just like those dentists." Bonner had been hearing about "the dentists," so now he pursued the story. By 1965, conventions had become routine in Las Vegas, although not the vast business of today. The owners had persuaded the county to build the vast Convention Center (by agreeing to pay for it) and every hotel had salesmen trying to land the big affairs. But the city was still under a cloud. Millions still thought it was a Mafia-owned cesspool of gambling, liquor, and whores, and too dirty a place for a convention. Las Vegas had been snubbed royally, its invitations spurned by the American Bankers Association, by the American Medical Association—not even answered by church groups. So when the hotels learned that America's dentists were looking around, they went to work. The dentists took some wooing, but, in time, agreed to take a chance. They arrived, took over several hundred rooms, set up registration booths, and had pretty girls directing traffic. By evening of the first day, casino managers were calling each other, "Your dentists doing anything?"

"Why, yes, making peanut butter sandwiches in their rooms. Seen any in your casino?"

"Yes, a few. They like to watch. Particularly roulette."

"Hear about the Riviera? A guard saw a bunch of them in a corridor upstairs; they're lagging pennies at a spot in the carpet." By the third day the stories were a game. It was agreed that the dentists were the chintziest conventioneers so far, and they might as well get some laughs from a bad guess. "Did you hear that Danny Thomas moved out of the Sands? Some dentists were cooking hamburgers in the sink and his floor caught fire." "Dentists" became the opposite of big spender. Even the sheriff's men were using it. "Hell, you get only dentists, you've got prostitution licked. That week they lowered the trick average 50 percent."

Then Bonner heard about Mr. Bryce of Texas. A James Bryce (not really his name) had spent three days in Caesars, and had managed to get hurt and to irritate Sheriff Lamb, District Attorney George Franklin and officers of the hotel. Bryce was a Texas contractor, at the money level which most people call rich but which, in Dallas, is just comfortable, a man worth a half-million. In the mood for Las Vegas, and with about fifty dollars in his pocket, he made the plane connections that got him into town that evening. In Caesars, Bryce handed the cashier a check for $5,000 and waited while a clerk pulled out his card. He got the deferential, "Glad to have you back, sir. As you know, your credit is $25,000 any time you want." Bryce liked the club-like, man-among-peers feeling.

He drifted around for two days, getting the "sir" treatment at several hotels, but returned to Caesars for his gambling: he confined his play to line bets at craps. By the second day, he had won something like $11,000. It was his custom to carry his win with him and to hide his original stake in the breast pocket of a soiled shirt in his suitcase.

On the evening of his last day, he was feeling fine. He had several drinks in Nero's Nook and then asked for a table to catch the show of Juliet Prowse. At a table nearby, were two girls whom he described as breathtaking. They smiled. He stood up and asked them to join him, and the captain did some chair juggling. The girls told him it was their night off from the show at the Tropicana. They were maidenly shy and soft-spoken; one mentioned a year at the University of Oregon, and both spoke of divorced husbands. Bryce took them out on the town and, at the Sands, gave each two hundred-dollar bills to play with. Around six in the morning, Bryce proposed breakfast in his suite, strawberries in champagne. The strawberries came up around seven. It was after ten when he woke up. Trying to make his mind work through the nausea, he knew he had been drugged. However, the thing was to keep the police and reporters out of it, to get a doctor, and wait.

Bryce was one of the men who dread publicity, and so make things easier for the criminal whore and criminal pimp. Most men have reasons for not wanting to be identified with a whore, and Bryce had his. He was separated from his wife, and the two had recently agreed to go all the way and make it divorce. While it was amicable, he preferred that his wife not know he was so casual about money. Also, he hated to tell Caesars bosses that he had been taken by whores. A doctor gave him a mild purge and, by afternoon, he was feeling better.

The girls had taken his wallet, which he carried in a hip pocket, and whatever bills he had shoved into other pockets; he had won and lost and didn't know within a thousand dollars what he had. The wallet was found under a couch, and the $5,000 in the shirt was untouched. Bryce stayed an extra day and decided to confide in a Caesars shift boss. The boss found the story familiar; the Bryce-types would take almost any licking rather than sign a complaint. The girls were probably not known in Las Vegas, and so could not be traced through any bell captain or host. The chloral hydrate meant they were criminals. The shift boss told Sheriff Lamb. Even with no complaint, the police wanted a description; if they ever saw either girl, they would know what to do.

Bonner was having fun: he was chasing down a story in which, he could assure his wife, he simply had to pursue girls. But he had discovered that those who knew the prostitution story were not talking. The town, of course, was full of self-declared experts, and you could find waiters who could reveal how many girls were on the call list of the Sands and break them down by age, weight, and bust size. But police would beg off with explanations that they were deeply involved with real crime. Bonner got more confused when he heard the story about Moe and the forty-eight breasts.

Dalitz, as we know, is living legend, the driving force in creating the Desert Inn and the Stardust. Over the years he was the force back of the construction of the Convention Center, the YMCA, a Catholic church called the Guardian Angel Shrine, the Desert Inn Country Club, the United Fund, the University football team, to mention some of his ideas. He lives at a high whine, and when he gets too wound up he flees to Acapulco, to London, or to his yacht. When in Las Vegas, he takes a hand in the staging of the Lido Show.

In 1958, the Stardust's *Lido de Paris* was, in the words of Carl Cohen, the casino boss of the competing Sands, "The greatest show I have ever seen anywhere on earth." The Lido was extravaganza. It ran two hours, and when the last curtain was down, the audience was wrung out, emotionally exhausted. Each edition ran two years. The Lido of 1968 had been described by *Time* as the greatest revue in stage history, which was fine, except that the next would have to top it.

With this awesome assignment, in the spring of 1969, its producer, Donn Arden, spent his usual weeks in Paris and London recruiting girls and talking to people who were dreaming up new scenes. He was budgeted for what had become a standard figure, one million dollars, to get the new edition on stage. On opening night, Dalitz had several partners in his box, which is in dead center of the showroom, plus some five hundred VIPs who were jammed in as guests. When the last curtain came down, dozens of people tried to reach Moe's booth to tell him how wonderful, fabulous, indescribable, the new show was. Moe smiled at everyone, but he was impatient to give orders. In the preceding two hours there had been three slow descents down the great staircase, each by three lines of girls. The twenty-four girls were individually arresting, seemingly unaware of the weight of their breasts. The Lido had long been known for its ability to find that rarity, the girl who is slim and beautiful, with the breasts of a girl twice her size.[2] That night they came on with their ideas of breast makeup; some had tinted nipples purple, some red; some had enlarged the corona, and a few had sprayed their torsos with a blanketing copper. When, finally, the house had thinned out, Moe turned to an aide who was standing by. "It's Balaklava," he said grimly, "the advance of the damned infantry! All those breasts

[2] Sitting in the darkened showrooms, looking up at breasts which only a Jolly Green Giant could fondle, women have whispered to husbands that it must all be silicone. Las Vegas show producers, whether moved by gallantry or pride, admit that surgeons have done much to help, but that the nation still produces many girls with the lovely imbalance. Says Irwin, "Don't minimize what we were able to do in the 50s; a stage full of Jane Russells, when doctors couldn't even spell silicone."

pointed at you, every pair, like the slow bayonet advance in that movie . . . it's too damned much. Tell Arden to cover them up!" Before all the girls had left the hotel, wardrobe people were on the phone frantically discussing what leaf or gauze to put where.

Moe's caution was the rule. The policy of the great hotels was to suggest sex but not reach a point where anything can be called vulgar. Dalitz knew Paris, as did all owners, where it was raw. All knew the Paris where a man and wife entering a hotel must wade through a crowd of prostitutes, girls who might even give the man a tug at the sleeve. They knew the European cafés where, of ten girls sitting around, eight might be pros. For sound reasons, they tried to keep the girl traffic big enough to satisfy the men, and yet as unobtrusive as possible. Bonner had arrived thinking that Las Vegas was a great, ripe girl orchard. Now he was less sure, with doubts fed by such things as the two invitations he got from his friend, Eugene Murphy. Murphy was the public relations director of two of the "big five" hotels, the Desert Inn and the Stardust, and a man who made stories in his own right.

In 1948, when Dalitz opened the Desert Inn, he hired Murphy to handle publicity. Murphy was fired, sixteen years later. One of the town's jokes (all pro-Murphy) was that he found too many things too funny, and that the Desert Inn partners had wearied of his humor. He was one of the few Gentiles in an almost solidly Jewish house, so scholarly that partners like Kleinman, Kolod, and Tucker would go to him to check on the fine points of Hebrew liturgy. Whatever his original orders, Murphy soon found himself doing everything, a man swept downstream in a Niagara of developments, fighting to get a good image for a building that was creating its own. It was Murphy's lot to have to explain Las Vegas to possibly a thousand writers, editors, and newsreel men, and, understandably, he had to find things funny or crack. One time, when Bob Considine threw him a compliment and said, "Gene, your building is getting to be as famous as the Taj Mahal," Murphy replied, "Yes, but our courtesans aren't dead."

Bonner was having coffee in the Desert Inn one morning at the unlikely hour of seven, when Murphy walked in. Murphy explained that he was meeting a plane. "Most of the cast of the Lido show," he said. "They've been recruiting new gals in London and Paris." The Stardust had chartered two jets from Air France, one for the cast and one for costumes, and it was the "people" plane that would be landing in a half-hour. "Want to come? You'll see all the nudes with their clothes on."

Bonner went to the airport and stationed himself at the foot of the ramp. He said, "Romance fled. You could tell they were showgirls and dancers, of course, but you got the feeling that they had weathered a storm around the Horn. It seemed every other girl was carrying a baby. They came out, rumpled and bickering, and no question which bickerers were husband and wife. In the bus you would see a girl hand a husband a bag with the bottles while she fumbled with diapers."

Five weeks later, Bonner was again in Las Vegas, again as Eugene's guest, to see the Lido opening. When the curtain parted on the opening scene, a wing-to-wing expanse of beautiful people, Bonner recognized no one. Scene followed scene with no evidence of the drawn girls who had come down the ramp. "They were all out of one mold, beautiful bodies, beautiful faces, and those Lido breasts!"

Murphy had put Bonner in a booth with four other writers, one a *Variety* reporter, who had come with his wife. When the show was over, the group moved to the bar. Bonner saw that the *Variety* couple went in for some rather rough banter, a dialogue just short of quarreling. Apparently, the wife had told her husband many times that she didn't care to see these things with him. "He tries to look bored and indifferent," the wife explained, "but I know him, he's salivating."

They were a well-adjusted pair, their kidding quarrelsome but mild and apparently old stuff. The husband laughed. "I react the way all men react."

"How's that?" Bonner asked.

But the wife cut in. "Oh, performing a little mental cunnilingus on each damned one. Starting from the left," she added. Even this, apparently, was familiar stuff and did not lead to blows.

"Actually," the husband said dryly, "I was talking to Stan Irwin and he said that men are no more lecherous than women." Now he had to explain Irwin.

Stanley Irwin was the show producer who had staged some of

the great shows of the Sahara, centered around stars like Ray Bolger, Mae West, Marlene Dietrich, and Judy Garland. One time, trying to explain the mystique that makes one show great and another so-so, Irwin said that he would never aim an act solely at men. "In the whole creation, as you sweat it out with designers, choreographers, composers, you are as much concerned with women as men. The reason is that while women have a different sexual reaction, it's strong. As they sit there with their husbands, they are comparing themselves, improving, learning."

They considered Irwin's theory and someone asked, "How many girls were up on that stage tonight?"

"Oh, maybe fifty."

"So, how many of the fifty are available? How many can you buy?"

Everyone reached for the same laugh and said, "Fifty." But Bonner remembered the troupe that had come down the ramp had included husbands and lovers. This would mean that every man who came down the steps would have to be an accommodating pimp which, of course, was nonsense. When Bonner left, he had given up on the girl story.[3]

He did know that the ladies of the stage, when available, were by far the city's most expensive. All informants agreed that few showgirls were interested in the standard one hundred dollars, and that the price was several "bills." (A bill is $100.) But he could not get his sources to agree whether two to five bills would interest a few or all fifty ladies of the Lido; what percentage was buyable in the gorgeous platoon on stage at the Dunes, the Tropicana, or the Desert Inn.

Before he left, Bonner did spend an hour with one of the few men who could have told him, a man referred to as a "host" at the Desert Inn. Over the years, this man had been a broker between rich men and many ladies of the stage, but he had also handled

---

[3] Bonner quit because he got discouraged with the universal evasion, the same denials on prostitution that one gets on the subject of gambling, "skim," or absentee owners. Owners have been asked pleadingly and coaxingly by the nation's best reporters to give them the lowdown. The owners admit that prostitution is going on, admit that a man can get a girl, but they say it is handled by men far down the ranks, and that they themselves don't really know too much about it.

writers, and he was certainly not going to tell one of them that he was a procurer. The host stood Bonner to a pleasant lunch and explained things with a candor and frankness which, Bonner says, "Was the Goddamndest man-to-man crap I have ever heard." When Bonner left, he figured that money would get you about a third of the beauties of the Lido stage, that this was probably the percentage for every stage, which meant quite a choice. Someone once said that the only man who might see all the city's showgirls in a single night would have to be a schizoid fire marshal, a man determined to look in on every stage in one marathon, using a police escort for frenetic stops at the Hacienda, Tropicana, Flamingo, Dunes, Aladdin, Caesars Palace, Sands, Desert Inn, Hilton, Frontier, Stardust, Silver Slipper, Thunderbird, and Sahara.

The showgirl market was as complex as cotton futures. Las Vegas had more of them than Paris or New York, but you did not buy them like perfume. If a big player got a yen for the blond dream, three from the left, on the Dunes stage, he could wind up having her, but it would involve wooing before triumph. If you asked a pit boss, chances were he would try to steer you elsewhere; pit men might not know her and, almost certainly, the bellman wouldn't either. The lovely creatures wanted introductions, arranging, brokerage—different in every case. This class of lady[4] was not as casually available as a girl in Joe's, and not the merchandise of bellmen.

---

[4] In one of his Toynbeean moments, Eugene Murphy gave a picture of the showgirl:

"She is a girl," he said, "who was being told that she was beautiful when she was ten, and who was permanently changed by the fact. She started getting passes earlier, had her first affair earlier and, because of her beauty, she got into theatre. In the theatre everything is faster. She got married earlier and had babies earlier. I believe the figures show that showgirls get inseminated twice before marriage, and that they will average two and one-sixteenth children each before they are twenty-one. I believe that showgirls have the lousiest judgment on men possible to the sex; they are gorgeous losers and pick bums who leave them, and leave them with children. The showgirl who has been abandoned makes a good mother. She will support the child with no thought of bothering the man, or suing him or even seeing him. She will mail her child-support check to whoever is taking care of the child before she pays her rent."

W. E. "Butch" Leypoldt, Sheriff of Clark, before Ralph Lamb, once said that the best way to find out about the girl exchange—who is in on it, who is not, its prices, kickbacks, policies, the mysteries of a subtly managed business—would be to fall heir to a hotel. Overnight, every soul in it would be your employee. You could summon bartenders, pit bosses, guards, and demand to know how things work. You would be briefed by men—some of whom earn $200,000 a year—on how the "cage" works, the "count," gambling credit, the mysteries of management, as no reporter or FBI man could ever know. Butch made his joke, never dreaming it would be acted out by Robert Maheu.

Robert E. Maheu, as the world knows, was once chief expediter for Howard Hughes in the years when Hughes was based in Los Angeles. He was in his sixteenth year as factotum when Hughes decided to abandon Los Angeles for Boston. In Boston, Hughes had Maheu exploring new moves, possible new landings, in five parts of the world, Canada, Mexico, the Bahamas, Lake Tahoe, and Las Vegas. Las Vegas won. Three months after their arrival, Hughes had bought the Desert Inn, with the result that Maheu found he had become its boss, one man replacing the Desert Inn's eleven former owners. A few months later, Maheu became the boss of the gorgeous Sands, now replacing fourteen former owners. That December, Bob inherited the Frontier.

After the stormiest boss-employee relationship of modern times, Maheu was fired. He is now a modest figure in Las Vegas and has finally adjusted to not working for Hughes, though he can still jump at the sound of a phone. He plays tennis, lunches at the country club, fights a weight problem, and spends part of each day on memoirs. He prefers to avoid reporters because he still chokes up at the mention of Hughes. It is doubtful whether, on taking office, Governors Reagan or Rockefeller were briefed on so many secrets as Maheu when he took over his hotels. He learned that the Sands should keep a million in cash at all times; not to worry about security because, while holdup men take on the Chase National, they don't take on casinos; that the membership of the Desert Inn Country Club was as rich as that of Pebble Beach; that Washington had two senators who went elaborately incognito when they visited the Sands, but that most Washington wheels leaned toward the rival Sahara. While he was trying to understand Las Vegas, Hughes had him on the phone ten to thirty times a day telling him to buy the ABC Network, the Airwest Airline, and much of Nevada. Which was why rival hotel owners prophesied Bob would fail in gambling, distracted as he was by his frenetic boss.

Bob did stumble. He is a church-going man, father of three, with an attachment to his wife, Eve, that caused gossip with a reverse twist. In a town where loyalty to a mate can look eccentric, Maheu was news. Everyone was watching, hoping to discover what chorus girl, what lounge singer would topple "Mr. M." But eventually, he was pronounced a square, which itself made gossip. Everyone wanted to know whether Hughes' hotels would ban the whores. Here was an unknown, working for a man who himself was sexually puzzling. Las Vegas had long wondered about Hughes' own sex tastes. "Howie," as they called him, was coming to the El Rancho well before Siegel built the Flamingo. The El Rancho had cottages, and one time Hughes rented five, one for himself and four for his girls. Hughes kept returning to Las Vegas for twenty years, and the girl stories grew. Every Hughes aide—from Noah Dietrich, through William Gay and Robert Maheu—has had to enlarge his job to take care of the Hughes women. Naturally, gambling Moguls wanted to know what Maheu himself would do about girls.[5]

---

[5] When the memoirs are in, Hughes' own sex story may take an unexpected turn. The record shows that he was probably the world's most deliberate, calculated exhibitionist, dating, courting, parading the reigning actresses of two decades. Whatever his psychic kinks, he wanted to be considered a ladies' man, and he pushed the image. Still, it began to emerge that Hughes might not be too virile or much of a stud, and that the parading was a cover.

One of his biographers, Noah Dietrich, did not believe that the sexual life of his boss was proper reporting, and in three hundred pages avoids the Hughes bedroom performance. But others did get into the subject. When Howard Hughes had the four girls in cabins at El Rancho, the staff noted that he made no use of them. The El Rancho orchestra leader (still in Las Vegas today) was a forthright stud and toppled two of them. Both girls told him that they had no reason to believe that Hughes slept with women. Since then, many writers have seen that the question will be open until someone manages to interview the twenty or forty ladies, who are still living, and who might tell.

William Gay, now top boss of Hughes' operations, could settle much spec-

Bob smiles in remembrance. What with trying to serve Hughes, to obey orders that defied reason—end America's nuclear testing, make Hubert Humphrey president—buy up Nevada—he had to let some things go. In three thousand phone talks with Hughes he never asked for instruction on whores.

Maheu spent days, off and on, with Dalitz, possibly the most astute man in the history of Nevada gambling, and who had sold him the Desert Inn. In what may be called the education of a czar, Maheu spent months with Carl Cohen as his tutor. (Don Digilio, editor of the Las Vegas *Review-Journal*, believes that if a popularity poll could be taken and extended back twenty years to include men now dead, the most votes would go to "big Carl.") Cohen was the boss of the Sands casino, the greatest money room in the history of gambling. Maheu had a long reach and located Dean Elson. The former boss of Nevada's FBI had been transferred, shortly after Hughes arrived. He had embarrassed J. Edgar

---

ulation because, in his early years, he was literally a chauffeur, escort, and harem-master for Hughes' women. But Gay, like Hughes, loathes reporters and won't talk.

When Al Benedict was hired by Maheu to become manager of all Hughes' hotels, he sat down one day for a cup of coffee with Jack Hooper, the boss of the huge Hughes' security structure.

Said Benedict, "Jack, I think I've seen enough homosexuals backstage to be able to tell. Now these Hughes aides . . ." Benedict was referring to the six men who served Hughes personally in the Desert Inn penthouse, the only men who saw Hughes daily, who waited on him, who were the secretary-buffers between him and the world. Benedict named three of the aides to Hooper and observed that they had some funny ways.

"You don't have to be so damned delicate," said Hooper, a former Los Angeles Chief of Police. "In Los Angeles, two of them have police files for soliciting in men's toilets."

Robert Maheu, after his years of arms-length service to Hughes, makes no bones about the fact that Hughes likes to have Mormon homosexuals as his intimate servants. But Maheu does not go so far as to hint that Hughes himself is one.

"I know that Howard does a lot of posturing about his sex ability, but I also know that, of his many, many girls, he definitely did sleep with some. One of my first problems in Las Vegas—when we were buying the first hotels—was to take care of one very angry gal. She was," says Maheu, "the most beautiful girl I have ever seen in my life." Maheu pauses, and repeats, "The greatest beauty I have ever known. This one really thought she was going to marry Howard, and Howard begged me to get her off his back. Well, I got to know her. We became friends. She settled the question; she told me that Howard's love style is masculine enough."

Hoover when his wire-tapping was discovered and, in its deadpan way, the FBI gave him a "well done," and sent him off to await retirement. Maheu pulled him out of retirement and added him to his coaching staff. Finally, the man whom Maheu talked to most was Alvin Benedict, whose rise in gambling dwarfs that of any man in Nevada history.

Benedict's career began when the Desert Inn group decided that there would be no end to the press attacks, those lurid blasts that dogged the Desert Inn partners, and that press hostility would be a way of life. They decided to groom a man for top management who could not be accused of any gang background. Benedict was a good pupil. He started in the food department of the Stardust and soon became its general manager. As the attacks continued, the Desert Inn owners moved farther back into the shadows, moving Benedict forward, from the Stardust to management of the Desert Inn. When they sold the Desert Inn to Hughes, several of the partners decided to get out of Las Vegas entirely. They moved Benedict back to manage their remaining property, the Stardust. A year later, when Hughes had acquired four hotels, Maheu asked Carl Cohen to take over their four casinos, with Benedict handling their other departments.

Maheu had almost as many advisors as Governors Rockefeller or Reagan—men who were earning between $50,000 and $300,-000 a year—men such as Jack Entratter, who controlled the Sands' "Stable of Stars." He had Grant Sawyer, who stepped down as Nevada Governor in January to become a Hughes attorney in March. He was briefed by two of the most sophisticated men in gambling history, the attorneys, Jack Donnelley and Bryant Burton. Burton was the veteran attorney for the Sands group, a man referred to as the "lawyer's lawyer" on gambling law. But no coach got into the girl part, and the reason goes to the heart of the Las Vegas story.

Bob waded in. He found time to look in on the rival Dunes and Riviera, where pretty girls batted their eyelashes. He crossed the street to catch the show of what he assumed would become another of his properties, the Stardust. In the Sands he looked in on the Celebrity Lounge where three minutes was enough to give you a girl awareness. Finally, since the Desert Inn itself was

Hughes' headquarters, he would herd his assistants into the Lady Luck Lounge. Girls were particularly obvious there because it was an exclusive room and at some hours, hard to get into. After ten, when shows let out, it was jammed, people pressing against the rope, happy to tip for a table. Yet the room had scattered singles and doubles. This bothered Maheu. "You see," he said, "we put in one hell of a police force. We wanted to end everything notorious, to stop all talk of "skim," stop cheating of players, stop cheating of the house, stop cheating of the state, we figured to fire any waiter whose cousin was a hood. Fine, but with that kind of army people would assume that any girl there had the sure-as-hell approval of Howard. And with everything else they were calling him, I didn't think he should be called a procurer too. So, I gave the order, 'No girl running.'" He hoped this would cover everything.

Now, presumably, no pit boss would help a big player, no bellman run girls, no mini-skirted pros work the swimming pools or dawdle over a drink. "OK," says Maheu, "I issued my edict and I could almost feel it when, walking through a casino, the waiters would make the square sign behind my back."

Managers of rival hotels smiled. Maheu was too good to be true. If this was Hughes' management, you could forget the scares of monopoly because, clearly, Maheu would shoo business away. For some months there was a girl drought in the two top Hughes hotels. Business fell off in the Desert Inn and the Sands, partly because of the girl embargo and partly because of the Gestapo feeling, the fear that any waiter could be a security man. It took time for Maheu to catch on to this and to reopen the doors to girls, though he never put it into words.

Bob Maheu, one time military counterspy for the CIA, one time FBI agent, one time head of a detective firm, a man who had seen Paris four times before he was thirty, a member of California's swank Balboa Yacht Club, boss of hotels that employed showgirls, hosts, and an army of bellmen, did not know much about girl-running. He was discussing his girl worries with one of his PR men one day, wondering how girls were handled by Hilton, Sheraton, the Waldorf. The PR man was startled to see that the big man should be so touchy about procuring. Bob obviously needed coaching so that PR man composed a memo:

Bob, if you get into the hotel business you back into the whore business. It's the inkeeper's lot. It was that way when Dickens stopped at those English inns where half topless wenches would pour his ale and ask if there would be anything more upstairs. Every man who enters the business must decide how he feels about pandering or, at least, supplying the furniture of love.

I think that we can accept, after what has happened in recent years, that man is sex-obsessed. The books, the movies, the ads, the pornography, should make it clear that nature and not hotels made man erotic. Now in most businesses an owner can decide whether to have any part of the sex business, but not the hotel owner. He has what men need for intercourse, rooms and beds.

We know that men are polygamous as hell, that most men have the secret goal of knocking off dozens of lassies without the wife knowing. It's hard to pull off in your home town, whereas it's easy when you leave town on business. But even in another town you need a hotel. Which is why in every hotel the man away from home puts it to the bellboy. The girls, knowing this, use the hotel as a base. It would be hard to find a veteran hotel man who hasn't spotted a gal at a table, gone up to her, bought her a drink, and asked, 'Honey, how does it work?' This, in his first year. After talking to a hundred, he knows. Your employees educate you. If you have been a hotel man for twenty years, you have had more feed-in than the sex scientists. You get it from chambermaids (and, brother, that can be detailed), from waiters on room service, from cocktail waitresses.

You talk to the boys on the vice squad. You get it from the maitres and the showgirls. Every Las Vegas hotel has a sex authority, the wardrobe mistress. Every hotel has a Kinsey, he's the choreographer. So, when the original Vegas men got into the hotel business, they no more pioneered sex in hotels than Nixon pioneered Washington taxicabs. When they opened, there was such a run of whores to Las Vegas, such a nation-wide assumption that this was the Mecca, that the owners actually tried to keep the numbers down.

The education of Robert Maheu was a cram course. Bothered by that troublesome sex sideline, he got still more man-to-man briefing from one of his top executives, a man whose income was half again that of President Nixon. This man explained, "Bob, you're in a rough business; in these places it can go a half-million either way in an hour; it takes men with balls. Now, about the owners, your colleagues. None of 'em graduated from Holy Cross (Maheu's school). Most of them had a rough past, they took a lot of humilitation to make the top. But the fact remains that 'procure' is still a dirty word. It's still a world where a man will perjure himself rather than admit he runs girls. What you must understand is that the big owners do not like to procure. Just about every big point-holder[6] is now a rich man.

"Some owners won't remember when it was that they crossed over into their first million. Whatever the hustling of the past, they are now executives. They hate to be involved in getting girls. In these hotels, where you might have twenty or thirty go upstairs at the Sands one night, the top guys don't like to be in on it. They let others do it, the men at other levels. But everyone, so help me, will deny it."

The formula invented by Siegel, and adopted by all hotels, could be put this way:

There must be girls, as many as the men demand. If this gets you into the astronomy of how many girls are needed for three or six million men a year, well, accept the figures. But never forget Kefauver. Never forget Kennedy. Never forget the Diatribe. You can't be so vulgar that you offend middle-class America which fills your hotels. It must not become so open, so raw that it hurts the real business, which is gambling. Separately, since so many of the babes are criminals, who will black-

---

[6] In the earlier days of the business, most hotel-casinos were partnerships and the share of any partner was expressed as a percentage of the whole; a man with eleven "points" owned eleven percent of the operation.

mail, rob, or maim a customer, the hotel, the sheriff, the
D.A. must protect him from consequences. But the town,
the state itself, must accept the fact that it is in the sex
business, and that all must push the sex image.

Man has many groupings. In gazetteers he is Caucasian,
Mongol, or Negro; in hospitals, a blood type; in law, an adult or
minor. In Las Vegas he divides into "big player" and "ordinary
man." The "big player" has amazing perquisites: he is Nevada's
nobleman and he can lay his head on such breasts as other men
only dream of. Since there are so few big players, their story
comes first.

It is one in the morning, and as you enter the Dunes you see a
crowd, people gathered around a table staring, motionless and
intent, at a big player (let's call him Les Clark, or LC as everyone
will know him). LC, too, is intent and quiet, aware of the crowd,
but not playing to it, a man who is so good that his play is
admired even by the bosses. He has been throwing dice since six
PM, obeying impulses that make him put down about $2,000 on
each play in a rhythm of one or two per minute. If he is $30,000
ahead, the gossip all over the hotel will have it $50,000 to $100,-
000. But the owners know that in a marathon yesterday, and
another the day before, LC lost $40,000. They know, too, that he
seldom leaves town ahead of the game. The Dunes think he is
wonderful. The markers which he will leave behind this time are
only one of two or ten sets that year.

Every hotel had its list of LCs, men who fly in from all over
America with one thing in common, money, and an unexplained
fascination for the tables. They come for long stretches at one
game and most of them are loyal to a particular hotel, even to a
particular casino boss. They may end the night with a win or loss
of one thousand dollars or one hundred thousand dollars. A win
hardly upsets the owners because they know LC will be back. As
the joke has it, the LCs should be listed among assets in the event of
a sale. He has almost the status of owners; he seldom sees a bill
and he signs for everything, though not always, as the story has it,
for girls.

Every year the Sands has had a three-day "anniversary party" to coddle its big players. Invitations go to all parts of America and to Europe. There are the same big-player gatherings at the Dunes, Sahara, Riviera, Tropicana, and Flamingo. A high roller checking into his hotel will be given credit for $25,000 without a phone call to his bank. Staff instructions are simple, "Give him anything he wants." When, at one or five in the morning, Les is suddenly tired of dice and decides he wants a girl, like the one on the cover of *Vogue,* he gets her.

But as to how it works, there is no pattern. Many big players take care of themselves. A high roller is a man who knows that the gorgeous ones may cost $500—whether he pays or the hotel pays. He has had them; he knows the way. His arrival may be conveyed to showgirls by dealers or bartenders. Girls are ringing his phone before he unpacks. Girls who knew him before will stroll by his table. Sometimes, he may phone ahead to tell a particular girl to keep herself free, and keep her in his suite three days watching TV, waiting while he throws dice.

Most reports on Las Vegas say that the casino bosses procure for the big player. They do, but the simple fact is that most of them are hip deep in girls and need as much help as Frank Sinatra. Still, the affluent society does produce new millionaires, new to luxury, new to Las Vegas and to its ways and, not realizing what creatures they could have by blinking an eye, they do ask the pit.[7]

Still, as Carl Cohen once explained to Robert Maheu, few players have the nerve to ask a major owner to procure a girl, but it can happen. When approached personally, the big owners do different things. Here is a typical exchange: a big player, highly valued by the house, will hail an owner and suggest a drink. After a time, the player will drop the bomb: "Jake—or Sam—I've just made another donation to your place of, let's see, it's thirty-three big ones so far (a "big one" is a thousand-dollar bill). You sup-

---

[7] The word "pit" is often misused. What most people mean is the playing area, the gambling floor, the casino, of which a pit is only a part. A casino has several; crap pit, roulette pit, 21 pit, areas with their own crews and bosses. In a large hotel the casino may have twenty supervisors spread through several pits. In three shifts, counting dealers, boxmen, shift bosses, there may be one hundred casino men handling players.

pose you can help me meet a gal? She's in the show, the one three from the end on the left." Some owners go chilly and would refuse the service if the plea came from Kissinger. Del Webb, the tall, ascetic, inarticulate, wooden man, given to halting monosyllables, would cut you dead if you should wink and imply that he, self-declared friend of five presidents, might arrange a date with any of the nudes on his stages. Webb maintained the executive posture—that he was above it all. In the same way, William Weinberger, millionaire boss of Caesars Palace, would stare you down with the hauteur of a Dean Rusk for the same suggestion. Most of their subordinates, at the vice-president level, show the same shock at a suggestion that they procure. The answer might be, "Oh, I'm sure if you talk to Frank, he may know her." It is a putdown and intended as such.

"Frank" is a host—and every hotel has one or two or three, pleasant men who are arrangers in residence. From here on Frank will handle things on his own, and so absolve the owners of procuring. He will possibly arrange the introduction, or, if the girl, three from the left, should turn out to be married to a deputy sheriff, point the player at someone else.[8]

But when the big player goes to the lesser bosses in the pit, he will wind up with a girl who is reached in many different ways.

To deal first with the most exotic, the showgirl, she is pretty much a pit property. The pit is the biggest exchange for stage beauties. But for how many? Assuming that Las Vegas has six hundred of them, the number that can be bought is not six hundred. Some are lost to any pit because they are Lesbians. Some are married and caught up with baby sitters, diapers, and detergents. Some are single, but career-minded, aiming at the stage, and they think prostitution is no detour. This leaves those willing to succumb to the staring men in the vast audiences. If Bonner's percentage is close, the city total of gorgeous availables is only two hundred.

But the showgirl must "register," that is, tell the men in the pit

---

[8] The only physical beating ever sustained by the accident-prone Howard Hughes came when that all-American forager got stubborn about a girl who was betrothed to a celebrated football player.

that she is available. Some "register" in several hotels, and some talk with the hotel host. As a class, they will not go to a man's room on call. They want to be introduced and to be with him for a while —dining, gambling—demanding time to make an assessment. Bed will follow, but only after the civilities. Early in the courtship she will convey that she is not a production-line type and that he should not be thinking of any one hundred dollars. Some split their fees with whoever did the arranging, but the extent of such rebate is lost in the anarchy of the town's casually malicious gossip.

The pit also has a "card file" on another girl who has become typed, the cocktail waitress. The girl who, in fact, is the biggest earner of all the girls of Nevada. Her tips range from $1,000 to $40,000 a year, with few at either extreme, but with many earning $20,000 a year. Legend says that most of them double as whores, which is nonsense, because for years the Sands had three who were grandmothers, women who made no secret of aching feet and who could not be swingers by any rule of common sense. For some reason, reporters have failed to explain that they come in grades, in a ranging order of types as different as boy scouts, mail desk sergeants, and combat marines.

There are the leggy kids who serve the swimming pools. It is their lot to serve the gender that is known for low tipping, the women who spend hours taking the sun, groups that play Canasta and order six lemonades, two with maraschino and one with Sucaril, and cause the girl to scurry two hundred yards to and from the bar for a 25-cent tip. She is always on the run—chocolate malts for the kids, Alka-Seltzers for the universe—and she must be healthy enough to make a swimming team. This girl never gets near the pit or the big player, and she is no worry to the Internal Revenue. A little better off are the girls who serve the coffee shops and restaurants, where tips are better. A notch higher are those who serve the lounges, where customers may sit for hours, get glassy-eyed, run up big checks, and tip well.

But the girl of the legend is the one they all envy, the "pit girl," the one who is allowed behind the tables, the girl who gets as close to players as a nurse taking a pulse. She serves men who taunt fate, who equate money with courage, who go into the gambling trance; that ecstasy in which a man believes that his wisdom is greater than that of the house. She serves men who are never asked to pay for a drink. She is an accessory to the world's most sophisticated, most flattering larceny. She has top clearance and is, without question, the most informed of all the girls of Nevada. She has an inside view envied even by the FBI. In her eight hours she is elbow-to-elbow with the dealers and bosses who build up the figure of Nevada's gambling win. She sees the complexities of credit, the imperceptible, whispered conference that decides whether the pit will agree to a player's demand for another $20,000 or to cut him off. She senses the unspoken order of a pit boss to bring more Scotch to a frenzied player, just as she catches his invisible "no" when a drunken player demands the drink that will make him a stretcher case. She sees the concern of the whole house when five or fifteen players are simultaneously ahead by five to fifty thousand each. She sees the occasional attempt of a player to cheat. She sees the man who is suddenly aware that he has gambled away all he owns, and she may catch the wild expression of a dice thrower who contemplates suicide. She is there, smiling, when a disheveled player decides to quit, looks at her, and says, "Honey, I'm dead beat and lonesome." Players confide in her when they won't confide in a dealer. She has been stopped by the happy player who wants cigarettes and who drops a twenty in her tray, and she remembers the despondent loser, whom whiskey did not help, who gave her his remaining chips and walked away. She sees players who are being clutched by gorgeous showgirls, the elite of prostitution, and players who picked up a street tramp who would not be too welcome in the coffee shop. She sees procurement with such intimacy as is not seen by vice-squad men. She sees all this while holding the tray that gives her invisibility. Players get so used to the pretty, pleasant girl and her sympathetic sounds that they find her presence essential to environment. When such a girl decides that she herself wants to dip into it she needs no broker to pick her man. She doesn't need bellmen. When she weakens it is generally with a man who doesn't care much about money.

If around dawn when she goes home, a neighbor parts the

curtains to see whether the pretty hussy has a man with her, the neighbor might see: (1) a divorced girl coming home to a tract house where her first moves are to pay off the baby-sitter, take out the garbage and start ironing; (2) a girl who enters the house quietly so as not to waken a husband who also has weird hours and whom she sees only for the few hours when each is at home and awake and off-shift; (3) a girl who uses her hotel as a dating bureau to spot her man of the night, for assignations that may total two or ten a week, but not in her house. If one could label those available only to big players and those who are available through bellmen, the ratio might be twenty to one for the selective ones.

Everyone concedes that the "big player" makes no problem. He tosses out the down payment on a house on every play. But, for all his ability to buy the high-priced girl, he is statistically nothing, an oak tree in a wheat field. Compared to this elite group, the ordinary men run to the millions, men with no standing at the cashier's cage, no credit. Yet they are the money, the faceless armies who account for possibly 90 percent of all Nevada revenue. They too want girls, and these are the lads who lift bedroom statistics to the levels of Hong Kong.

There are other types, who serve the great armies of the "ordinary guy"—the call girls.

Once, a judge asked attorney, Tom Pursel, "Just what is a call girl?" Pursel's answer was that it might be best to tag the other whore types first so as to know what a call girl is not. After some thought, Pursel said he could discern eight types, provided you didn't get stuffy about overlap. For it can happen that a girl working in Sheri's in March can be a Las Vegas call girl in June and a Flamingo cocktail-swinger by December.

Some girls are so far out on the edge that they should be listed just to get them out of the way. Thus the "Utah Lolita." This little almost-prostitute is a kid who could be a precocious thirteen but whose age bracket generally runs fourteen to sixteen. A girl who, impressed by today's magazines and movies, decides she, too, can make money. She may tell her folks that she is off for an overnight stay at a friend's house and then, three or four in a car, streak for

Las Vegas. There they find things hard. Only the sleaziest motel will give them a room. Pimps won't handle them because pimps lose all police tolerance if they handle minors. Besides, for every Lolita who looks like a movie starlet, ten have acne and sticky hair. They are permitted to wander through the hotels because they might be the children of guests, but they are under the scrutiny of guards who learn to spot them fast. For the run of their sin weekend, they will solicit on foot or from cars parked at the curb. When love occurs, it might be in the motel or in the back of a station wagon.

A more successful type is the girl who is called (in harsh libel of the women of California) the "California secretary." The neighbor state has always produced girls—secretaries, school teachers, nurses, stewardesses—who slip into Las Vegas for a toe-dip into prostitution. They meet men, tell them the truth, team up and see a few shows. Some girls will have two or three such dates before being back on the job Monday, a few hundred ahead. They know that Las Vegas has tens of thousands of males who are hotel-hopping, and they come to swell the girl army. The professionals hate them because they feel they are unfair competition. They range from plain healthy-nice to gorgeous. They come with the clothes for each setting and, having the immunity of guests, they can use them—the bikini at pool-side, the skimpy halter thing at lunch, the little sequined nothing in the showroom. They have the quality that makes men think they are toppling something only slightly used and non-commercial. They come in enormous variety . . . girls who talk the patois of the campus, the stewardess with the shrewd ability to judge men, the office girl whose radar selects only the types she knows to be safely married and monied. Among the "secretaries" is the recently divorced lady who talks children and schools to men, setting up an empathy with those who find this reassuring. She is a vast cross-section, "The girl next door," or "Next office," except that she will suggest that it would be nice if her date helped with the rent.

Tom Pursel, scanning the mini-skirted horizon, can discern eight types who charge for love; they are:

1. The "house-girl," the girls in residence in the Mustangs, Mabels, and Sheris of today.
2. The "showgirl-swinger." Swinger, incidentally, is the qualifier which, attached to any woman, accuses her of occasional whoring. While no one has ever heard of a Salvation Army-lady-cornetist-swinger, it has been attached to almost every other female profession. Conforte even found "army-nurse-swingers" on Guam.
3. The cocktail waitress swinger.
4. The occasional adolescent, sometimes called the "Utah Lolita."
5. The "call girl," who is called by hotel bellmen or pitmen, but who has no pimp.
6. The "call girl," reachable only through her pimp.
7. The "California secretary," that great, blanketing catch-all name for every woman who gets the idea to try it and find out what it is like.
8. The "streetwalker," the girl who is at least temporarily unconnected and who strolls around in Europe (the boulevards and sidewalk cafés), in New York (with special density, Times Square), in Las Vegas (on the foot-tiring miles of the Strip and its many bars). In many cities she has taken to the automobile, and men returning from France report that the Bois de Bologne has more girls in prowling Citroens than it has gendarmes.

These, with much overlap, are the divisions.

As was seen by every owner since Siegel, men don't come for gambling alone. They come for the "Las Vegas Total," for the hours when they match egos with a grave, courteous dealer, for the magic moment when the great curtains part on the Las Vegas stages, and for the moment when they snap off the light and turn in bed to a new girl. On arriving, they spread out into thirty thousand hotel rooms, and a certain number will proceed to the business of finding a girl. Now the hunt takes all directions. Men can find that, after some hours they have not made any progress with a non-pro, and they settle for a pro.

It is part of the American way that, in his first minutes in a hotel, an arriving male will reach some intimacy with a bellboy —or bellman, as he prefers to be called. The man registering in Claridges in London, the Ritz in Paris, or the Grand in Rome is escorted to his room by a functionary in swallow-tail coat. Later, a tired porter will rap softly on the door with his baggage. These dispirited older men could no more procure a girl than they could explain their country's balance of payments.

American ways are chummier. When the desk clerk taps the bell, a smiling bellman appears. He may ask cheerfully if the weather was nice coming in from "Ellay." This brings the reply that the visitor is from Minneapolis, but it starts the talk. In the elevator, the good bellman opens with whatever sport is in season, and by the time they are in the corridors he may confide that his name is Mike. As he fiddles with the thermostat he conveys that he is the man to call, whether you need an introduction to the Governor or a girl. "Of course," says one, "if the guy looks like Governor Rockefeller, you play it cool. But don't write him off, because he may still want a broad. If he's got the look, give him a card."

Still, those who have not received a bellman's pitch can hesitate to call one. Some men are queazy about asking, not sure if that is the way. They have heard that in almost any hotel he is the boy to see, but what if he sneers? So, as a starter, men will call room service, order a newspaper or a bottle and, with the bellman in the room, start throat-clearing. A veteran bellman feels the question coming before he has closed the door. Since every deal means as much as twenty or thirty baggage tips, he handles things like a car salesman. "You let him know," says one, "that only last week you fixed up the police commissioner of New York." The deal is made, that is, the time is set.

Pursel defines the call girl as anything: a swinging housewife, a showgirl, a cocktail waitress, a former streetwalker. Her basic quality is standing. She has proved she is dependable, discreet— and never dangerous. This need for reliability has been felt by every man who procures, for his own protection.

The rules are set, commercial vows exchanged. The house man will call on her, and he will expect her to come. She is to provide sex and protect the man, which is to say, protect the house and the arrangement. If the man is asleep when she leaves and his wallet is on the dresser, she would be wise to place it under his pillow. When the many details are agreed upon—how to handle the phone, how the fee is split—they have a call girl arrangement. To talk to waiters, bellmen, newsmen, or detectives is to learn that the call girl spectrum runs wide, that it ranges from the high school student to the married dowager. The range of men who do the calling is as wide. In the hotels there are handsome, expensive hair-stylists who will procure a girl. In taxis, men talk to the drivers, who drop them off and go to a pay phone to call one. The old figure, used by the authors, Reid and Demaris—that 10 percent of the population of Las Vegas is engaged somehow in procuring—was always considered grotesquely high, but the fact remains that sheriff and D.A. know that there are a few dilettante procurers even among Las Vegas university students.

Somehow the call girl has acquired an image that is prettier than life. In the stories she can endure for decades, have a fairly predictable year, have a certain security, and wind up owning property. People who like their images round say that she retires and marries well. Some do, but most call girls have the security of a stray cat. For every one who winds up with money, fifty cannot put together a good year. Attrition is vicious. Gonorrhea in repeated bouts is hell on looks, and heavy antibiotics almost as bad. The men who call her are changeable, men who worry about their own file in the sheriff's office, and who will drop a girl because she is getting too visible, too careless, too independent, too pockmarked from VD, too stingy with freebies, too generous with them, or too fat.

There is, of course, the limbo of the "top call girl," a girl used over and over by bell captains or pit men because she is reliable. The girl who makes this grade has proved several things; that she is attractive enough to suit selective men, and reliable enough to be bondable. She will never be caught in narcotics, or get drunk and boast about her customers. She will not become a lounge fixture or become obvious to the Vice Squad. She must fall into the Las Vegas way, which is to shut up and fight all impulse to confide that she served a governor or a U.S. senator. There are call girls who bestir themselves only when the caller is a casino boss who is helping a stage celebrity, and there are call girls who go running, on call from the bellmen of a half-dozen hotels.

Here is a scene which has intrigued many people. A taxi discharges a pretty girl in front of a hotel. Mr. and Mrs. Sioux Falls, standing there, don't know whether she is a showgirl headed for rehearsal, the wife of Elvis Presley, the mistress of an owner, or, just possibly, that mysterious thing, the call girl. Generally, she will go to the house phones to call the man's room, to check whether he has changed his mind or got drunk or was unexpectedly joined by his wife. In most cases she is told to come upstairs, though some men want to come down and buy a drink to look her over. Upstairs, a door opens and two people face the preliminaries of strangers who will soon be in mankind's most intimate act. She will ask for payment before they start, and the amount, in most hotel-based affairs, was, for a long time, one hundred dollars. Prices in today's changing market vary enormously and, on a slack Wednesday afternoon, when even dealers are yawning, a man who wants to bargain might pay only thirty-five dollars.

However, while thousands leave it to the bellman, and devour anything that walks through the door, others won't. Many men think it is stupid to let another man pick a girl, knowing that when she walks in he is committed. Of course, even after making the bellman a broker, the customer may refuse. Men have said, "Look, honey, it's off. Here's twenty, and I'll take care of the bellboy myself." But it is awkward. A man can arrange with the bellman to meet the girl in the bar to have a size-up drink, but that still leaves the problem of explaining a "no." Upstairs, it is a lottery. The girl who steps in may show mannerisms that make him gag. "Well, allrightee, shall we do a little lovin'?" or "What's your name, dear?" and on hearing the fictional "Bill," use it endearingly fifteen times in five minutes. There is the girl who hides a slight burp and covers with a refined "Pardon, those damn tamales over at the Horseshoe always give me gas." Men who are cheating on wives of chic and taste may lose appetite if the girl who walks in has put together a harmony of red dress, red pumps, gloves, and bag. So thousands take the long evening hunt, going from hotel to hotel, buying drinks for a half-dozen girls before finding one with the chemistry.

The textbooks say that any girl seen fondling a daiquiri in a lounge is there with the approval of guards, lounge captains, or head bartender; in effect, with the OK of management. This is true at some hours on some days in some hotels. But it couldn't apply to Caesars Palace at 10 P.M. unless Caesars has processed much of the girl population of California! At certain hours the girl movement in and out of the big hotels is like that of Columbia University. When shows have let out and all humanity seems on the move, the guards of the Stardust, Hilton, or MGM could no more screen the pros than they could pick girls of Scottish blood. The lounge is the hunting ground of every type. The only safe generalization is that some girls are there with the nod of a maitre or captain. She can stay for hours, and even become conspicuous as the only single in the crowded room. A man smiles and gives her the "May I buy a drink?" When he leaves with her, the captain knows that she will be back and that in due course he can count on her envelope. But this is true only in some lounges, on some days. In thousands of other pickups the captain is relieved because it vacates a table and means a new tip.

Who then are the girls in the lounges? The jokes change with the times. When the Thunderbird was new, detectives spoke of the "clinical eye," the ability to look at a girl and tell whether she was a veteran, a beginner, or what is called the honest woman. But in the Las Vegas of today, when fifty may wander through Caesars between ten PM and four AM, the variety makes the "clinical eye" a silly conceit. As one detective says, "Any girl who is not a fall-down drunk or waving a machine gun must be served in a public place." She may be a call girl who is not getting many calls, or a secretary. She may be one of two thousand straight gals who are in town to see Presley or Tom Jones. She may be job hunting, a girl who will take anything, waitress, bus girl, shill, cocktail waitress, and who goes through the lounges hoping for a lead from a bartender or lounge captain. So, while the lounge is the home of the prostitute, it is also the place where girls stop to rest their feet. "And it can get interesting," says Ray Gubser, Chief Deputy. "What do you do about the beautiful babe who's maybe quit her job as showgirl, and who is married to a dealer and waiting for him to come off shift? She's got the roving eye so a plainclothesman asks if he can buy her a drink, and she says, sure.

So he buys her four. Then he suggests they go to his hotel, and she's still sweet as hell, and she says, soft and smiling, 'Look, you dumb prick, I know you're a cop, so if you're through buying I'll go home and start supper for the kids.' "

Some men like to sit at a table and size up each new female silhouette that appears in the half light, but others like to go to the bar and chat with a bartender. But men can hesitate to ask another man how to get a girl. The bar procedure is to toss down a few drinks, debate whether the bartender will laugh or snarl, have another and ask anyway. Reaction varies, since there are several thousand bartenders, with differing views on procuring. The first major hotel, as you enter Las Vegas from the Los Angeles end is the Hacienda, with three bars. The number of bars soars to fifty before you reach the Sands and to seventy before the Sahara. So there can be six hundred bartenders on a swing shift and fourteen hundred at work during twenty-four hours. They have no single attitude on procurement. If a visitor hits one who is sympathetic, the bartender may solve his problem by asking what he thinks of the little redhead six stools down. But the man mopping the bar may be one of the great majority who is content with his $220 a week and irritated that so many glassy-eyed jerks think he will pimp. He may shrug and explain, dead-pan, that being married himself, he often wonders just what the hell you *do* do. Again, he may be one of a few who work a quiet second business with a string of girls, or even one who, after long, friendly discourse with a customer, figures him good for a few hundred and goes to a phone to call his wife.

What makes Las Vegas such a delight is that prostitution should be so huge and so illegal. Everything is outlawed—fixed houses, free-lance girls, call girls, house girls, streetwalkers, pimps, procurers, panderers—not by one law but by many. It has been a consistent and enduring lobby of all owners, from Siegel, through Dalitz, to the conglomerates, that prostitution must be outlawed to avoid federal problems.

But although this attitude helped the image, it did not solve the problem of millions of male erections each year. The men wanted girls. It mattered little whether people like Houssels and Maheu were as agreeable as Conforte or as hostile as Baptist ministers—the men wanted girls. So the gambling industry set about perfecting the procedures, the rules for girl management, which would allow infinite fornication without identifying the owners too closely as procurers. This has meant operating orders to every man in the chain of command, and particularly clear operating orders for that emir of coitus, the hotel's head bellman, an understanding between casino manager and his pit bosses, and harmony between bar manager and his captains and waiters. It meant rules for the security men, waiters, maitres and vice presidents.

But how does all this square with law? The law bars all prostitution, but as Jack Golden saw, the Sands elevators keep dropping them off at every floor. Does Sheriff Lamb simply say there is none? Would the sheriff arrest a Richard Danner, a Del Webb or a Kirk Kirkorian on seeing, say, twelve girls in the Sands' Celebrity Lounge, the Sahara's Congo Room or MGM's Lion's Den?

Many writers would like to do a book about Sheriff Lamb. J. Edgar Hoover said that Lamb knew more about Las Vegas than any man living or dead. But Lamb seldom discusses his town and when a reporter manages to corner him, he stalls with easy platitudes.

Lamb, now forty-eight, was born on a desert ranch eighty miles from what would become Las Vegas. He has been in police work all of his adult life. He was a detective or a deputy sheriff during the years that saw the creation of the Strip. He saw the years when the "Diatribe" inferred corruption of its police. He saw the U.S. Senate anger when Kefauver wanted to close Nevada gambling. He was sheriff when the nation read *Green Felt Jungle*, the book that called Nevada the nation's most depraved state. Lamb cringed during the years when FBI boss, Dean Elson, installed over a hundred phone taps in Las Vegas. During all of this, he was contemptuously dismissed by the news media as indifferent to gang owners, a man who maintained law and order at the fist-fight level, while gangs ran the gambling.

While this was the judgment of outside writers, it was not home opinion. The local view was that any share-holding by gangsters was the business of the FBI, of the Department of Justice, of the IRS, and of Nevada's huge State Gaming Board. Lamb, they said, had enough with internal worries—murder, robbery, fraud, arson, rape, blackmail and, when they got out of hand, whores.

When any strong candidate decides to run for Nevada office, he can be financed in amounts that are impressive. From the beginning, every man who ran for office has known that if he did not applaud gambling he was dead. Any man who questioned the morality of slot machines, 21, or dice could not raise one thousand dollars. Should he persist, he could find that rumor had made him an embezzler or a homosexual, or that his wife is a whore he met in Macao. But no anti-gambling candidate ever appears. To the contrary, at election time, hundreds of men emerge to fight for offices, and all try to reach the owners to assure them of their fealty, of their deepest respect for gambling and willingness to defend it. For the owners, it is not a question of choosing the most valiant Horatio, but rather, picking those who show the most common sense. There have been campaigns, of course, when word did go out to back a particular man, but in most cases, if the candidates are OK, if they are sound on gambling, the decision can be left to the voters. Since the days of Siegel, virtually every office holder has received most of his campaign money from the owners. It has been called the "partnership of power," the arrangement wherein owners finance the men who make the laws. Again, this is less sinister then it sounds, because the owners are more sophisticated than native politicians, more aware of the need for prudence. They are more Washington-conscious, more image-conscious than any Nevadan could be. In all areas of crime they want governors and sheriffs to run a tight ship.

For years Lamb has had good relations with the long succession of owners running from Siegel and Goffstein, through Dalitz and Houssels, through Maheu and Kirkorian. He runs and wins, largely because the owners feel he fits the needs of a complicated city. And Nevada voters seem to accept the fact that the owners, however imperious, run things with inner wisdom. (How else explain the survival of gambling itself, its new popularity, its new summits of volume, despite the "18-year Diatribe"?)

So, for Lamb, campaigns are not complicated; no plausible candidate ever takes him on. He has never figured in scandal and no opponent has ever charged corruption. Now and then, when killings seem epidemic, he will put on a shoulder holster and, in old sheriff tradition, be in on a shoot-out but generally, he stays with administration. At election time most owners agree that "Ralph" should have another four years. Lamb, whose needs are modest, doesn't bother much about campaigning: one call to about forty gambling houses—calls made by friends—and he knows that TV time is paid for.

What then is Sheriff Lamb's position on prostitution?

It is a position he has never been asked to state. Essentially, it is that the huge call girl traffic must be accepted. The owners want it, the customers want it, and to end it would be to cut Nevada tourism and slash Nevada income. Similarly, the hotels must be allowed a roaming girl population in their lobbies and lounges because they "dress up the house.'" Men must feel that their own hotel offers foraging or they will go to other hotels. But the understanding is that, though girls may roam, the count must never be too great or the parading too much, or the sheriff will be criticized, and sheriffs do not like to be criticized. As for the pit, the source of the wealth of Nevada, it would never occur to Lamb to stop any of some two thousand pit men who may service a player.

This amounts to saying that the laws are there, not to interdict prostitution, but to be used only when something becomes too much—to be applied only when it becomes rampant, obvious, crude, defiant, tasteless. It imposes on the sheriff's office a judicial role that causes bothersome decisions almost every day. Finally, there is the problem of the "bad girls."

There is something about undressing for a stranger and discovering his ways that turns some girls into man-haters. Madams spot this and waste little time: they tell her to keep moving. But in the great market of Las Vegas there can be little screening of a changing girl army each month. The hater can be jailed only after she has shown it through robbery, homicide or some fascinating form of sadism. The madams have handled many and a composite view it might be this: so many girls who became hard-core pros have a low IQ as a starter, an inability to manage life. They turn to prostitution with bitterness because nothing else has worked. All of them have known intercourse with men who used them, who gave nothing, and left them to make their way. To them, all men are self-serving bastards. Says Sally Conforte, "If I were a man I'd be scared to death of some of those 110-pound cuties. They're walking anger. For them, life has been shit. Most street whores have had men who roughed them up, took back their money, and told them to go call the cops. Some have had taxi drivers who, on top of wanting their cut, make the girl pay off on the back seat. Even when they are arrested they run into bail-bond types who want a screw or a French, on top of bail. I've seen girls whose idea of happiness was to personally castrate men with a razor.

"Well, after a while, they decide that whoring is a sucker's game, but that it does provide the chance for the big score. They become selective and look for the man with money. They team up with men of the same type. Pimps can be man-haters who love the idea of hitting a guy who is horny. There is a type of criminal who thinks it's fun to clip a man who's on the make; its another form of sadism. They get him into a room excited, eager, a place where it's impossible to get help, where the pimp, or two or three of them, can come in, beat him up, take his money, and leave him cold. So that is the risk in Las Vegas. The city is getting hundreds of girls every month and it's a grab bag. How many are harmless weekend girls and how many have a rap sheet, who can tell?"

The bad girl? She is a sophisticated, divorced, white woman with a sex hatred of men. She is a tawny Latin who has had a hate since puberty for the light-skinned men who speak of greasers, spicks, wetbacks. She is an adenoidal white cretin who thinks that astral forces started the Vietnam war, and that a penis in erection is a man's real self. She is a white woman who shuns narcotics, and who will give a man knockout drops for a hit of twenty dollars; who will not be upset to find that the drink killed the jerk who happened to have a bad heart. She is a Negro with an enduring hatred for whites who caused the humiliation of her race, a girl who runs with Negro men who have the same hatred, who likes to steer sex-hungry whites into a parking lot where her black friends can pound them to a pulp. She is a female who, in uncomprehending hatred of a rough world, is determined to take it out on men. She runs with criminals who have discovered the vulnerability of men inflamed by sex hunger, and who have evolved, in effect, a new sub-species of crime; muggings, thefts, holdups, blackmail, homicides, and miscellaneous evils.

When the hordes of visitors descend on the city, neither the hotels nor the police can hope to handle more than a fraction of the night's events. In an orderly world, the Vegas visitors would go through the bell captain structure, accept the girl delivered, and pay for the screening that eliminates "bad" girls. But thousands of men insist on the manly right of getting a girl their own way. So Lamb and the owners are in no conflict on philosophy, and in harmony on the need to control, roust, stop the criminality which surrounds prostitution.

Discussing this latitude, former D.A. George Franklin laughed. "Well, I suppose the story would hardly bother anyone now, so I can tell it. A couple of years back we hosted the national convention of American D.A.s. We had six hundred in town. As host, I got the figures and I saw where only two hundred had come with their wives. I got to figuring how many of the other four hundred might tie into a bad girl, so I called their hotels. The system is different in different houses, and in some cases I called the bell captain and in some the casino boss. I told them it would be bad if some D.A. got rolled or mugged or overcharged or had his picture taken. You know, some of these pictures you wouldn't believe. A guy has passed out, from either drinking or knockout drops, and a man who was never closer to an orgy than buying *Penthouse* Magazine is propped up, one girl nursing him—not with her breasts—and another . . . Oh, God, they must have prop men just to hold the lights!

Anyway, I told the hotels to give these guys the same protection that our State Department gives a horny visiting general. Well, as no reporter has really pointed out, the management of the Strip hotels is great. For weeks afterward I might be in a hotel and some grinning bellman holds up his hand, the A-OK sign, indicating that with his D.A.s everything went fine!"

No one, not the Webb, Hughes, Recrion, or Hilton managements questions that men must have their girls. What they want for their men is safe coitus, with a minimum of sex-connected crime. This is quite an order because the index includes:

1. Armed robbery by pimps or whores, or by teams
2. Hotel room theft by thieves tipped off by whores
3. Blackmail by pimp and/or whore
4. Physical assault (mugging) by pimps or thug associates
5. Narcotic sales to whores by their pimps
6. Narcotic pushing by addict whores

The hotels and the police are jolted to see that America is on three sprees, a crime spree, a sex spree, and a narcotics spree, and that so many whores and pimps should have worked out a business that combines all three.

11

It will probably come, dear Lord, another movement, another great debate. Several states have groups pushing for legalization.

But who wants to be first? Those who are pushing it would appreciate it if good old Nevada led the way and came up with another breakthrough. But Nevada doesn't want any more firsts. It will sit back and legalize it after other states get their own noses bloodied, after others have shown the way. I would guess, though, that Nevada might come in third or fourth, the state just hates to lag too far behind in anything.

Don Digilio, Editor,
Las Vegas Review-Journal

Who'll Be the First?

NEVADA, RICH, booming, nervous, counts its blessings, and would drown all boat-rockers.

Its gambling no longer revolts the nation and the Diatribe is down to an occasional sneer. In the summer of Watergate, one of TV's most popular games, CBS's *Jokers Wild*, centered around the slot machine. CBS, NBC, and ABC have found that the stay-home Americans have the same hunger for stage celebrities as people who go to Las Vegas. So they have reshaped television. It has become the era of talk shows and panel shows, and the wildest dream of any Siegel or Dalitz could not have imagined such wholesale, free Las Vegas promotion. Johnny Carson, star of the *Tonight Show*, and headliner at the Sahara, plays host to hundreds of stage figures every year. He goes into easy banter with Danny Thomas, Sammy Davis, Jr., Joey Bishop, any of a hundred stage people who speak of Las Vegas as home, the showcase, the place to be.

Again, on another network, Merv Griffin reached millions with more talk about Las Vegas, drawing on the same theatrical *Who's Who*—Pamela Mason, Wayne Newton, Lorne Greene, Peter Lawford, people who speak of the goings on at Caesars Palace or the Hilton, who explain that they are just finishing at the Sands or starting at the Desert Inn. Mike Douglas also brought on people

257

whose stage lives center on Las Vegas. It is all graceful and exciting, the gossipy talk that has decided still more millions to try the
fabulous city. The most hostile reporters have thrown in the
towel. Mention of the boys—Bugsy, Lansky, Stralla—the violent
ones of other times—produces no quiver; they are dead or dying
and their story, recreated in *The Godfather*, is history. American
crime may be bigger than ever, but people feel it is silly to try to
tie the Mafia to the towers of Hughes, Webb, and Hilton. The columnists and the TV hosts have made an easy apostasy. They have
turned to using Las Vegas for its rich name-dropping, for its theatrical vibrations alone. The owners built taller than they knew.

Nevada listens to distant sounds, alert, like a nervous deer, to
the breaking twig that may signal danger. It no longer has the
dread of the 50s and 60s, the fear of a federal crackdown. The
owners wonder, instead, how long it will be before other states
steal their gambling. They think this is still a distant danger but,
when, or if, it happens, they plan to outdo the competition by
keeping Las Vegas the theatrical center of the world. Should trag-
edy hit and gambling become legal elsewhere—Atlantic City,
Saratoga, Miami or Hawaii—they are prepared to open hotels in
those places. Anticipating this, the Nevada legislature has
repealed the law that prohibited branching out. Today, Webb,
Hughes, Hilton, MGM, any of them, may open up their branch
banking in whatever state beckons.

But what about legalizing prostitution? What chance of Nevada
going all the way, doing now what some states will do, inevitably?
The story turns to Joe Conforte once more, for it was he who
opened the curtain that showed how many in Las Vegas are ready
for such a step now.

When Joe was beginning to do well at Mustang, he met a
younger man, Roy Woofter, who became his friend, a man who
was broke, where Joe was becoming rich. Young Woofter wanted
to enter law school and Joe staked him. When Woofter passed the
bar he became the first Nevada lawyer who had made it because
of Joe. Woofter went into practice and then, with an audacity to
match Joe's, ran for one of the highest offices in Nevada, the office
of Clark County District Attorney. He won. It would be ridiculous
to say Joe planned it that way—that he could be that prescient in

picking winners—but the fact was that the most powerful D.A. in Nevada was now his close and grateful friend. Less than two weeks after taking over the job, Woofter acknowledged his friendship. He wrote an ordinance to legalize prostitution in Clark County and somehow prevailed upon two of the Clark commissioners to support it. Any ordinance must have several hearings before a vote and, on first publication of this one, Clark County exploded. Some people roared because something so revolutionary had been introduced as a sleeper, without the slightest warning. Others were angry at the proposal, and still others because it was so obviously a move by Joe. But the real surprise was that so many people should ask a laconic "Why not?" It was a town topic for some weeks. In the Women's Clubs there were those who argued that since Las Vegas was already one of the whore centers of the world, why not legalize it? But the strength was with the owners, who said "no" once again. This time, not because of fear of Congress, but because of a new situation.

The total of the Las Vegas conventioneers now varies between ten to thirty thousand males per month. Las Vegas has some two thousand men who do nothing but court America's convention business. When the convention managers heard about Woofter's idea, they wailed. If Las Vegas should do something so stupid as to have open whorehouses, America's wives would scream like banshees. Nothing would hurt conventions more than if women learned that their men were off to a town that had open twenty-dollar parlors. "You can't do it," said the convention bosses, "you will wreck Las Vegas." Woofter's law did not get a second reading. Reporters found Woofter quite candid. "I can't turn my back on a man who helped me so much," he said, "and as for the issue, I think legal houses are certainly better than the present foulup—narcotics, syphilis, muggings—to name a few blessings."

Joe and Roy showed courage; they had tried a coup in a city that had passed to impressive bosses. It was now the city in which Hughes had decided to keep his holdings, and whose new team, headed by William Gay, ran six operations. It was the city of MGM, a company which had upped the ante for a hotel's cost to 110 million, a company now run by men with a thousand times the political power of Joe. It was a city of great corporations more than ever dedicated to the gambling industry, a city in which even the clergy was finding new ways to bless and protect it.

Still, to the amazement and irritation of so many, Joe, who can be odiously boastful, turns out to be a prophet.

In October 1971, when crime had hit awesome summits, President Nixon named a commission to assess the new crises. The National Advisory Commission on Criminal Justice, Standards and Goals gave its findings in five volumes. In one, it recommended that prostitution should be "decriminalized." This amounts to advice to the fifty legislatures to do what Storey did —legalize girls. Joe never saw the report, and only recently heard about it, but he continues to irritate Nevadans by saying that a movement has started, and that his stumbling idea, which dated so far back, may become American doctrine.

Of course, movements move like glaciers. The income tax, woman's suffrage, national prohibition, repeal, abortion, all had gestation periods of quarter-centuries. But what was long an untenable, outrageous idea picks up converts by the month.

Many owners believe that some change must come, that considering all the miserable throw-off of prostitution—the criminal whores, the brokerage of pimps, the ties with narcotics, girls so ridiculously overpriced, sex merchants corrupting government— some state will decide to try something else. The state has thoughtful people who watch the sexual revolution and the widening American tolerance. But it will not be Nevada! Nevada has observers but no crusaders (except Joe). The owners are content to live with the structure as it is, however grotesque. Outright legalization must come elsewhere first.

For the foundation of Nevada rests on gambling, not prostitution. When, on a booming midnight, Dunes boss Major Riddle strolls over his acres of carpet, he knows that each nickel machine yields $7,000 a year and each dollar machine about $20,000, and that on a good day the casino will record a $400,000 drop, of which $80,000 is that day's gross win. When one big player or 10,000 small ones get girls into their rooms, the house makes nothing. Sex is a side transaction that does not get into the accounting pipeline. The money that changes hands goes only to the girls and to lower-rung employees who help procure; none of it goes to owners.

So, no one is crusading for Joe's idea (for Nevada's two gambling cities) as an income idea. The owners will accept it for Nevada only when it has been adopted elsewhere, in at least two states—when it would not be another Nevada first.

As to how fast the country itself may be moving toward the idea, every man must be his own Toynbee. The arguments carry some irony. Who dares imagine the sexual needs of today's fifteen-year-olds when they are thirty-five? Sex may be so uninhibited that today's unremitting, famished search for it will seem as picturesque as that of the colonial man who went hunting for his Thanksgiving turkey. This view is favored by many whores. They are particularly sensitive to free love on the outside today, and they incline to think that what they are doing now will soon become so common that the man with a whorehouse will have little to sell. All that can be proved now is the speed of change.

A glance at each month's *Time* or *Penthouse* shows what new jolt awaits people over forty. There must be some meaning to the fact that *Cosmopolitan* ran an article that explained not only that is masturbation good for you, but how women should practice it, with what use of the heel of the hand, and how much digital insertion.

As to some of the people whom we have met in this story, each remains grooved to his ways.

Carol Smith never saw Bart again. She married after some years of travel. Her man is an instructor in a California college, a man who was reading Kant and Schopenhauer when he was eighteen, and who is detached from almost everything in the human condition. He has a deep love for Carol, and leaves it to her whether to discuss her past. Carol was closing her apartment door one morning when she saw the postman wave. The letter was from the San Francisco law firm of her Uncle Bart. Standing on the sidewalk, she read that he had died in a car crash in Utah. It had taken police some time to connect him to his nearest relative, Laura.

After some confusion, he had been buried in California. The attorney was sorry that Carol could not have been told in time for the funeral. He advised her that Bart had left everything to her and suggested that, when convenient, she should come to San Fransco.

Margaret Grey had left Joe's and, in effect, disappeared without trace. Nevada's little houses are inconsistent about identification. In some towns, girls are fingerprinted by local police, but in others, they may work for years under assumed names without acquiring a police file. Since they are contractors and not employees, they do not use the universal identification, the social security card. When they leave a place they can frustrate even the FBI, and Margaret had left no forwarding address.

As for William Raggio, his story went into a troubled, political spin, influenced not by Joe Conforte but by Howard Hughes.

When Hughes was dominating Nevada—and dickering for no fewer than thirteen of Nevada's ranking hotels—he made serfs of quite a few Nevada officials, in particular, Nevada's Republican Governor, Paul Laxalt. Laxalt turned himself into a broker trying to help Hughes buy anything he wanted. He was assured that when he left the governor's office, he could count on being named chief counsel of all Hughes' operations in Nevada.

At the end of his four years, Laxalt decided not to run for re-election. Unfortunately, there was no hope of joining Hughes' organization, because Hughes had fled. Instead of quitting politics entirely, Laxalt decided, as ranking Republican, that he would become the state's kingmaker, the man who decides on Republican candidates for the office of governor, U.S. senator, and congressman. Bill Raggio, now in his twentieth year in office, wanted to run for governor. He quit the D.A. job when polls showed that he would be a strong candidate. But Laxalt said no.

Laxalt had picked Edward Fike to run for governor. He persuaded Raggio to run for the U.S. senate instead. This meant taking on the popular incumbent, Senator Howard Cannon, who, the polls said, was unbeatable. Reluctantly, Raggio got into a race he knew he could not win. With his entry, people assumed that his old enemy, Joe, would pile in with whatever money was necessary to beat him. "And I was sure as hell going to," says Joe, "except that when I see the first polls, and see the poor guy's already dead, I figure to just sit back and watch him buried. I don't lift a finger." Raggio was defeated badly, and he turned bitter for having agreed to such humiliation at the hands of Laxalt. He joined a new law firm. Later, he ran for the state senate and won. In autumn of 1974 he was running for Lieutenant Governor.

Joe has dark moods when he feels that history may give him a kick in the groin and pass him by. He is sure that girl-houses will become legal, even commonplace, and that they will evolve their own architecture and traffic-flow as supermarkets evolved theirs. But it may be for other men. "Hell, I may be like them Wright Brothers, or Hughes with the wooden plane, a guy who develops an idea for somebody else." The best assessment of Joe was made by George Franklin, former D.A. of Clark County, who doesn't like Joe particularly, but who understands him. "In the handling of Joe," says Franklin, "Nevada is not very perceptive. Joe's great, enduring dream is not to conquer Las Vegas, not to make another million, but to be approved, applauded, accepted. Joe's Everest is not money or power; what he really wants is to be invited to the home of a college dean for dinner. I believe that for an invitation to join Rotary or the Prospectors Club, he would agree to get out of the business, or, considering his bent, open three more whorehouses and commit their earnings to the boy scouts, girl scouts, and the University of Nevada."

Joe was off on his annual pilgrimage to Sicily, to the little town of Augusta. He goes there every year to make an offering at the ritual of the Procession of the Madonna. He has made the trip every year since his gross first went into the hundred thousands. In Augusta, people speak of him as the nice man from "L'America del Nort," so modest and humble. They are certain that he makes this atonement for any slips in his duties to God. The priests invite him into the sacristy, where they accept the $100 bills, and then ask him to join their little sacerdotal group for food and the light red wine of the region.

In the month that Joe was visiting Augusta, a new face surfaced in Nevada, that of the district attorney of obscure Lyon County, on which Joe had trespassed so long ago. This was Ronald Banta, whom Nevada reporters put on TV because his county had passed an ordinance that legalized houses, making Lyon the second American county to make history. Speaking with some pride for the law, Banta explained that he had just received a phone call from the city attorney of Seattle asking for a copy.

In the summer of Watergate, Joe had become a minor celebrity and was getting invitations to address Rotarians, Lions, Elks, college seminars, and women's clubs from all parts of America— even a few in Canada.

One talk was before the Rotary Club of Chico, California, a farming town that could serve as a model of the all-American, all-average everything. But Chico still retains the character of Sinclair Lewis' *Main Street*, and some Rotarians rose to ask questions that were quite hostile. One man asked him whether he could ever really hope to get the respect of decent people, and Joe, momentarily stung, replied, "Yes. Just a few months back we served the next president of the United States."

There were gasps, but with shrewd, collective judgment, the merchants of Chico dropped the subject. No one prodded Joe into naming the eminent American. The meeting broke up. Outside, someone asked, "You're pretty sure you had the next president?"

"Well, yes," said Joe. "The way they are being eliminated by Watergate—yes, I'd say he's a strong possibility."

"Wasn't he nervous? Wasn't he worried about being recognized?"

"No," said Joe, lowering to the soft, intense voice he uses to express things deeply felt, "That's the point, the whole, central fucking point. He picks out a girl who is so impressed she don't ask him to pay in advance. Afterwards, he asks her how they stand, and she says it's twenty bucks. He busts out laughing. 'Honey, we're in the same business, but I'm richer than you,' and he hands her a fifty. He's a hell of a guy and he'll make one hell of a president."

Nevada reporters picked up the story and drove Joe crazy trying to make him name the notable. But Joe fell back on the old rule of not betraying customers. "Besides," he said, "us politicians should stick together. I've just decided to run for the legislature."